Did Jesus Speak Greek?

Did Jesus Speak Greek?

The Emerging Evidence of Greek Dominance
in First-Century Palestine

By
G. SCOTT GLEAVES

Foreword by
RODNEY EUGENE CLOUD

PICKWICK *Publications* · Eugene, Oregon

Pickwick Publications
An Imprint of Wipf and Stock Publishers
199 W. 8th Ave., Suite 3
Eugene, OR 97401

www.wipfandstock.com

ISBN 13: 978-1-4982-0433-0

Cataloging-in-Publication data:

Gleaves, G. Scott

    Did Jesus speak Greek? the emerging evidence of Greek dominance in first-centu-
ry Palestine / G. Scott Gleaves.

    xxvi + 204 p. ; 23 cm. —Includes bibliographical references and index(es).

    ISBN 13: 978-1-4982-0433-0

    1. Jesus Christ—Historicity. 2. Bible. New Testament—Language, style. I. Title.

BS2545 L3 G65 2015

Manufactured in the U.S.A.   05/06/2015

A project of this kind could not be achieved without the help of a very capable and talented research assistant. I dedicate this book to my friend and PRA,

Betty K. Lamberth
(aka BB)

Contents

Foreword

IT IS A SPECIAL privilege to be invited by Dr. G. Scott Gleaves to contribute a foreword to *Did Jesus Speak Greek? The Emerging Evidence of Greek Dominance in First-Century Palestine.* This topic is an engaging one for those who have an inquiring mind and who desire to dig deeper into the world of the New Testament. As I began considering what needed to be said, my mind kept returning again and again to the account of the crucifixion in John 19:20–22. John's account is the only place in the New Testament that informs the reader that the inscription placed on the cross where Jesus died was written in three languages: Hebrew (Aramaic), Latin, and Greek. The text is also the sole source that identifies Pilate as the author of the statement attached to the cross. The appearance of these languages in a public place at this specific time reveals the multilingual character of Roman Palestine. In addition, an inquiring mind may desire to understand how these languages intersect. Are they equally distributed among the population? Are they associated with certain geographical regions, ethnic and religious peculiarities, or national identities? Is there a particular language that may be dominant and therefore serve as a primary means of communication? Consider this analogy: If a traveler, fresh from a trip to the exact same area of the Middle East in 2015, left a statement in a travel diary that a large number of signs in what we today classify as modern Israel were written in Hebrew (Israeli), English, and Arabic, some were only in Hebrew and Arabic, and a number of others were only in Hebrew and English, what conclusions would one reach upon discovering such information in 4015? Additionally, if somehow that researcher also knew that only a tiny portion of the population back in 2015 were English-speaking, what inferences could be drawn?

At the time of Jesus and his disciples, the inhabitants of Palestine lived in a land where Latin was present only because the Romans were present and in control of the region. Few Jews spoke in Latin, except to speak of Caesar, Caesarea, a centurion, or a denarius. Hebrew was well-known primarily to those who studied the Hebrew Scriptures. Aramaic was widely spoken by the native population, as is reflected in the New Testament, but Greek was the *lingua franca* of the Mediterranean world, appearing in a surprising number of places throughout Galilee, Samaria, Judea, and other neighboring territories. Though Aramaic was without question the native language of many who lived in first-century Palestine, was it the dominant or primary language of Jesus and his disciples? Dr. Gleaves argues that the historical and archaeological evidence (ossuaries, papyri, parchments, building and stele inscriptions, and inscribed pottery) may very well paint a different picture than the one presented by academia. Despite the fact that several important and learned scholars hold that Aramaic was overwhelmingly the language spoken in New Testament Palestine (with a few denying that Jesus spoke Greek at all), Dr. Gleaves argues his case from what the evidence reveals and therefore counters positions that may rely more upon tradition.

When Scott was in our doctoral program at Amridge University, he enrolled in a course called *Historical and Archaeological Research of the New Testament*. I encouraged him to do a thorough study—dealing with whether or not Jesus spoke Greek, and if so, to what extent. My plan was to show him that here was a fascinating and meaningful topic which could grow into a dissertation and possibly someday be worthy of publication. He obediently began the research, but with much less excitement than I had hoped. However, by the time he had completed a lengthy paper on the topic, he had become passionate about investigating the question in much greater detail. How excited I was when he jettisoned his original dissertation topic and energetically took up the present study. My plan had succeeded. I was blessed to function as the chair of his committee. I am convinced that the overall approach of Dr. Gleaves is unique. His reasoning is sound. His conclusions answer adequately the part played by the Greek language in the formation of the New Testament. He gives plausible reasons why the books of the Greek New Testament show signs of being original compositions rather than translations from Aramaic. He interacts with differing viewpoints as he builds a case for his own conclusions.

Scholars in the field of biblical studies need to read this work and carefully weigh its findings. This effort is one filled with long hours of hard work and is, in my opinion, one of the best academic achievements produced to this point by our students at Amridge University. The motive behind this work goes beyond a mere fulfillment of an academic requirement. Such is not the case with most of the dissertations I have read in my fifty-five years as a college and university professor. Many, no doubt, began as a means to an end, including my own at Hebrew Union College in Cincinnati, but happily became a labor of love that blessed and enhanced my own study. Yet my dissertation and those of many others, however beneficial, fall short when compared to what Dr. Gleaves has accomplished.

The conclusions he puts forth, if correct, have far-reaching implications, but I must allow him to make his own case within the pages of this book and to permit the readers to judge the quality of his work for themselves. I am excited to recommend this work and obviously am convinced it will lead to a better understanding of the place of Greek in the world in which Jesus lived.

Rodney Eugene Cloud, PhD
Dean, Turner School of Theology
Amridge University

Acknowledgments

I AM INDEBTED TO many professors, family members, friends, and colleagues who have mentored, guided, and encouraged me during this adventurous journey. Rodney Cloud, my mentor and friend, offered enthusiastic, helpful, and patient assistance. Daniel Fletcher and Paul Watson also provided valuable insights that improved the quality and substance of my research. My friend and gifted scholar, David Warren, has positively impacted me in ways that I can never repay. My association with Randall Bailey, one of my professors in graduate school and now a friend and colleague, has been a personal and professional blessing.

I thank the executives, the board members, the administration, and the faculty of Amridge University for the education that I received. Additionally, I acknowledge the generous and loyal support of the Faulkner University board members who comprise the college of biblical studies committee (Billy Lambert, Dale Kirkland, E. R. Brannan, Harrell and Carlton Freeman, Jess Hall, Jim Campbell, and Mike Houts), the president of the university (Billy Hilyer), and the faculty and staff of the V. P. Black College of Biblical Studies and Kearley Graduate School of Theology of Faulkner University (Carl Cheatham, Kevin Ellis, Todd Brenneman, Paul Tarence, Floyd Parker Jr., Don Myers, Martel Pace, Matthew Conley, Richard Trull, Terry Edwards, David Hester, James Gee, Bruce Morton, Jeanette Stubblefield, Jane Fletcher, and Will Freeman). Jack Tucci and Cecil May Jr. offered me an opportunity of a lifetime for which I will be forever grateful.

I must also make known my gratitude to the elders and members of the Granny White Church of Christ in Nashville, Tennessee, where my adventure began, for allowing me to pursue a dream.

I thank my mother, Sally Bushnell, and my father and stepmother, Jerrell and Linda Gleaves, for having confidence in me. My in-laws, Charlie and Mackie Boddy, are springs of encouragement. My children, Lindsay Gibson (also her husband, Brian, and daughter, Amelia), Nathan Gleaves, and Taylor Gleaves, are blessings beyond measure. And above all, my wife, Sherri, deserves the highest praise for her loving support and sacrifice. She is the wisest person I have ever known.

Abbreviations

GENERAL ABBREVIATIONS

2d ed.	second edition
3d ed.	third edition
4th ed.	fourth edition
ANF	*Ante-Nicene Fathers*
ℵ	Greek manuscript (uncial), fourth–sixth centuries CE
θ	Greek translation (Theodotion), second century CE
B	Greek manuscript (uncial), fourth century CE
b. B. Bat.	*Babylonian Talmud, Baba Batra*
BCE	before common era (correlates to BC)
BHS	*Biblia Hebraica Stuttgartensia* (4th ed.)
ca.	*circa*, about
CE	common era (correlates to AD)
c.	century
cf.	*confer*, compare
ch(s).	chapter(s)
D	Greek uncial manuscript, sixth–seventh centuries CE
DSS	Dead Sea Scrolls
e.g.	*exempli gratia*, for example
ed.	edited by
ed(s).	editor(s)
Eng.	English
esp.	especially
ET	English Translation
et al.	*et alii*, and others

etc.	*et cetera*, and the rest
ex.	example
exp.	expanded (edition)
*f*13	Greek manuscript (minuscule family 13)
frg.	fragment (of document)
gen.	genitive, genitival
Gk.	Greek
GNT	Greek New Testament
Heb.	Hebrew
ibid.	*ibidem*, in the same place
i.e.	*id est*, that is
lit.	literally
LXX	Septuagint (Greek translation of the Old Testament)
m. Avot	Mishnah, *Avot*
m. Meg.	Mishnah, *Megillah*
m. Ned.	Mishnah, *Nedarim*
m. Sotah	Mishnah, *Sotah*
m. Yad.	Mishnah, *Yadayim*
mg	*in margine*, in the margin
MS(S)	manuscript(s)
MT	Masoretic Text (standard Hebrew text of the Old Testament)
Mur	Murabba'at
NA[28]	*Novum Testamentum*, Nestle-Aland, 28th ed.
NASB	New American Standard Bible
n.d.	no date
NPNF[2]	*Nicene and Post-Nicene Fathers, Series 2*
NT	New Testament
OT	Old Testament
P[46]	Greek papyrus, second century CE
P[75]	Greek papyrus, early third century CE
p(p).	page(s)
Q	hypothetic "sayings source" of Jesus, agreements between Matthew and Luke
repr.	reprint

rev.	revised (by)
ser.	series
Sifre Deut.	*Sifre to Deuteronomy*
suppl.	supplement
syh	The Harclean Syriac version
Syr.	Syriac
Tg(s).	Targum(s)
trans.	translated by
V	verbatim
v(v).	verse(s)
vol(s).	volume(s)
x	no. of times a form occurs
§	section number(s)
#	number

PRIMARY SOURCES

Old Testament Books

Gen	Genesis
Exod	Exodus
Lev	Leviticus
Num	Numbers
Deut	Deuteronomy
Josh	Joshua
Judg	Judges
1–2 Sam	1–2 Samuel
1–2 Kgs	1–2 Kings
1–2 Chr	1–2 Chronicles
Neh	Nehemiah
Esth	Esther
Ps/Pss	Psalm(s)
Prov	Proverbs
Eccl	Ecclesiastes
Song	Song of Songs (of Solomon)

Isa	Isaiah
Jer	Jeremiah
Lam	Lamentations
Ezek	Ezekiel
Dan	Daniel
Hos	Hosea
Obad	Obadiah
Mic	Micah
Nah	Nahum
Hab	Habakkuk
Zeph	Zephaniah
Hag	Haggai
Zech	Zechariah
Mal	Malachi

New Testament Books

Matt	Matthew
Rom	Romans
1–2 Cor	1–2 Corinthians
Gal	Galatians
Eph	Ephesians
Phil	Philippians
Col	Colossians
1–2 Thess	1–2 Thessalonians
1–2 Tim	1–2 Timothy
Phlm	Philemon
Heb	Hebrews
Jas	James
1–2 Pet	1–2 Peter
Rev	Revelation

Apocrypha and Septuagint

Bar	Baruch

Add Dan	Additions to Daniel
Pr Azar	Prayer of Azariah
Bel	Bel and the Dragon
Sg Three	Song of the Three Young Men
Sus	Susanna
1–2 Esd	1–2 Esdras
Add Esth	Additions to Esther
Ep Jer	Epistle of Jeremiah
Jdt	Judith
1–2 Macc	1–2 Maccabees
3–4 Macc	3–4 Maccabees
Pr Man	Prayer of Manasseh
Ps 151	Psalm 151
Sir	Sirach/Ecclesiasticus
Tob	Tobit
Wis	Wisdom of Solomon

Greek and Latin Works

1 Apol.	Justin, *Apologia i*
Ag. Ap.	Josephus, *Against Apion*
Ant.	Josephus, *Jewish Antiquities*
Arch.	Cicero, *Pro Archia*
Claud.	Suetonius, *Divus Claudius*
Comm. Os.	Jerome, *Commentariorum in Osee libri III*
Dem. ev.	Eusebius, *Demonstratio evangelica*
Conf.	Philo, *De Confusione linguarum*
Epist.	Jerome, *Epistulae*
Geogr.	Strabo, *Geographica*
Haer.	Irenaeus, *Adversus haereses*
Rom. Hist.	Dio Cassius, *Roman History*
Hist.	Tacitus, *Historiae*
Hist. eccl.	Eusebius, *Historia ecclesiastica*
J. W.	Josephus, *Jewish War*
Mos.1, 2	Philo, *De vita Mosis I, II*

Praep. ev.	Eusebius, *Praeparatio evangelica*
Pan.	Epiphanius, *Panarion (Adversus haereses)*
Paneg.	Isocrates, *Panegyricus (Or. 4)*
Pelag.	Jerome, *Adversus Pelagianos dialogi III*
Verr.	Cicero, *In Verrem*
Vir. ill.	Jerome, *De viris illustribus*
Sat.	Juvenal, *Satirae*

SECONDARY SOURCES

Arch	*Archaeology*
BA	*Biblical Archaeologist*
BAIAS	*Bulletin of the Anglo-Israel Archeological Society*
BAR	*Biblical Archaeology Review*
BASOR	*Bulletin of the American Schools of Oriental Research*
BIOSCS	*Bulletin of the International Organization for Septuagint and Cognate Studies*
BJRL	*Bulletin of the John Rylands University Library of Manchester*
BRev	*Bible Review*
CBQ	*Catholic Biblical Quarterly*
EvQ	*Evangelical Quarterly*
ExpTim	*Expository Times*
HTR	*Harvard Theological Review*
IJNA	*International Journal of Nautical Archaeology*
IEJ	*Israel Exploration Journal*
JArch	*Jesus and Archaeology*
JBL	*Journal of Biblical Literature*
JETS	*Journal of the Evangelical Theological Society*
JNES	*Journal of Near Eastern Studies*
JSNT	*Journal for the Study of the New Testament*
JTS	*Journal of Theological Studies*
NovT	*Novum Testamentum*
NovTSup	*Supplements to Novum Testamentum*
NTS	*New Testament Studies*

ResQ	*Restoration Quarterly*
TSK	*Theologische Studien und Kritiken*
TynBul	*Tyndale Bulletin*
WTJ	*Westminster Theological Journal*
ZNW	*Zeitschrift für die neutestamentliche Wissenschaft und die Kunde der älteren Kirche*

Introduction

EARLY IN MY ACADEMIC studies I assumed that the dominant language in first-century CE Palestine was Aramaic and that Jesus and his disciples, therefore, taught and spoke in Aramaic. The problem I encountered in accepting the dominance of Aramaic related to my understanding of the relationship between the GNT and the teachings of Jesus. Did the gospel accounts represent accurately what Jesus taught, or were they misrepresentations of the historical Jesus? Was the Jesus of history different from the Christ of Scripture?[1]

Additionally, based upon the primacy of Aramaic, would not the legitimacy of Christianity be linked to the Aramaic sources underlying the GNT? G. R. Selby accurately describes the dilemma of many Christians who are confused about the nature of the NT: "Not only is there uncertainty about the validity of late twentieth-century life of what these documents say, but also, the historical accuracy of that which is contained within the pages of the Gospels is often challenged."[2]

I began to view the Aramaic Hypothesis[3] as an inadequate solution for many of my questions: (1) If Aramaic was the dominant language in first-century CE Palestine (and throughout the Roman Empire), why were all the NT documents written in Greek? (2) If Aramaic was the dominant

---

1. Schweitzer provides a review of the initial development of the idea of the quest for the historical Jesus, stating that "modern historical theology, therefore, with its three-quarters skepticism, is left at last with only a torn and tattered Gospel of Mark in its hands . . . It is evident, therefore, that this professedly historical Jesus is not a purely historical figure, but one which has been artificially transplanted into history" (*Quest*, 307). For a summary of the current thinking regarding the quest for the historical Jesus, see Brown, "Historical Jesus," 326–41. Evans provides a helpful bibliography of works related to studies regarding the historicity of Jesus in *Life of Jesus*.

2. Selby, *Jesus*, 2.

3. The designation "Aramaic Hypothesis" has become a technical term often connected to studies relating to the historical Jesus and to studies relating to Gospel/NT origins.

language, why was Greek the common language (*koinē*) of the period? (3) If Aramaic was the dominant language, why was Greek so prevalent in the literature, the architecture, and the culture of both Galilee and Judea in the first century CE? (4) If Aramaic was the source behind the Gospels (and the NT), why do the documents of the GNT show signs of being original compositions rather than translations? (5) If Aramaic was the dominant language, why would the Jews be bilingual (some even trilingual)? (6) If Aramaic was the dominant language, why were many cities (e.g., Ptolemais and Scythopolis) and regions (e.g., Decapolis and Idumea) called by Greek names? (7) If Aramaic was the dominant language, why did many Jews adopt Greek names (e.g., Andrew, Philip, Nicodemus, and Theophilus)? (8) If Aramaic was the dominant language, why were Greek customs and practices adopted by the culture (e.g., measurements, pottery, and Greek loanwords)? (9) If Aramaic was the dominant language, why would Jews inscribe words in Greek on ossuaries?

These questions led me to consider the validity of Aramaic's dominance as a language in the first century CE. Stanley Porter makes a very important point about the presuppositions of the Aramaic hypothesis:

> [I]t seems to me that the evidence regarding what is known about the use of Greek in ancient Palestine, including the cosmopolitan Hellenistic character of lower Galilee, the epigraphic and literary evidence, including coins, papyri, literary writers, inscriptions and funerary texts, but most of all several significant contexts in the Gospels, all points in one direction: whereas it is not always known how much and on which occasions Jesus spoke Greek, it is virtually certain that he used Greek at various times in his itinerant ministry . . . This says nothing about the overall linguistic competence of Jesus, nor do we know the frequency with which he used the languages at his disposal. But this conclusion at least opens up the possibility of further exploration of this topic, since it must be recognized that this conclusion has a solid foundation and cannot be ruled out on the basis of presupposition alone.[4]

In the study that follows, I will explore further the possibility that Greek was more widely used in both written and oral form by Jesus, his disciples, and the Jews who inhabited first-century CE Palestine. My thesis is that within the region of Galilee in Roman Palestine in the first century CE, Greek became the *dominant* language spoken among Jews and Gentiles.

---

4. Porter, "Did Jesus Ever Teach in Greek?," 199–235.

Many scholars have argued since the late nineteenth century that the written sources behind the Gospels were Aramaic and that there might have been Aramaic originals of the Gospels themselves.[5] Nigel Turner, however, suggested that though Aramaic might lie behind the Gospels, it is more likely that they were composed in Greek, mimicking in many ways a Semitic syntax and style.[6]

> Since the quality of New Testament Greek is decidedly Semitic in varying degrees, there may well have been a spoken language in common use among these trilingual Jews which would render superfluous the hypothesis of source-translation as an explanation of certain phenomena in New Testament Greek.[7]

Therefore, what we may have in the NT is a *Palestinian* Greek containing Aramaic words and Semitic expressions as were spoken by both Jesus and his disciples. The methodology of research, therefore, will be to examine the archaeological, literary, and biblical evidence that pertains to the languages spoken in Roman Palestine during the first century CE. Such predominance leads to the conclusion that the composition of the GNT writings generally and the Gospel of Matthew specifically were not dependent upon written Aramaic originals. The motivation behind the study was precipitated by an observation made by Joseph A. Fitzmyer:

> If asked what was the language commonly spoken in Palestine in the time of Jesus of Nazareth, most people with some acquaintance of that era and area would almost spontaneously answer Aramaic. To my way of thinking, the defense of this thesis must reckon with the growing mass of evidence that both Greek and Hebrew were being used as well. I would, however, hesitate to say with M. Smith that "at least as much Greek as Aramaic was spoken in Palestine." In any case, the evidence for the use of Aramaic has also been growing in recent years.[8]

The "growing mass of evidence" has now become a convincing witness to the wide use of Greek in Palestine even among the members of the inner circle of disciples who followed Jesus.

This study will focus upon three significant areas. First, the primary geographical area that will be investigated is the land of Palestine, which is defined as that area of land located between the Mediterranean Sea and the

---

5. Wise, "Languages of Palestine," 443.

6. Turner, *Style*, 5–10.

7. Ibid., 7.

8. Fitzmyer, "Languages of Palestine," 501–31.

Arabian Desert and between Sinai and the mountains of Lebanon, within the southern portion of the Temperate Zone situated at the eastern end of the Mediterranean Sea, located at the southwestern end of the Fertile Crescent, and comprising an area including Syria, Lebanon, and Palestine or Israel.[9] Second, the primary focus of the study will be limited to the first century CE, specifically to the lives of Jesus and his closest disciples, namely the apostles and half brothers of Jesus. Third, the primary intent of this study is not exhaustive but only representative in regard to the evidence that is currently available. Emerging issues of minor relevance will be noted in footnotes that reference sources for further review and study.

This study could potentially have a monumental impact upon the currently accepted presuppositions in regard to the gospel tradition and NT studies. I will challenge the presumption that the only linguistic historical connection with Jesus and his disciples is through Aramaic. On the contrary, I will show that in many respects the GNT contains the very words that Jesus and his disciples spoke in Greek.[10]

---

9. Lasor, "Palestine," 632–48.

10. Since the introduction of form criticism in the late eighteenth and early nineteenth centuries, many scholars have detached the composition of the NT documents from historical reality. For example, Koester states, "Whatever Jesus said and did has been refracted in various ways like through a prism in the process of being formed into a tradition of the community. The original life situation of a saying or story in the life of Jesus is no longer accessible, because the formation of all traditions is deeply embedded in communal life situations" (*History and Literature*, 62).

CHAPTER 1

Did Jesus and His Disciples Speak Greek?

WHAT LANGUAGES WERE SPOKEN in first-century Palestine? Did Jesus and his disciples speak and teach in Greek? If so, do we have in the NT historical preservations of their actual communication? These questions have generated a rich debate through the years. It has been the general consensus among scholars that in order to recover the real Jesus of history it is necessary to uncover the Aramaic behind the Greek. For example, Maurice Casey makes this statement:

> If therefore we wish to recover the Jesus of History, we must see whether we can reconstruct his sayings, and the earliest accounts of his doings, in their original Aramaic. This should help us to understand him within his own cultural background.[1]

Greater recognition, however, should be given to the fact that many languages were current in Palestine during the time of Jesus. While it is generally agreed that Aramaic and Hebrew were key languages of the period, it is my purpose to demonstrate the widespread use of Greek and to argue that Jesus not only spoke Greek but also taught in Greek. Consequently, the Gospels may contain the very words that Jesus spoke instead of translations into Greek of Jesus' original words in Aramaic.[2]

1. Casey, *Aramaic Sources*, 1.

2. Wise notes that since the late nineteenth century scholars have held two basic assumptions regarding the influence of Aramaic upon the NT. First, scholars have assumed that Jesus spoke only in Aramaic. Second, they have also assumed that since Jesus spoke only in Aramaic his disciples preserved a record of sayings in Aramaic. See Wise, "Languages of Palestine," 434–44. This record or source is often identified in Synoptic studies as "Q," used by both Matthew and Luke (but not by Mark) in the

Joseph Fitzmyer argues that there are three important stages in the gospel tradition. First, stage one refers to the *Aramaic period* of the actual ministry and teachings of Jesus (1–33 CE), a period before the Gospels were written. Second, stage two represents the *Apostolic period* when the disciples and apostles taught and preached about the words and deeds of Jesus (33–66 CE). Third, stage three (66–95 CE) represents the canonical *Gospel period* reflecting a development of Greek writing. Fitzmyer's point is to remind readers not to confuse later Greek tradition with the early Aramaic of stage one. To do so is to "fall into the danger of fundamentalism."[3]

I find Fitzmyer's stages of gospel tradition unconvincing. They may reveal a bias toward a history-of-religions approach by incorrectly presupposing that Aramaic was the dominant language of Palestine and that the Greek compositions of the Gospels represent an advancement (stage three) in gospel tradition. If Jesus did indeed speak Greek, then we may have "direct access to the original utterances of our Lord and not only to a translation of them."[4] Consequently, much more than just a few Aramaic words and expressions can be connected to the Jesus of history. Porter's observation is therefore insightful:

> It is not possible to settle the various issues regarding the linguistic milieu of first-century Palestine, as Fitzmyer rightly notes, except to say that the archaeological, linguistic and sociological evidence seems to indicate that the region was multilingual, including at least Aramaic and Greek in widespread and frequent

composition of their respective gospels. Scholars like C. H. Weisse (1838), G. H. A. Ewald (1848), H. J. Holzman (1863), Sir John C. Hawkins (1899), and B. H. Streeter (1924) were early proponents of the existence of "Q." See Stein, *Synoptic Gospels*, 97–123; see also Stein, "Synoptic Problem," 784–92, and Michaels, "Apostolic Fathers," 203–13. Turner observed, "If Greek was understood well enough in Palestine to warrant issuing the Gospels in that language, it is strange that Palestinians who later became Christians needed to have their Scriptures in a Palestinian Aramaic version, the 'Palestinian-Syriac' which was provided by Byzantine emperors of the Christianized Palestinians." See Turner, *Style*, 5–10. Additionally, what drives the assumption that Aramaic lies behind the Greek, especially in regard to the Gospel of Matthew, is the statement by Papias (second century CE) preserved by Eusebius stating that "Matthew collected the oracles in the Hebrew language, and each interpreted them as best he could" (*Hist. eccl.* 3.39.15). Lamsa argues that the entire NT is dependent upon Aramaic sources (*New Testament Origin*). Scholars like Torrey (*The Four Gospels*), Black ("Recovery," 305–13, and *Aramaic Approach*), Butler (*Originality*), and Parker (*Gospel*) argue for a more modest position of confining Aramaic dependency to the Gospels. Rife asserts that in actuality "Matthew shows less evidence of being a translation from a Semitic original than does Mark." See Rife, "Greek Language," 571.

3. Fitzmyer, "Did Jesus Speak Greek?," 58–77.

4. Argyle, "Did Jesus Speak Greek?," 92–93.

use. . . . Therefore, the likelihood that Jesus, along with most Gentiles and Jews, was multilingual himself is strong.[5]

A GENERAL OVERVIEW OF THE LANGUAGES OF PALESTINE IN THE FIRST CENTURY CE

There is no doubt that Jesus spoke Aramaic. Jesus would have spoken a form of Middle Aramaic called Palestinian Aramaic. Fitzmyer indicates that there were five dialects of Middle Aramaic: (1) Palestinian, (2) Nabatean (around Petra in modern Jordan), (3) Palmyrene (central Syria), (4) Hatran (eastern Syria and Iraq), and (5) Syriac (northern Syria and southern Turkey).[6] Prior to 1947 CE, the date when the DSS were discovered, Palestinian Aramaic was supported only by a meager number of inscriptions on tombstones and ossuaries. Consequently, Gustaf Dalman argued that though Jesus may have known Hebrew and more than likely spoke Greek, he nonetheless certainly taught in Aramaic.[7]

However, since 1947 CE, many literary texts have been discovered that shed light on the dialect of Aramaic spoken by Palestinian Jews prior to and contemporaneous with Jesus.[8] The DSS reveal that Aramaic may have been the dominant language,[9] but the evidence reveals that it was not the only language spoken.[10] Therefore one cannot conclusively argue that Jesus spoke *only* Aramaic.[11] Palestine was multilingual in the first and second

5. Porter, *Language*, 27.

6. Fitzmyer, "The Phases of the Aramaic Language," 57–84.

7. This observation is from Porter, "Did Jesus Ever Teach in Greek?," 199, who relied upon the work of Dalman, *Jesus–Jeshua*.

8. Interestingly, Greek documents were also found at Qumran. Millard states that "while these Greek texts are very much in the minority among the Hebrew and Aramaic scrolls, they indicate an awareness of Greek and, presumably, the presence of people who could read them, even if they were not copied in the Qumran region but had been brought into the country from outside." Millard, *Reading and Writing*, 113.

9. Smelik observes that "Aramaic is widely held to have been the vernacular most commonly used by Jews throughout the Roman period. That Aramaic was widespread in Hellenistic and Roman Palestine seemed obvious to scholars even before the Qumran discoveries because of the Aramaic texts, quotations, loanwords, and names referred to above." See Smelik, "Languages," 126. Wise also states that "it would seem that Aramaic was the best-known and most widely used language among Jews of all classes in Galilee and in Judea also, at least in the larger urban areas" ("Languages of Palestine," 439).

10. "Given modern analogies, it is likely that Palestine in Jesus' day was a welter of dialects and languages, many of which have left no written record at all" (ibid., 434).

11. Selby, *Jesus*, 4. Sevenster writes, "it has become practically a generally accepted tradition that the mother tongue of Jesus, the language he knew best and therefore

centuries CE.[12] Hebrew was the language employed by the Essenes who settled at Qumran (adjacent to the caves where the DSS were found) in order to preserve the sacred Law (i.e., the Torah) of the Jews.[13] Hebrew by this time had become the language associated with temple rituals and worship in synagogues where the Law and Prophets (the Torah and the *Nevi'im*) were read. The majority of the Jews no longer understood Hebrew.[14]

Aramaic, the sister language of Hebrew, was by necessity learned by Jews in Babylonian captivity (sixth century BCE) because it was the *lingua franca* of the empire.[15] Fitzmyer stated that "the use of Hebrew does not seem to have been widespread" as a spoken language after the Jews returned home.[16] Hebrew was customarily translated orally into Aramaic by a person called the *meturgeman* ("translator"). These translations from Hebrew were eventually written in Aramaic and were called *targumim* (singular, *targum*).[17]

Scholars have argued since the late nineteenth century that the sources behind the Gospels were Aramaic and that there might have been Aramaic

---

usually spoke, was Aramaic." See Sevenster, *Do You Know Greek?*, 33.

12. This chapter does not give an overview of Latin because it seems to have been "used primarily by the Romans in political and administrative matters." See Porter, *Language*, 27.

13. Opinions among scholars vary as to the identity of those who authored the DSS. In addition to the Essenes, connections have also been made to both Pharisaic and Sadducean sects. See Buchanan, "Essenes," 152.

14. There is the belief, however, from more recent evidence that Hebrew was not as scarce among the spoken languages as many scholars had previously argued. See Sevenster, *Do You Know Greek?*, 34. However, Dalman argued that "Aramaic became the language of the Jews to such an extent that the Gospel of St John as well as Josephus found it possible to designate such Aramaic words as *beza'ta, golgolta, gabbeta, asarta, rabbuni* . . . as Hebrew." See Dalman, *Jesus—Jeshua*, 15.

15. "[A]lthough Imperial Aramaic was the *lingua franca* and served for many official purposes, the Jews continued to use Hebrew in connection with the government and Temple." See Wise, "Languages of Palestine," 435. Dalman noted that "the spread of Aramaic in the originally Hebrew Palestine must already have begun in the year 721 B.C., when Samaria was peopled by Mesopotamian colonists. Through the influence of the Babylonian and, later, the Persian Governments it continued to spread: finally reaching Southern Palestine, when the leading classes were deported from there and supplanted by the alien element" (*Jesus—Jeshua*, 9).

16. Fitzmyer, "Did Jesus Speak Greek?," 58; see also Emerton, "Vernacular Hebrew," 1–23. It is the assumption of many scholars that "the 'Hebrew'-speaking Jews of Palestine actually spoke Aramaic, and not Hebrew. Hence it is assumed that, wherever mention is made of the Hebrew language . . . in the New Testament . . . Aramaic is what is actually meant." See Sevenster, *Do You Know Greek?*, 34.

17. Three *targumim* were discovered among the DSS—the *targum* of Job from cave 11 and the *targumim* of Leviticus and Job from cave 4.

originals of the Gospels themselves.[18] Nigel Turner, however, suggested that though Aramaic might lie behind the Gospels, it is more likely that they were composed in Greek, mimicking in many ways a Semitic syntax and style.[19]

> Since the quality of New Testament Greek is decidedly Semitic in varying degrees, there may well have been a spoken language in common use among these trilingual Jews which would render superfluous the hypothesis of source-translation as an explanation of certain phenomena in New Testament Greek.[20]

Therefore, what we may have in the NT is a hybrid *Palestinian* Greek containing occasional Aramaic words and Semitic overtones.

Greek was widespread and was spoken by even the Romans and the Jews. Most scholars have recognized that "Greek was the *lingua franca* of the Greco-Roman world and the predominant language of the Roman Empire."[21] Consequently, as the Jews were compelled to learn Aramaic during captivity and the years following it, they were similarly pressured "to learn Greek in order to communicate broadly within the social structure" of their larger communities.[22]

Further evidence of the dominance of Greek among Jews is found in rabbinic sources that contain provisions for those who did not speak Hebrew. For example, the Mishnah[23] allows the following accommodation regarding the recitation of certain passages of Scripture:

> These are said in any language: (1) the pericope of the accused wife [Num 5:19–22], and (2) the confession of the tithe [Deut 26:13–15], and (3) the recital of the *Shema*, [Deut 6:4–9], and (4) the Prayer, (5) the oath of testimony, and (6) the oath

18. Wise, "Languages of Palestine," 443.

19. Turner, *Style*, 5–10.

20. Ibid., 7.

21. Porter, "Did Jesus Ever Teach in Greek?," 205.

22. Ibid., 209. Different forms of a language develop as communities assimilate to cultures and languages. *Diglossia* is a process by which a language develops into forms—a classical or high form and a rudimentary or lower form. The high form becomes the language of literature and the low form is the vehicle of everyday communication. This phenomenon is also referred to as "code switching." It is my contention that the lower form of *koinē* Greek contained a Palestinian dialect that included Aramaic words and expressions. See also Wise, "Languages of Palestine," 434.

23. The Mishnah is a compilation of sixty-two tractates of rabbinical teaching or "philosophical law code" that addresses various theoretical and practical topics. It was produced around 200 CE, though much of the content refers to the oral teachings of famous rabbis of an earlier time. See Neusner, *Rabbinic Literature*, 97–128.

concerning a bailment. And these are said [only] in the Holy Language: (1) the verses of the firstfruits [Deut 26:3–10], (2) the rite of *halisah* [Deut 25:7, 9], (3) blessings and curses [Deut 27:15–26], (4) the blessing of the priests [Num 6:24–26], (5) the blessing of a high priest [on the Day of Atonement], (6) the pericope of the king [Deut 17:14–20]; (7) the pericope of the heifer whose neck is to be broken [Deut 21:7f.], and (8) [the message of] the anointed for battle when he speaks to the people [Deut 20:2–7] (*m. Sot.* 7:1, 2).[24]

Additionally, other rabbinic writings contain specific instruction regarding the recitation of Deut 26:1–11:

There is a provision here for "responding," and elsewhere there is an equivalent provision [at Deut 27:14]. Just as "responding" at that other passage requires use of the Holy Language, so "responding" stated here requires use of the Holy Language. In this connection sages have said, "In earlier times whoever knew how to recite [in Hebrew] would make the recitation, and whoever did not know how to recite—they would recite in his behalf. Consequently people refrained from bringing first fruits [out of shame]. Sages made the rule that [priests] would recite in behalf of both those who knew how to make the recitation as well as those who did not know how to make the recitation. They ruled upon the verse of Scripture, "And you shall then respond" . . . maintain that "responding" is solely to what others say (*Sifre Deut.* 301).[25]

Although certain sections of Hebrew Scripture were only to be recited in the Holy Language, the fact remains that, by necessity, the religious leaders adapted in many respects to the cultural milieu of their people. Interestingly, according to another tractate of the Mishnah, a Torah scroll could also be written in Greek:

There is no difference between sacred scrolls and phylacteries and *mezuzot* except that sacred scrolls may be written in any alphabet ["language"], while phylacteries and *mezuzot* are written only in square [Assyrian] letters. Rabban Simion b. Gamaliel says, "Also: in the case of sacred scrolls: they have been permitted to be written only in Greek" (*m. Meg.* 1:8).[26]

---

24. Neusner, *Mishnah*, 457.

25. Neusner, *Sifre to Deuteronomy*, 276.

26. Ibid., 318.

This ruling appears to be at odds with other stipulations, most notably the requirement of using the Hebrew square script for the writing of Torah scrolls:

> The Aramaic [passages contained in Scriptures] written in Hebrew, or a Hebrew [version] written in Aramaic or [passages written in archaic] Hebrew script do not impart uncleanness to hands. [Holy Scriptures] impart uncleanness to hands only if written in Assyrian characters, on parchment, and with ink (*m. Yad.* 4:5).[27]

Although the Mishnah was composed around 200 CE, the philosophical foundation and interpretation of the Torah found within it are based upon the interpretations and teachings of rabbis of an earlier period. This is highly significant in demonstrating the extent to which Greek had made deep advances into the very heart of Jewish culture.

Greek was the language of both secular and sacred literature. Outside of Palestine, Jews wrote regularly in Greek. One of the most prolific Jewish writers was Philo (ca. 20 BCE to 40 CE), a contemporary of Jesus.[28] In his book, *De Confusione linguarum*, Philo compares the tower of Babel to the one that Gideon swore to destroy during the period of the Judges (Judg 8:9) as the place where people turn from God:

> That name is in the Hebrew tongue (Εβραῖοι) Penuel, but in our own "turning from God." For the stronghold which was built through persuasiveness of argument was built solely for the purpose of diverting and deflecting the mind from honouring God (*Conf.* 126 §129 [Colson and Whitaker, LCL]).

Notice how Philo defines the meaning of the Hebrew name *Penuel* by giving the translation in his own tongue which of course is Greek. Philo's references to the "Hebrew tongue" and "our own" reveal how significantly Greek had eclipsed Hebrew as the common language among both the Jewish educated class and the Jewish common people outside of Palestine. It would seem that if the educated leaders of the Jewish population were already writing and speaking in Greek outside of Palestine, much of the Jewish population in Palestine must have been losing the ability to read, write, and speak in Hebrew.

Alexandria, Egypt, was known as the center of intellectualism and Hellenistic influence among the Jews. In this city, the Hebrew Scriptures were translated into Greek (ca. 250 BCE), and the Septuagint (LXX), the "Bible"

27. Ibid., 1130; see also Smelik, "Languages," 125.

28. Millard, *Reading and Writing*, 112.

of the Jews, was produced. The textual evidence reveals that the Scripture more often quoted by NT writers was the LXX translation, not the Hebrew text. In fact, Everett Ferguson asserted the following:

> Much of the grammar, vocabulary, and thought-world of the New Testament finds its best parallel and illustration in the Septuagint. The distinctive religious meaning of many New Testament words (e.g., *ekklēsia, baptisma, presbyteros, psallō, cheirontonia*) is to be found not from etymology or classical usage but from the adaptations already made by Greek-speaking Jews, as known from the Septuagint, Philo, Josephus, the Apocrypha, and the Pseudepigrapha. On such theological and religious terms and on ways of things, the influence of the Septuagint on New Testament vocabulary and theology is extensive.[29]

The weight of the evidence appears to point to Greek as the spoken and written language of Gentiles *and* Jews without and within Palestine, as will be shown in the next section.

A GENERAL OVERVIEW OF THE EVIDENCE OF GREEK IN PALESTINE

The penetration of Greek into Palestine had already begun before the conquests of Alexander the Great (fourth century BCE).[30] However, the hellenization of Palestine accelerated afterwards, especially under the Seleucid monarch Antiochus IV Epiphanes (second century BCE), and continued under Ptolemaic, Seleucid, Hasmonean, and Herodian kings. By the third and fourth centuries CE, Greek had practically replaced the Semitic languages of Palestine.[31]

The Edomite-Greek ostracon (277 BCE), found at Khirbet el-Kôm in 1971 CE, is the earliest Greek text discovered in Palestine.[32] This ostracon

29. Ferguson, *Backgrounds*, 437–38.

30. "[T]he Jews of Palestine had long known of the Greeks and perhaps some of them had had reason to learn some Greek, but the real advance followed upon Alexander." See Wise, "Languages of Palestine," 439.

31. Hengel provides a detailed analysis of the archaeological and literary data that demonstrates the advances of Hellenism in Palestine from the fourth century BCE to the first century CE. See Hengel, *Judaism and Hellenism*. See also Wilson, "Hellenistic Judaism," 477–82.

32. Khirbet el-Kôm, located between Hebron and Lachish, is the modern Arabic name of the village that rests upon an ancient site dating back to the Early Bronze Age. Ostraca numbers 1, 2, 4, and 5 are written in Aramaic, ostracon number 6 is Greek, and number 3 is a nine-lined bilingual ostracon. See Geraty, "Kôm, Khirbet El-," 99–100.

is a receipt dated "year 6," presumably the sixth year of Ptolemy II Philadelphus.[33] Although this discovery does indicate the presence of Greek, it does
not indicate how widely Greek might have been used at that time. Louis
Feldman states that "the bilingual character of the Edomite-Greek ostracon
would appear to indicate that Greek was not the primary language of the
inhabitants."[34] The purpose, however, in mentioning the ostracon is not to
argue for Greek as a dominant language of the period but to illustrate the
use of Greek in ordinary human affairs. Wise makes the following important observation:

> This ostracon, a bilingual Aramaic and Greek record of a loan,
> shows that Greek loanwords had already begun to invade Ara-
> maic, even for mundane concepts and matters for which per-
> fectly good words already existed in Aramaic.[35]

The presence of Greek in the ostracon provides evidence of Greek in common communication. Feldman further observes that "if we ask why Greek
was employed at all, we may reply that perhaps it was intended to deter
non-Jewish passers-by from molesting the graves."[36] Though Feldman sees
no real evidence from this discovery to substantiate the common usage of
Greek by the Jews of Judea, one could argue that efforts were made by Jews
to communicate in Greek with their Greek neighbors, thus revealing the
close contact that Jews had with the Greek language.

Much early Jewish literature was written in Greek by historians, poets,
and military generals.[37] Justice of Tiberias, a bitter enemy of Flavius Josephus (ca. 37–100 CE), had received a Hellenistic education.[38] He was also a
historian during the First Jewish Revolt against Rome (66–70 CE). Justice
wrote the "History of the Jews against Vespasian."[39] In response to Justice,
Josephus wrote his first version of the *Jewish War* in Aramaic and then the
final form in Greek.[40] In another work called *Jewish Antiquities*, Josephus
makes an interesting comment about the Greek language:

> My compatriots admit that in our Jewish learning I far excel
> them. But I labored hard to steep myself in Greek prose [and

---

33. Geraty, "Bilingual Ostracon," 55–61.

34. Feldman, *Jew and Gentile*, 14.

35. Wise, "Languages of Palestine," 439.

36. Feldman, *Jew and Gentile*, 14.

37. Fitzmyer, "Did Jesus Speak Greek?," 59; Holladay, *Fragments*.

38. Schreckenberg, "Josephus," 132–33.

39. Holladay, *Fragments*, 371–76.

40. Millard, *Reading and Writing*, 113.

poetic learning], after having gained a knowledge of Greek
grammar; but the constant use of my native tongue hindered
my achieving precision in pronunciation. For our people do not
welcome those who have mastered the speech of many nations
or adorn their style with smoothness of diction, because they
consider that such skill is not only common to ordinary freedmen, but that even slaves acquire it, if they so choose. Rather,
they give credit for wisdom to those who acquire an exact
knowledge of the Law and can interpret Holy Scriptures. Consequently, though many have laboriously undertaken this study,
scarcely two or three have succeeded (in it) and reaped the fruit
of their labors (*Ant.* 20.12.1 [Feldman, LCL]).

Although Josephus admits his own difficulty of mastering Greek, he does
not imply that Greek was sparsely spoken. He had a command of the language even if spoken in a "broken form of Greek."[41] Josephus was also the
interpreter for the Roman general Titus when he spoke to the Jewish popu-
lace near the end of the war. Such a post provided Josephus the opportunity
to sharpen his abilities to speak on behalf of Roman authorities, write historical accounts of Roman activities, and serve as a translator. He described
the strategy of Titus as follows:

Blending active operations with advice, and aware that speech is
often more effectual than arms, he not only personally exhorted
them to seek salvation by the surrender of the city, already practically taken, but also delegated Josephus to parley with them
in their native tongue, thinking that possibly they might yield
to the expostulation of a fellow-countryman. Josephus, accordingly, went around the wall, and, endeavoring to keep out of
range of missiles and yet within ear-shot, repeatedly implored
them to spare themselves and the people, to spare their country and their temple, and not to display towards them greater
indifference than was shown by aliens. (*J.W.* 5.9.2–3 §361–62
[Thackeray, LCL]).

Josephus therefore appears to have been overly modest about his Greek
language skills.[42]

Inscriptions solely in Greek and bilingual inscriptions in Greek and
Hebrew/Aramaic were used on ossuaries near the vicinity of Jerusalem. At
one particular excavation at Mt. Olivet, twenty-nine ossuaries were found
containing inscriptions in Hebrew (seven), Aramaic (eleven), and Greek

---

41. Fitzmyer, "Did Jesus Speak Greek?," 59.
42. Wise, "Languages of Palestine," 440.

(eleven). These ossuaries date before the Jewish war with the Romans (66–73 CE). Robert Gundry makes the following observation:

> One would think that in the presence of death a language of the heart would have been used, a language in which people habitually thought and spoke. Yet all three languages in question appear on the ossuary finds in roughly equal proportions.[43]

Evidence of this kind would appear to counter Matthew Black's assertion that the dominant linguistic setting of the first century was Aramaic:

> Greek was the speech of the educated "hellenized" classes and the medium of cultural and commercial intercourse between Jew and foreigner; Latin was the language of the army of occupation and, to judge from Latin borrowings in Aramaic, appears also to some extent to have served that purpose of commerce; Hebrew, the sacred tongue of the Jewish Scriptures, continued to provide the lettered Jew with an important means of literary expression and was cultivated as a spoken tongue in the learned coteries of the Rabbis; Aramaic was the language of the people of the land and, together with Hebrew, provided the chief literary medium of the Palestinian Jew of the first century; Josephus wrote his *Jewish War* in Aramaic and later translated it into Greek.[44]

Based upon the archaeological evidence, Black's assertion seems exaggerated. What we find is that all three languages—Hebrew, Aramaic, and Greek—were commonly used in the first century. As Gundry notes, "We are not dealing with an either/or, but with a both/and."[45]

The longest Greek inscription is the Theodotus Inscription dating in the first half of the first century CE. The inscription reads as follows:[46]

ΘΕΟΔΟΤΟΣ . ΟΥΕΤΤΕΝΟΥ . ΙΕΡΕΥΣ . ΚΑΙ
ΑΡΧΙΣΥΝΑΓΩΓΟΣ . ΥΙΟΣ. ΑΡΧΙΣΥΝ[ΑΓΩ]–
Γ[Ο]Υ . ΥΙΟΝΟΣ . ΑΡΧΙΣΥΝ[Α]ΓΩΓΟΥ . ΩΚΟ–
ΔΟΜΗΣΕ . ΤΗΝ . ΣΥΝΑΓΩΓ[Η]Ν . ΕΙΣ . ΑΝ[ΑΓ]ΝΩ–
Σ[Ι]Ν . ΝΟΜΟΥ . ΚΑΙ . ΕΙΣ . [Δ]ΙΔΑΧΗΝ . ΕΝΤΟΛΩΝ ΚΑΙ
ΤΟΝ . ΞΕΝΩΝΑ . ΚΑ[Ι . ΤΑ] . ΔΩΜΑΤΑ . ΚΑΙ . ΤΑ. ΧΠΗ–

43. Gundry, "Language Milieu," 406; see also Hughes, "Languages Spoken by Jesus," 133.

44. Black, *Aramaic Approach*, 15–16; Hughes, "Languages Spoken by Jesus," 127–28.

45. Gundry, "Language Milieu," 405.

46. Dots have been added to the inscription to indicate word breaks, and hyphens have also been added to denote line breaks. See Hanson and Oakman, "Theodotus Inscription," lines 1–10.

Σ[T]ΗΡΙΑ . ΤΩΝ . ΥΔΑΤΩΝ . ΕΙΣ . ΚΑΤΑΛΥΜΑ . ΤΟΙ–
Σ . [Χ]ΠΗΖΟΥΣΙΝ . ΑΠΟ . ΤΗΣ . ΞΕ[Ν]ΗΣ . ΗΝ . ΕΘΕΜΕ–
Λ[ΙΩ]ΣΑΝ . ΟΙ . ΠΑΤΕΡΕΣ . [Α]ΥΤΟΥ . ΚΑΙ . ΟΙ . ΠΡΕ–
Σ[Β]ΥΤΕΡΟΙ . ΚΑΙ . ΣΙΜΩΝ[Ι]ΔΗΣ

Theodotus, son of Vettenus, priest and synagogue ruler, son
and grandson of a synagogue ruler, (re-)built the synagogue for
reading the law and teaching the commandments, also the guest
room and upstairs rooms and the water supplies as an inn for
those from abroad in need, which his ancestors and the elders
and Simonides founded.[47]

The importance of this inscription cannot easily be underestimated. The
existence of an inscription of this kind in Greek indicates that Jewish leaders
and synagogue attendees had accommodated themselves to, or had assimilated, the language of their Greek neighbors. The inscription may imply that
the Jews who were Jesus' contemporaries were already using Greek in their
everyday communication, further substantiating a multilingual presence in
Palestine.

The period between the destruction of Jerusalem/temple in 70 CE and
the Second Jewish Revolt (Bar-Kokhba revolt) in 135 CE has yielded many
archaeological discoveries. Numerous Greek papyri have been unearthed
during this period. The discoveries include letters, marriage contracts, legal
documents, literary texts, and some undeciphered Greek shorthand.[48] One
of the more fascinating discoveries is the Letter of Bar-Kokhba written in
Greek to his lieutenants. The translation reads as follows:

Sou[mai]os to Jonathe,
(son of) Baianos, and Ma-
[s]abbala, greetings!
S[i]nce I have sent to
You A[g]rippa, make
H[ast]e to send me
B[e]am[s] and citrons.
And furnish th[em]
For the [C]itron-celebration of the
Jews; and do not do
Otherwise. Not[w] (this) has been writ-
Ten in Greek because
a[de]sire has not be[en]

47. Albright, *Recent Discoveries*, 112; Thompson, *Bible and Archaeology*, 332; Millard, *Reading and Writing*, 110.

48. Fitzmyer, "Did Jesus Speak Greek?," 77.

found to w[ri]te in Hebrew. De[s]patch
him quickly
fo[r t]he feast,
an[d do no]t
do otherwise.
Soumaios.
Farewell.[49]

Fitzmyer makes an insightful observation in regard to this letter:

> Thus, at a time when nationalist fever must have been running high among the Jews, the leader of the revolt—or someone close to him—frankly preferred to write in Greek. He did not find the *horma*, "impulse, desire," to write *hebraisti*.[50]

If Greek had not by this time emerged as the dominant language, one wonders why a Jewish nationalist would have written and perhaps would have spoken predominantly in Greek. Even if one argues that Aramaic is to be understood when the term Hebrew is employed, the point still remains that Greek had upstaged Aramaic by the first quarter of the second century CE.

The Herodian Temple Inscription found in 1935 outside the wall around Jerusalem's Old City near St. Stephen's Gate (the Lion's Gate) warns Gentiles in Greek that they must keep out. The nineteen-inch-high limestone fragment dates back to the time of Jesus. A complete version of the same inscription was found in the late nineteenth century CE. A translation of the full version reads as follows:

> Let no Gentile enter within the partition and barrier surrounding the Temple, and whosoever is caught shall be responsible for his subsequent death.[51]

The inscription confirms what Josephus wrote in his *Jewish War*:

> Upon [the partition wall of the Temple court] stood pillars, at equal distances from one another, declaring the law of purity, some in Greek, and some in Roman letters, that "no foreigners should go within that sanctuary." . . . (*J.W.* 5.5.2 §193–94 [Thackeray, LCL]).

These inscriptions are extremely valuable because they demonstrate the use of the Greek language by Jews to communicate with their Gentile neighbors; though in the above case, the communication was less than cordial.

49. Fitzmyer, *Wandering Aramean*, 36.
50. Fitzmyer, "Did Jesus Speak Greek?," 60.
51. Ibid., 61.

A GENERAL OVERVIEW OF THE BIBLICAL EVIDENCE THAT JESUS AND HIS DISCIPLES SPOKE IN GREEK

The evidence so far considered has been extrabiblical evidence in regard to the use of the Greek language in Palestine in the time of Jesus. Nothing about the extrabiblical evidence is conclusive, but when such evidence is corroborated with the biblical record it becomes much more convincing that Jesus spoke and taught in Greek. The biblical record attests to the multilingual environment in which Jesus and his disciples lived.

In Luke's history of the early church, Jewish Christians are referred to as both Ἑβραῖοι and Ἑλληνιστάι:

> Ἐν δὲ ταῖς ἡμέραις ταύταις πληθυνόντων τῶν μαθητῶν ἐγένετο γογγυσμὸς τῶν Ἑλληνιστῶν πρὸς τοὺς Ἑβραίους, ὅτι παρεθεωροῦντο ἐν τῇ διακονίᾳ τῇ καθημερινῇ αἱ χῆραι αὐτῶν (Acts 6:1; cf. 9:29).[52]

> On this day when the disciples were increasing, a complaint arose among the Hellenists against the Hebrews for their widows were being neglected in the daily serving.[53]

Hellenistic Jews may have spoken very little Hebrew or Aramaic.[54] Although Paul seems to imply that he was culturally and religiously an orthodox Jew—"Hebrew of Hebrews" (Phil 3:5)—he nevertheless is highly capable of writing and speaking in Greek (e.g., Acts 21:37–40). The reference to Hellenistic Jews may strictly refer to those who habitually spoke Greek, and the native Hebrew Jews were those more likely to have spoken in a Semitic language (Aramaic).[55] Despite the fact that Jews within and immediately surrounding Jerusalem may have conversed in Hebrew or Aramaic, they must have had the linguistic ability to converse with their Hellenistic counterparts, particularly since they were able to understand their "complaint." The prejudice may have been more about culture than language per se. The

---

52. All citations in Greek are from NA[28].

53. All English translations are mine unless otherwise indicated.

54. Koester states, "Jerusalem was a metropolis of worldwide significance, largely because of the Jewish dispersion, for which that city was still the true center of the cult and the symbol of the religion of Israel during the early Roman imperial period. But the vast majority of all adherents to this religion lived in the diaspora and had long since adopted the language and culture of their various places of residence outside Palestine, where most of them had lived for centuries, that is, they had become Hellenized" (*History and Literature*, 97).

55. Moule, "Who Were the Hellenists?," 100–102.

Greek-speaking Jews were fully assimilated by Greek culture. Their language was evidence of the assimilation.[56]

Although Latin was primarily used among Roman officials for administrative purposes, it is highly unlikely that Pilate, the Roman Prefect, would have conversed with Jesus in Latin (or in Aramaic, for that matter) during Jesus' trial. Greek would have been the natural conversational medium (see Mark 15:2–5; Matt 27:11–14; Luke 23:3; John 18:33–38). Paul once urged Timothy to ἀγωνίζου τὸν καλὸν ἀγῶνα τῆς πίστεως ("fight the good fight of faith," 1 Tim 6:12) consistent with τὴν καλὴν ὁμολογίαν ("the good confession") that he had made in the presence of many witnesses. Such action, Paul argued, would be following the model of Jesus, τοῦ μαρτυρήσαντος ἐπὶ Ποντίου Πιλάτου τὴν καλὴν ὁμολογίαν ("the one who testified before Pontius Pilate the good confession," 1 Tim 6:13). Jesus and Pilate did converse with one another, but it is not likely that a Roman like Pilate would have been able to speak Hebrew or Aramaic or that he would have wanted to do so.[57] Additionally, there is no indication in the text that a translator was involved. Since the common language shared between them would have been Greek, would it not be reasonable to assume that both of them conversed in it?[58]

In fact, the Synoptic parallels of the interaction between Pilate and Jesus when compared with the Gospel of John may indicate that the very words of Jesus have been preserved. There are multiple attestations in all four Gospels regarding the question Pilate asked Jesus:

σὺ εἶ ὁ βασιλεὺς τῶν Ἰουδαίων;[59]
Are you the king of the Jews?

The Synoptic Gospels agree and record Jesus' response to Pilate's question with the following words:

σὺ λέγεις.
You say.

---

56. Bruce states, however, that "the main distinction between the two groups was probably linguistic: The Hellenists were Jews whose habitual language was Greek and who attended Greek-speaking synagogues; the Hebrews spoke Aramaic (or Mishnaic Hebrew) and attended synagogues where the service was conducted in Hebrew." Bruce, *Acts*, 120.

57. As a Roman governor, Pilate would have had disdain for Jewish customs and certainly may have thought it beneath his dignity as a Roman to talk in a Semitic language. See Wise, "Languages of Palestine," 442.

58. The use of Latin in Palestine will be addressed in chapter 2.

59. Cf. Mark 15:2, Matt 27:11, Luke 23:3, and John 18:33.

However, the Gospel of John provides an extended response seemingly to clearly indicate that Jesus claims to be a king:

σὺ λέγεις ὅτι βασιλεύς εἰμι.[60]
You say that I am a king.

The Greek phrase σὺ λέγεις does not occur in any other place in the Synoptic Gospels and as such would not likely have been the result of an act of redaction on the part of some author. The multiple attestations by both the Synoptic Gospels and the Gospel of John coupled with the complete dissimilarity of wording when analyzed within the text of the Synoptic Gospels argue favorably that at least two words—σὺ λέγεις—may have been the actual words that Jesus spoke.[61] This observation on the surface may seem trivial; however, if these are the actual words of Jesus, then the premise that the Gospels are simply translations of Aramaic originals cannot stand.

During his Galilean ministry, Jesus entered Capernaum where he met a desperate man who had an ill servant βέβληται ἐν τῇ οἰκίᾳ παραλυτικός, δεινῶς βασανιζόμενος ("a paralytic was cast down in the house, being tormented terribly," Matt 8:6). Matthew identifies the man as a ἑκατόνταρχος ("centurion") while John chooses the Greek term βασιλικός ("royal officer"). This soldier obviously held a position of some authority. After the encounter, Jesus complimented the insight of the centurion and held him up before the Jews as an example of great faith. The centurion likely would not have been able to converse in Hebrew or Aramaic and, as I have attempted to show, Greek would have been the most common language spoken among the people who lived in the Galilean region (cf. Matt 8:5–13; Luke 7:2–10; John 4:43–46).

Mark records an event while Jesus was in the region of Tyre in which he conversed with a woman described as being of the Syrophoenician race. The woman had a daughter who was possessed by an unclean spirit. After hearing Jesus, the woman came and fell at his feet, pleading for him to cast out the demon. Jesus responded with what seemed to be some rather harsh words:

καὶ ἔλεγεν αὐτῇ· ἄφες πρῶτον χορτασθῆναι τὰ τέκνα, οὐ γάρ ἐστιν καλὸν λαβεῖν τὸν ἄρτον τῶν τέκνων καὶ τοῖς κυναρίοις βαλεῖν.

And he said to her, "Permit first the children to be satisfied, for it is not good to take the children's bread and to cast it among the little dogs."

60. John 18:37.
61. Porter, *Criteria for Authenticity*, 204–5.

The woman appeared to be unshaken by Jesus' words and voiced a humble protest in verse 28:

ἡ δὲ ἀπεκρίθη καὶ λέγει αὐτῷ· κύριε· καὶ τὰ κυνάρια ὑποκάτω τῆς τραπέζης ἐσθίουσιν ἀπὸ τῶν ψιχίων τῶν παιδίων.

But she replied to him, "Lord, the little dogs also eat from the crumbs of the children under the table."

Impressed with her determined spirit and faith, Jesus told her to return home where she would find that the demon had been cast out of her daughter. When she arrived home, the woman εὗρεν τὸ παιδίον βεβλημένον ἐπὶ τὴν κλίνην καὶ τὸ δαιμόνιον ἐξεληλυθός ("found the child lying on the bed and the demon gone," v. 30) just as Jesus had said.

What language would Jesus have used to speak to the Syrophoenician woman? Mark identifies her as a Ἑλληνίς—a Greek ("Gentile" NASB).[62] Consequently, it would be reasonable to assume that what we have recorded in Mark's gospel is the actual conversation between Jesus and the woman. As a Gentile, the woman would have spoken Greek and probably would not have conversed with Jesus in Hebrew or Aramaic.

Jesus would have also conversed with the Greeks who sought him (John 12:20–22) in their native tongue. If Jesus intended to teach the Greeks among the Diaspora as some jested hypothetically, would he not have done so in Greek (John 7:35)? The language used in the synagogues of the Diaspora was "as a rule Greek."[63]

The prophetic voice of Isaiah indicates that the appearing of the "great light" among the Gentiles would be seen among people dwelling in "Galilee of the Gentiles" (Matt 4:15; Isa 9:1 NASB). Jesus' home town of Nazareth was in close proximity to towns like Sepphoris[64] and other cities of the Decapolis which were Hellenistic-Roman cities where Greek culture flourished.[65] Surely Tiberias (built by Herod Antipas around 20 CE) was more bilingual than Jerusalem.[66] While growing up, Jesus would have been

---

62. France notes that though the term Ἕλλην like Ἑλληνιστής "might in a different context refer to language and culture rather than strictly to racial origin, there is no doubt that here it carries its normal biblical connotation of Gentile (as opposed to Jewish)," France, *Mark*, 207.

63. Argyle, "Did Jesus Speak Greek?," 93.

64. Herod Antipas rebuilt Sepphoris and made it the capital of Galilee and his royal residence. Josephus referred to the city as "the ornament of all Galilee," probably a reference to its fortifications (*Ant.* 18.2.1); See McRay, *Archaeology*, 175.

65. Achtemeier et al., *New Testament*, 39.

66. Batey, "Sepphoris," 50–64. Though Draper argues that the reference to Greek speaking Gentiles "does not mean that these people spoke only Greek, but that in the

exposed to and would by necessity have had to learn Greek in order to be an active participant in the carpentry trade if he were to conduct business with Gentiles in nearby towns, especially Sepphoris. Many of Jesus' parables show that he was familiar with Palestinian trade and government.[67] Would not his disciples also have spoken Greek since they would have most likely conducted business as fishermen or as a tax collector with their Gentile neighbors?[68] Sevenster states that "Hellenistic culture, which implied the use of Greek, dominated every aspect of life and society."[69] Consequently, H. C. Kee draws this conclusion:

> This means that for Jesus to have conversed with inhabitants of cities in the Galilee, and especially the cities of the Decapolis and the Phoenician region, he would have had to have known Greek, certainly at the conversational level.[70]

The NT's use of the LXX indicates that Jesus and the disciples alluded to it often and quoted from it.[71] For example, Jesus appears to be quoting the LXX on three different occasions in Matthew's temptation narrative. Each reference coincides with the three separate temptations:

First Citation Regarding Stones Turned to Bread

> Matt 4:4
> ὁ δὲ ἀποκριθεὶς εἶπεν· γέγραπται·οὐκ ἐπ᾽ ἄρτῳ μόνῳ ζήσεται ὁ ἄνθρωπος, ἀλλ᾽ ἐπὶ παντὶ ῥήματι ἐκπορευομένῳ διὰ στόματος θεοῦ.

> But he replied, "It is written, 'Man shall not live by bread alone but by every word that proceeds from the mouth of God.'"

---

midst of a population where the everyday language was Aramaic these Gentiles were bilingual." See also Draper, "Did Jesus Speak Greek?," 317.

67. Argyle argues that though Jesus spoke Aramaic "it is a mistake to assume that there must be Aramaic behind all His words. Some Aramaists in their enthusiasm for the theory of Aramaic in His sayings overstate their case and produce doubtful arguments" ("Did Jesus Speak Greek?," 93).

68. Ibid., 92.

69. Sevenster, "Do You Know Greek?," 96. Porter also argues that "it is not legitimate to think of Jesus as growing up in linguistic and cultural isolation. Nazareth was situated along a branch of and had a position overlooking one of the busiest trade routes in ancient Palestine, the Via Maris, which reached from Damascus to the Mediterranean." See Porter, "Did Jesus Ever Teach in Greek?," 211.

70. Kee, "Early Christianity," 21; quoted in Porter, "Did Jesus Ever Teach in Greek?," 212–13.

71. See Argyle, "Did Jesus Speak Greek?," 92.

Deut 8:3

καὶ ἐκάκωσέν σε καὶ ἐλιμαγχόνησέν σε καὶ ἐψώμισέν σε τὸ μάννα ὃ οὐκ εἴδησαν οἱ πατέρες σου ἵνα ἀναγγείλῃ σοι ὅτι οὐκ ἐπ᾽ ἄρτῳ μόνῳ ζήσεται ὁ ἄνθρωπος ἀλλ᾽ ἐπὶ παντὶ ῥήματι τῷ ἐκπορευομένῳ διὰ στόματος θεοῦ ζήσεται ὁ ἄνθρωπος.

And he distressed you and caused you to hunger and fed you manna with which your fathers were not familiar in order to announce to you that *man shall not live by bread alone but* man shall live *by every word that proceeds from the mouth of God.*

Second Citation Regarding a Jump from the Temple's Pinnacle

Matt 4:7

ἔφη αὐτῷ ὁ Ἰησοῦς· πάλιν γέγραπται·οὐκ ἐκπειράσεις κύριον τὸν θεόν σου.

Jesus answered him, "Again it is written, '*You shall not tempt the Lord your God.*'"

Deut 6:6

οὐκ ἐκπειράσεις κύριον τὸν θεόν σου ὃν τρόπον ἐξεπειράσασθε ἐν τῷ Πειρασμῷ.

You shall not tempt the Lord your God in the manner you tempted him in the Temptation.

Third Citation Regarding the Worship of Satan

Matt 4:10

τότε λέγει αὐτῷ ὁ Ἰησοῦς·ὕπαγε, σατανᾶ·γέγραπται γάρ·κύριον τὸν θεόν σου προσκυνήσεις καὶ αὐτῷ μόνῳ λατρεύσεις.

Then Jesus said to him, "Be gone, Satan, for it is written, '*You shall worship the Lord your God and serve him only.*'"

Deut 6:13

κύριον τὸν θεόν σου φοβηθήσῃ καὶ αὐτῷ λατρεύσεις καὶ πρὸς αὐτὸν κολληθήσῃ καὶ τῷ ὀνόματι αὐτοῦ ὀμῇ.

You shall fear God and serve him and cleave to him and by his name you shall swear.

Matthew also records Jesus' citing primarily Isa 9:1–2 (MT 8:23—9:1–2) from the LXX when announcing the commencement of his ministry.[72]

If Luke is providing a reliable historical record, Peter cites from the LXX repeatedly in his speeches in Acts. For instance, according to Acts 2:25–28, Peter demonstrates how David prophesied about the Messiah in one of his psalms:

Δαυὶδ γὰρ λέγει εἰς αὐτόν·

προορώμην τὸν κύριον ἐνώπιόν μου διὰ παντός, ὅτι ἐκ δεξιῶν μού ἐστιν ἵνα μὴ σαλευθῶ. διὰ τοῦτο ηὐφράνθη ἡ καρδία μου καὶ ἠγαλλιάσατο ἡ γλῶσσά μου, ἔτι δὲ καὶ ἡ σάρξ μου κατασκηνώσει ἐπ᾽ ἐλπίδι, ὅτι οὐκ ἐγκαταλείψεις τὴν ψυχήν μου εἰς ᾅδην οὐδὲ δώσεις τὸν ὅσιόν σου ἰδεῖν διαφθοράν. ἐγνώρισάς μοι ὁδοὺς ζωῆς, πληρώσεις με εὐφροσύνης μετὰ τοῦ προσώπου σου.

For David says about him:

I foresaw the Lord ever before me, for he is at my right hand in order that I may not be shaken. On account of this my heart rejoiced and my speech exulted and yet even my flesh also shall dwell in hope for you have not abandoned my soul in Hades nor have you allowed your holy one to see corruption. You have made known to me the way of life; you fill me with gladness with your presence.

The above quotation is identical to the LXX in Ps 15:8–11 (Eng 16:8–11):

προωρώμην τὸν κύριον ἐνώπιόν μου διὰ παντός ὅτι ἐκ δεξιῶν μού ἐστιν ἵνα μὴ σαλευθῶ διὰ τοῦτο ηὐφράνθη ἡ καρδία μου καὶ ἠγαλλιάσατο ἡ γλῶσσά μου ἔτι δὲ καὶ ἡ σάρξ μου κατασκηνώσει ἐπ᾽ ἐλπίδι ὅτι οὐκ ἐγκαταλείψεις τὴν ψυχήν μου εἰς ᾅδην οὐδὲ δώσεις τὸν ὅσιόν σου ἰδεῖν διαφθοράν ἐγνώρισάς μοι ὁδοὺς ζωῆς πληρώσεις με εὐφροσύνης μετὰ τοῦ προσώπου σου . . . .

I foresaw the Lord ever before me, for he is at my right hand in order that I may not be shaken. On account of this my heart rejoiced and my speech exulted and yet even my flesh also shall dwell in hope for you have not abandoned my soul in Hades nor have you allowed your holy one to see corruption. You have

---

72. Nolland writes that "Matthew follows the overall structure of the LXX" though some of it appears to be an independent reading of the Hebrew (*The Gospel of Matthew*, 172). These allusions to the LXX are significant in view of the Jewishness of Matthew's gospel.

made known to me the way of life, you fill me with gladness with your presence. . . .

If Luke's record is accurate, as the preface to his composition certainly implies (cf. Luke 1:1–4), it is curious as to why he would preserve passages from the LXX if it were not because of the fact that Greek was the dominant means of communication among Jews and Gentiles. It must be borne in mind that the LXX was in many respects the "Bible" of the Jews.

James cites the LXX according to Acts 15:16–17 (cf. Amos 9:11–12) and could not have made his point if he had referred to the Hebrew text. Notice the italicized words below:

NA²⁸

μετὰ ταῦτα ἀναστρέψω καὶ ἀνοικοδομήσω τὴν σκηνὴν Δαυὶδ τὴν πεπτωκυῖαν καὶ τὰ κατεσκαμμένα αὐτῆς ἀνοικοδομήσω καὶ ἀνορθώσω αὐτήν, ὅπως ἂν ἐκζητήσωσιν οἱ κατάλοιποι *τῶν ἀνθρώπων* τὸν κύριον καὶ πάντα τὰ ἔθνη ἐφ᾽ οὓς ἐπικέκληται τὸ ὄνομά μου ἐπ᾽ αὐτούς, λέγει κύριος ποιῶν ταῦτα. . . .

LXX

ἐν τῇ ἡμέρα ἐκείνη ἀναστήσω τὴν σκηνὴν Δαυιδ τὴν πεπτωκυῖαν καὶ ἀνοικοδομήσω τὰ πεπτωκότα αὐτῆς καὶ τὰ κατεσκαμμένα αὐτῆς ἀναστήσω καὶ ἀνοικοδομήσω αὐτὴν καθὼς αἱ ἡμέραι τοῦ αἰῶνος ὅπως ἐκζητήσωσιν οἱ κατάλοιποι *τῶν ἀνθρώπων* καὶ πάντα τὰ ἔθνη ἐφ᾽ οὓς ἐπικέκληται τὸ ὄνομά μου ἐπ᾽ αὐτούς λέγει κύριος ὁ θεὸς ὁ ποιῶν ταῦτα . . . .

BHS

ביום ההוא אקים את־סכת דויד הנפלת
וגדרתי את־פרציהן והרסתיו אקים ובניתיה כימי עולם:
למען יירשו את־שארית **אדום** וכל־הגוים אשר־נקרא שמי
עליהם נאם־יהוה עשה זאת:

"In that day I will raise the booth of David which has fallen and wall up its breaches and I will cause its ruins to rise and rebuild it like the days of old. So that they may possess the remnant of *Edom* in order that all the nations who are called by my name among them," declares the Lord who is doing this.

The translators of the LXX must have misread אדום (*'edom*, "Edom") in Hebrew as אדם (*'adam*, "man") because of the obvious similarity in spelling and sound. The LXX translators therefore chose the Greek term ἀνθρώπων ("mankind" NASB). James, however, referred not to the Hebrew text but to the LXX translation in order to make the case that no obstacles should be placed before those ἐπιστρέφουσιν ἐπὶ τὸν θεόν ("return to God") from among the Gentiles (Acts 15:19).[73] Consequently, this citation reveals the wide use of Greek among the writers of the NT and provides substantial evidence that the Bible commonly used by them was not the Hebrew text but the Greek translation.

An area of peculiarity that relates to the language that Jesus spoke is found in the Gospel of Mark. On three occasions Jesus uttered Aramaic phrases. If Jesus spoke Greek, what is the significance of these Aramaic phrases? In Mark 5:22 Jesus encountered a synagogue official named Jairus. The man fell at Jesus' feet and entreated him earnestly:

> καὶ παρακαλεῖ αὐτὸν πολλὰ λέγων ὅτι τὸ θυγάτριόν μου ἐσχάτως ἔχει, ἵνα ἐλθὼν ἐπιθῇς τὰς χεῖρας αὐτῇ ἵνα σωθῇ καὶ ζήσῃ (v. 23).

> And he implored him earnestly saying, "My little daughter is at the point of death, come and lay hands upon her so that she might get well and live."

On the way to the house of Jairus they received news that the man's daughter had died. Jesus encouraged him to believe. After they arrived Jesus took the child's father and mother and his companions into the room where the child was. And taking the girl by the hand Jesus said these words to her:

> ταλιθα κουμ, ὅ ἐστιν μεθερμηνευόμενον· τὸ κοράσιον, σοὶ λέγω, ἔγειρε (v. 41).

> "*Talitha cum*," which is translated, "little girl, I say to you, arise!"

It seems apparent that Mark's account assumes that his readers would need a translation of the Aramaic phrase ταλιθα κουμ into Greek. This would of course verify that his readers would not understand the meaning of the

---

73. There is some dispute as to whether the text was corrupted or repointed by the Masoretes. Marshall notes, "We can thus understand the LXX text as arising from a different version of the Hebrew text of Amos, with similar words being substituted for the original text. . . . 'Edom' was often understood as Rome in the Targumim, and therefore it is possible (though beyond proof) that an original 'Adam' was repointed by the Masoretes as 'Edom' to reflect Jewish hopes at this time, and consequential changes were made to the rest of the text." Marshall, "Acts," 590–91. Archer and Chirichigno argue that the MT should be amended because it has been corrupted despite the lack of supporting evidence for making such an emendation. Archer and Chirichigno, *Old Testament Quotations*, 154–55.

Aramaic. Similarly, in Mark 7:34, Jesus healed a deaf man when he said in Aramaic, Εφφαθα ("Be open!"), which was translated for his Greek readers as ὅ ἐστιν διανοίχθητι ("which is, 'Be open!'"). Would it not be odd for Mark to have preserved the Aramaic words that Jesus spoke if it were his *custom* to speak in Aramaic?[74] This may indicate that Jesus accommodated people who only spoke Aramaic. Turner makes the following observation based upon the words of T. K. Abbott:

> As long ago as 1891 T. K. Abbott argued effectively in favour of Greek as the dominical language, and one of his best submissions was that if Jesus regularly taught in Aramaic it is difficult to explain why St Mark adopted the curious practice of reproducing only some, and not all, of his sayings in Aramaic. . . . One would think that the evangelist's reason for reproducing this particular selection of transliterations is that, contrary to his usual way, Jesus spoke in Aramaic on these occasions. The reason why is not so clear, but on some of them he may have been addressing individuals whose sole language was Aramaic.[75]

Mark 15:33–34 records another instance in which Mark provides a translation for the reader of an Aramaic expression uttered by Jesus while on the cross:

> Καὶ γενομένης ὥρας ἕκτης σκότος ἐγένετο ἐφ᾽ ὅλην τὴν γῆν ἕως ὥρας ἐνάτης. καὶ τῇ ἐνάτῃ ὥρᾳ ἐβόησεν ὁ Ἰησοῦς φωνῇ μεγάλῃ·ελωι ελωι λεμα σαβαχθανι; ὅ ἐστιν μεθερμηνευόμενον·ὁ θεός μου ὁ θεός μου, εἰς τί ἐγκατέλιπές με;[76]

> And being the sixth hour, darkness came upon the whole land until the ninth hour. And in the ninth hour Jesus cried out with a loud voice, "*Eloi, eloi, lema sabachthani?*" which is translated, "My God, my God, why have you forsaken me?"

Bystanders thought that Jesus was calling to Elijah for help (v. 36). Obviously, those who heard Jesus did not understand the meaning of his words. The Greek term for Elijah is Ἡλίας (*ēlias*) and would likely be pronounced differently than the Hebrew name אליהו (*'eliyah or 'eliyahu*), though the latter would sound similar to the Aramaic words that Jesus uttered. Consequently,

74. See Mark 1:25, 41; 2:5; 4:39; and 5:8–9.

75. Turner, "Language of Jesus and His Disciples," 182.

76. See parallel account in Matt 27:46. Archer and Chirichigno state that the NT does not follow the LXX in this narrative but "adopts an Aramaic paraphrase . . . which Matthew directly transliterates and then translates using a vocative inflection" (*Old Testament Quotations*, 65).

the Aramaic words spoken by Jesus were recorded for a Greek speaking audience. Otherwise, the reader would not understand why some were confused about what Jesus said. It is no surprise that Jesus would have used his native tongue during his most desperate hour.

Why then does Mark record the above Aramaic phrases and their Greek translations? There are basically two reasons. First, Jesus seemed to speak Aramaic on *rare* occasions when those to whom he spoke would not know Greek, thus accommodating them by speaking their language.[77] Second, the greater audience would not understand these infrequently used Aramaic expressions and therefore would need an explanation. Turner's observation is compelling:

> [T]he isolation of *talitha* cum and *ephphatha* and the like, as Aramaic phrases surviving in the Greek gospels, might then be explained as rare instances where patients of Jesus comprehended only Aramaic.[78]

These examples do not necessarily prove that Jesus predominantly spoke Greek, but they do strongly infer the possibility.

The scholarly consensus has been that Jesus and his disciples would not have spoken in Greek, since Aramaic was their native language and the dominant language of Palestine. Therefore, the writers of the GNT were dependent upon Aramaic oral and written sources. The matter is not settled, and many scholars stand on opposite sides of the issue.

SEMINAL STUDIES

In any area of research, certain scholars lead the field. Biblical and linguistic studies addressing the languages of Palestine during the first century CE and their relationship to Jesus, his disciples, and the GNT are abundant. However, I have identified the scholars below as the most influential ones relating to my study. In order to gain an informative overview of the languages related to the NT, I recommend as a good primer Stanley E. Porter's book, *The Language of the New Testament: Classic Essays* (1991). Porter serves as the editor, and many of the major issues relating to the Semitic nature of the NT are addressed by key scholars in the field: Stanley E. Porter, Adolf Deissmann, James Hope Moulton, Charles C. Torrey, Matthew Black, Joseph A. Fitzmyer, Henry S. Gehman, Nigel Turner, Lars Rydbeck, and Moisés

---

77. Wise notes that "Jesus certainly spoke Aramaic on occasion" ("Languages of Palestine," 442).

78. Turner, *Style*, 9.

Silva. Porter's purpose is stated as follows: "This anthology brings together a number of what I consider to be classic essays regarding the Greek language of the NT; that is, what kind of Greek is it: Semitic, koine, transitionary, and so on? Many positions have been advocated, refuted, and debated. This gathering of spokesmen is designed to give some idea of the history and progress of this continuing discussion."[79]

Gustav Hermann Dalman (1855–1941 CE)

Gustav H. Dalman was a German Protestant theologian closely associated with the Missionary Church Brotherhood at Herrnhut. Dalman taught for fifteen years at the Institutium Judaicum in Leipzig. He was the first director and head of the Evangelical Institute for Antiquity in Jerusalem (1902–1917).[80] Two works that Dalman published relate to the languages of first-century CE Palestine, focusing specifically upon Aramaic and the sources upon which the GNT may be based.

Dalman's first contribution to the study of Jesus and the Aramaic language was his pivotal book, *The Words of Jesus: Considered in the Light of Post-Biblical Jewish Writings and the Aramaic Language.*[81] Dalman's objective was to "ascertain the meaning of the words of our Lord as they must have presented themselves to the ear and mind of His Jewish hearers."[82] By evaluating extant Jewish, Aramic, and Hebrew sources, Dalman sought to demonstrate the dominance of the Aramaic during the time of Jesus and his disciples. Dalman stated in regard to the Greek writers of the Synoptic Gospels that the "groundwork of the material elaborated by them had been originally created in Aramaic. And this holds equally true whether their basis presented itself to the authors directly in its Aramaic form or already through the medium of Greek tradition, oral or written."[83] Additionally, in regard to the Semitism in the GNT, Dalman made this comment:

> [T]here can be no doubt that the Semitisms of the Gospels ought
> first to be looked for in the sphere of the Jewish Aramaic, and

---

79. Porter, *Language*, 8.

80. Biographical information can be found on the following webpage: http://www.jewishvirtuallibrary.org/jsource/judaica/ejud_0002_0005_0_04821.html (accessed July 15, 2013).

81. Dalman, *Words of Jesus*.

82. Ibid., v.

83. Ibid., 17–18.

that only where this does not suffice for explanation, need it be asked how far Hebrew is to be held responsible for Semitisms.[84]

Dalman's premise is based upon certain fundamental ideas in the GNT that connect directly to Aramaic—the sovereignty of God, the future age, eternal life, the world, the Lord, the Father in heaven, the Son of Man, the Son of God, the son of David, etc. Dalman operates upon the premise that Aramaic was the dominant language in Palestine; however, he offers a cautionary statement: "It might seem as if the linguistic basis presupposed in our work were indeed highly uncertain. To a certain extent this is true. Any investigator who will be conscientious and sure of his steps, must take into consideration the whole field of linguistic possibilities lying between biblical and the Galilean dialects of Aramaic."[85] Dalman's book paves the way for further Aramaic studies that address gospel origins.

Dalman's second contribution to the study of gospel origins is a book that builds upon his previous work. In 1929 CE, Dalman published his acclaimed study, *Jesus—Jeshua: Studies in the Gospels*. Dalman addresses more specifically the language that Jesus spoke and seeks to understand "what were the linguistic forms into which His thoughts shaped themselves."[86] Interestingly, Dalman acknowledges the multilingual makeup of Palestine and its impact upon Jesus: "To the two languages which our Lord knew (Aramaic, His mother-tongue, and Greek, the language of the government and of the foreign inhabitants of the land), must also be added *as a third*— Hebrew, the language of His Bible."[87] After Dalman establishes the primacy of Aramaic, he seeks to recover the Aramaic sources behind the gospel tradition that relate to the words spoken by Jesus primarily in the synagogue, during the Passover meal, and at the crucifixion.

Charles Fox Burney (1868–1925 CE)

Charles F. Burney was associated with the Anglican Church. Early in his academic career, Burney lectured at Oxford and also served as the librarian from 1897 to 1908 CE. He became Oriel Professor of the Interpretation of Holy Scripture in 1914, and in that position he wrote *The Aramaic Origin of the Fourth Gospel* (1922). Burney states that "the problem of the origin and authorship of the Fourth Gospel had . . . always attracted him . . . and had

84. Ibid., 18.
85. Ibid., 82.
86. Dalman, *Jesus—Jeshua*, 1.
87. Ibid., 37.

been impressed . . . with the Semitic character of its diction."[88] Burney explains that in his analysis of the Fourth Gospel he was convinced more than ever that the Gospel was a translation of Aramaic. He provides a synopsis in the Introduction that supplies the central foundation for his thesis. In the following sections, he explores more deeply the Semitic nature of the GNT through the lens of Aramaic. He identifies in the GNT what he believes to be Aramaic syntactical, grammatical, and translational characteristics that are found in the Hebrew text, Aramaic Targums, Syriac, and the writings of Ignatius. In the Epilogue, Burney offers the following conclusion:

> We arrive, then, at the impression that the Gospel was not written at an earlier date than A.D. 75–80, nor from Palestine; yet on the other hand our theory of an Aramaic original seems to demand that it should have originated in an Aramaic-speaking country. Thus Syria is indicated, and if Syria, then Antioch.[89]

Matthew Black (1908–1994 CE)

Matthew Black was a Scottish minister and biblical scholar, spending much of his academic career at the University of St. Andrews in St. Andrews, Scotland. Black also served on the editorial committees for the *Novum Testamentum Graece* (26th ed.) and *The Greek New Testament* (UBS[3]). Black's most influential book that relates to the languages undergirding the GNT is *An Aramaic Approach to the Gospels and Acts* (1946). The popularity of Black's book is noted by the book's three editions (1946, 1954, and 1967) and three reprints (1971, 1977, and 1979).

Black's book is a continuation of the works of Burney and Dalman but with more refinement where he felt they were deficient in regard to the "linguistic side" of Aramaic.[90] Black states his hypothesis as follows:

> The Gospels were written in a predominantly Hellenistic environment, and they were written in Greek. But Greek was not the native language of the central Figure, nor of the earliest apostles, if it was not unfamiliar to them. Jesus must have conversed in the Galilean dialect of Aramaic, and His teaching was probably almost entirely in Aramaic. At the basis of the Greek Gospels, therefore, there must lie a Palestinian Aramaic tradition, at any

---

88. Ibid., 1.

89. Ibid., 129.

90. Ibid.,1.

rate of the sayings and teaching of Jesus, and this tradition must at one time have been translated from Aramaic into Greek.[91]

Black extends the Aramaic Hypothesis to include not only the Gospels but also the book of Acts. Since Black's book was originally written before the discoveries of the DSS, the new editions contain a chapter entitled "Recent Discoveries and Developments in Palestinian Aramaic." However, Black notes that the Aramaic manuscripts that were found do not necessitate "any far-reaching modification" of his original views.[92]

Black's book addresses the influence of the elements of Aramaic semantics, grammar, syntax, vocabulary, and poetry upon the GNT. He admits that many of the sayings of Jesus are not "literal translations of Aramaic, but translations which have passed through the minds of the Greek Evangelists and emerged as, for the most part, literary productions."[93] Consequently, the GNT (esp. the Gospels) is more about how the writers interpreted Jesus than about capturing the very "mind" of Jesus.[94]

Joseph Augustine Fitzmyer (1920 CE–)

Joseph A. Fitzmyer, an American Catholic priest of the Society of Jesus, is the professor emeritus at the Catholic University of America in Washington, DC. He is a prolific writer, and he also served as one of the editors for *The New Jerome Biblical Commentary* (1990). His most significant contribution has been his studies in the languages of Aramaic. He and Daniel J. Harrington published *A Manual of Palestinian Aramaic Texts* (1978; repr. 1982, 1994, and 2002) that date from the second century BCE to the second century CE. This publication is an extremely helpful resource in linguistic studies.

Two other significant studies in Aramaic relate to the linguistic background of the NT. First, Fitzmyer's book, *Essays on the Semitic Background of the New Testament* (1971; repr. 1974), explores the NT use of the OT and the Semitic background of NT passages in the Gospels, Pauline literature, the book of Hebrews, and the documents of early Christianity. Most helpful to Aramaic studies is Fitzmyer's treatment of the NT in light of the Qumran scrolls. Second, Fitzmyer published a compendium of essays of Aramaic studies in *A Wandering Aramean: Collected Aramaic Essays* (1979).

91. Ibid., 16.
92. Ibid., 35.
93. Ibid., 275.
94. Ibid.

These essays addressed specifically the relationship of Aramaic to the GNT. Fitzmyer argues that Aramaic was the language of Jesus and believes that an Aramaic substratum underlies the GNT. One of the most helpful chapters relates to the languages of Palestine in the first century CE. Within this chapter, Fitzmyer addresses the multilingual character of Palestine and analyzes the place of Latin, Greek, Aramaic, and Hebrew as they have impacted the first century CE. These two works have been recently combined in an edition entitled *The Semitic Background of the New Testament* (1997).

Maurice Casey (1942 CE–)

Maurice Casey is a British scholar and a professor emeritus at the University of Nottingham. Recently he published a book entitled *Jesus of Nazareth: An Independent Historian's Account of His Life and Teaching* (2010) that serves as his contribution to historical Jesus studies. The pivotal work, however, in the field of the linguistic backgrounds of the GNT is his *Aramaic Sources of Mark's Gospel* (1998). Casey states that since Jesus spoke in Aramaic, the only possible means of recovering the Jesus of history is to reconstruct his sayings in their original Aramaic. Consequently, Casey seeks to correct by retro-translating into Aramaic the mistranslations he finds in Greek of the Aramaic originals.

Stanley E. Porter (1956 CE–)

Stanley Porter is currently the dean and professor of New Testament at McMaster Divinity College in Hamilton, Ontario. He served previously as the professor of theology at Roehampton University in London. Porter proposed a new criterion for evaluating the historicity of the GNT based upon the multilingual environment of first-century CE Palestine. His study is entitled *The Criteria for Authenticity in Historical-Jesus Research: Previous Discussion and New Proposals* (2000). Porter observes that

> although much historical-Jesus research is concerned with determining what Jesus may have said or whether he said something that approximates what is recorded in the Gospels (the so-called *ipsissima vox*)—and this often suffices as "authentic" Jesus material—little of it is concerned with the actual wording that he may have used (the *ipsissima verba*) (since it is

maintained by many of these scholars that the words were uttered in Aramaic, but are now found in Greek Gospels).[95]

In response, Porter states three new proposals that form a deviation from
the current Aramaic hypothesis: (1) the criterion of Greek language and its
context; (2) the criterion of Greek textual variance; and (3) the criterion of
discourse features. Porter states the purpose of his presentation as follows:

> My hope is that my survey of this research will provide some
> impetus for opening up this discussion once again. However, a
> more important goal is to inject some new life into the discus-
> sion by taking a different approach altogether than has usually
> been taken. I attempt to do this by discussing the possible use of
> Greek by Jesus as providing a new set of criteria for discussing
> the authenticity of certain of his sayings.[96]

Porter maintains that in at least eight episodes in the life of Jesus Greek
would have been employed as the conversational medium. Seven out of the
eight episodes may very well contain the actual words that Jesus spoke in
Greek (John 12:20–28 is the exception):[97]

1. Jesus' conversation with the centurion (Matt 8:5–13; John 4:46–54)

2. Jesus' conversation with the Samaritan woman (John 4:4–26)

3. Jesus' calling of Levi/Matthew (Mark 2:13–14; Matt 9:9; Luke 5:27–28)

4. Jesus' conversation with the Syrophoenician woman (Mark 7:25–30;
   Matt 15:21–22)

5. Jesus' conversation with the Pharisees and the Herodians (Mark
   12:13–17; Matt 22:16–22; Luke 20:20–26)

6. Jesus' conversation with his disciples at Caesarea Philippi (Mark 8:27–
   30; Matt 16:13–20; Luke 9:18–21)

7. Jesus' conversation with Pilate (Mark 15:21–22; Matt 27:11–14; Luke
   23:2–4; John 18:29–38)

Porter asserts that the basis that forms the perceptual framework of historical Jesus studies and the quest toward authenticity is inadequate.[98]

Although the scholarly representation is selective, I believe that these
scholars provide an overview of the current state of linguistic studies im-
pacting gospel origins and the character of the GNT.

95. Porter, *Criteria for Authenticity*, 25.
96. Ibid.
97. Ibid., 158.
98. Ibid., 242.

SUMMARY

Since Roman Palestine was flanked by two dominant international languages—Greek and Latin—it naturally became a "linguistic border."[99] The linguistic situation in Roman Palestine was particularly influenced by its key geographical placement as the primary passageway for trade within the Fertile Crescent, thereby "attracting merchants who spoke foreign languages to an area already populated by various ethnic groups."[100] A poem dated in the early first century BCE captured the linguistic diversity of the day:

> If you art Syrian, then *Salaam*!
> *Naidios*! If Phenician . . . or
> *Chaere*! If a Grecian.[101]

Among such linguistic diversity Greek emerged as the dominant medium to disseminate the Christian message in both oral and written form.

---

99. Smelik, "Languages," 122.

100. Ibid.

101. Meleager, *Fifty Poems*, 101. Meleager came from the Hellenistic city of Gadara in Transjordan.

CHAPTER 2

The Emerging Dominance of Greek in First-Century CE Palestine

ACCORDING TO JOHN'S GOSPEL, after the Roman governor Pontius Pilate had Jesus scourged, he brought Jesus once again before the people and had him stand in their presence. Jesus stood before them wearing a purple cloak and a crown of thorns. Pilate announced to the crowd ἰδοὺ ὁ ἄνθρωπος ("Behold the man," John 19:5). The gathered crowd erupted, crying out, σταύρωσον σταύρωσον ("Crucify, crucify," v. 6). Pilate knew that their demands were unreasonable for he himself said that he had found no guilt in him. Though Pilate ἐζήτει ἀπολῦσαι αὐτόν ("sought to release him," v.12), he buckled under the pressure and handed Jesus over to be crucified. John continues the narrative and describes the crucifixion in John 19:16–20:

> Τότε οὖν παρέδωκεν αὐτὸν αὐτοῖς ἵνα σταυρωθῇ. Παρέλαβον οὖν τὸν Ἰησοῦν, καὶ βαστάζων ἑαυτῷ τὸν σταυρὸν ἐξῆλθεν εἰς τὸν λεγόμενον Κρανίου Τόπον, ὃ λέγεται Ἑβραϊστὶ Γολγοθα, ὅπου αὐτὸν ἐσταύρωσαν, καὶ μετ᾽ αὐτοῦ ἄλλους δύο ἐντεῦθεν καὶ ἐντεῦθεν, μέσον δὲ τὸν Ἰησοῦν. ἔγραψεν δὲ καὶ τίτλον ὁ Πιλᾶτος καὶ ἔθηκεν ἐπὶ τοῦ σταυροῦ· ἦν δὲ γεγραμμένον·Ἰησοῦς ὁ Ναζωραῖος ὁ βασιλεὺς τῶν Ἰουδαίων. τοῦτον οὖν τὸν τίτλον πολλοὶ ἀνέγνωσαν τῶν Ἰουδαίων, ὅτι ἐγγὺς ἦν ὁ τόπος τῆς πόλεως ὅπου ἐσταυρώθη ὁ Ἰησοῦς· καὶ ἦν γεγραμμένον Ἑβραϊστί, Ῥωμαϊστί, Ἑλληνιστί.

> So then, he handed him over to them in order to be crucified. Therefore, they took Jesus, and he went out bearing his own cross to the place called the Place of the Skull, which is called

in Hebrew *Golgotha*. There they crucified him along with two
others on both sides with Jesus in between. Pilate also wrote
an inscription and put it on the cross. It was written, "Jesus the
Nazarene, the King of the Jews." Therefore many of the Jews read
the inscription, for the place was near the city where Jesus was
crucified. And it was written in Hebrew, in Latin, and in Greek.

The above text contains two important items that relate to linguistic developments in the first century. First, it is important to note that Pilate ordered an inscription to be placed upon the cross. The Greek word for the
inscription is τίτλος, a Latin loanword derived from *titulus,* referring to a
public notice, announcement, or dedication.[1] Such inscriptions were not
uncommon, particularly in the above scenario involving Pilate's inscription
concerning Jesus. In fact, Eusebius described a similar situation involving
Christians who were led to wild beasts as sport before Roman spectators:

> But Attalus was himself loudly called for by the crowd, for he was
> well known. He went in, a ready combatant, for his conscience
> was clear, and he had been nobly trained in Christian discipline
> and had ever been a witness for truth among us. He was led
> round the amphitheatre and a placard was carried before him
> on which was written in Latin (Ῥωμαϊστί), "This is Attalus, the
> Christian" (*Hist. eccl.* 5.1.43–44 [Lake, LCL]).

These ancient inscriptions provide historical verification of what one may
read in the NT and illumination about societies long past. They also verify
important people and dates. This is especially true in tracing the linguistic
developments of a particular region like ancient Palestine.

Second, John's account of the crucifixion of Jesus says that the inscription attached to the cross of Jesus was written in three languages—Hebrew
(Εβραϊστί),[2] Latin (Ῥωμαϊστί), and Greek (Ελληνιστί). The three languages represented the trilingual society of first-century Palestine. Each
language served a unique purpose. Latin served as the official administrative language of the Roman Empire.[3] Hebrew or Aramaic, though once the
dominant language among the people of Palestine, began to slip as Greek
emerged as the common spoken language. Classical Hebrew continued its
reputation as the sacred language among those committed to preserving
ancient Jewish heritage.

1. Danker, "τίτλος," 1009.

2. The word "Hebrew" is probably a reference to Aramaic, a sister language of
Hebrew. See Howard, "John," 780.

3. Burge et al., *New Testament*, 85.

This chapter will explore each of the primary languages of Palestine in greater detail. Ancient inscriptions and related archaeological discoveries provide insight into the linguistic complexity in ancient Palestine. This chapter will also demonstrate that Greek was the common means of communication among Romans and Jews.[4]

THE LINGUISTIC MILIEU OF PALESTINE

Latin: The Administrative Language

Romans expanded their territorial conquests as leaders by a ceremony of *evocation*, which called upon the gods of their enemies to join them in their military campaigns. They promised the foreign gods that if they switched sides, the people of Rome would be more faithful and loyal in service than the people who were currently paying homage to them. "The appeal must have been effective," writes Ferguson, because "Rome always seemed to win."[5]

Rome's chief rival in the West was the city of Carthage. Rome fought three major wars, known as the Punic Wars, with Carthage. Rome succeeded in the First Punic War (264–241 BCE) to secure the islands of Sardinia, Corsica, and Sicily. A Roman general named Scipio Africanus defeated Hannibal during the Second Punic War (218–201 BCE), clearing the way for Rome to take control of northern Italy, southern Gaul, and Spain. Finally, after the Third Punic War (149–146 BCE), Rome extended its rule over all of the western Mediterranean.

Rome's dominance in the East was achieved after four Macedonian wars (214–205, 200–196, 171–167, 150–148 BCE). The people in the East both feared and respected Roman power and strength. Interestingly, unlike the hellenization of Alexander the Great, the Romans did not seek to latinize conquered territory:

> The intellectual life of Greece prevailed among the Romans, and in turn Roman power protected Greek culture and speculation and contributed to the uplifting and enlightenment of subsequent ages by both preserving and opening up to the world the spiritual qualities of Greece. The teachings of Socrates, Plato, and Aristotle went forth on their wide mission. Greek philosophy

4. Fitzmyer, "Languages of Palestine," 507.

5. Ferguson, *Backgrounds*, 21.

and theology trained many of the greatest leaders of the church, and since Greek was the language of scholars, the preachers of the Church used that language very frequently, particularly in the first two centuries.[6]

Rather than supplant Greek culture, Rome sought only to bring about a unified people who would think of themselves as Romans.

In the early days of the Republic, only inhabitants within the city of Rome were recognized as citizens. However, in order to achieve loyalty from distant territories, Rome developed a policy of dual citizenship in which citizen status did not require surrendering citizenship in one's home province. In this way, the Apostle Paul was a citizen of Tarsus of the region of Macedonia (Acts 21:39) and of Rome (Acts 22:26–27). Consequently, Roman citizenship requirements were relaxed and citizenship became more about honor than about political significance. Greek culture prevailed and the Greek language continued to be the dominant language in the East. Rome demanded order and respect for the rule of law.[7]

Since Claudius (41–54 CE) extended Roman citizenship to conquered territories, there was in place a process to obtain it. First, a birth certificate was issued by the empire if one had parents who were citizens. Second, slaves became citizens upon their emancipation by Roman citizens in Rome. Third, one became a citizen of Rome by performing some special acts of service. Finally, enlistment in the military opened the doors to Roman citizenship. During the reign of Claudius, bronze military diplomas (*diplomata civitatis*) were granted upon discharge from faithful military duty. A bronze diploma was awarded to one Marcus Papirius of Arsinoe (Philadelphia) on September 8, 79 CE, after his serving twenty-five years in the Roman navy. These diplomas were written in Latin and conferred all the rights and privileges of Roman citizenship.[8]

There were Romans who criticized Claudius for indiscriminately extending Roman citizenship.[9] However, it seems that Claudius tied the privilege of citizenship to knowing Latin, or he at least made knowing Latin a test to validate citizenship. Dio Cassius recorded an occasion when Claudius revoked citizenship because the one seeking it did not know Latin:

> [Claudius] reduced the Lycians to servitude because they had revolted and slain some Romans, and he incorporated them in the prefecture of Pamphylia. During the investigation of this

6. Angus and Renwich, "Roman Empire," 210.

7. Ferguson, *Backgrounds*, 22.

8. Fant and Reddish, *Lost Treasures*, 343–44.

9. Dio, *Hist.* 60.17.5.

affair, which was conducted in the senate, he put a question in Latin to one of the envoys who had originally been a Lycian, but had been made a Roman citizen; and when the man failed to understand what was said, he took away his citizenship, saying that it was not proper for a man to be a Roman who had no knowledge of the Romans' language (*Rom. Hist.* 60.17.3–5 [Cary, LCL]).

This action by Claudius seems to be inconsistent with statements in which he refers to both Latin and Greek as the mother tongues of the empire. The situation described by Cassius may be an exception since Claudius was dealing with some malcontents. Suetonius, while listing the many contributions that Claudius made to the empire, recorded a statement by Claudius that revealed the extent to which Greek had emerged as a common language in the empire:

[Claudius] gave no less attention to Greek studies, taking every occasion to declare his regard for that language and its superiority. To a foreigner who held forth both in Greek and in Latin he said: "Since you are ready with both our tongues"; and in commending Achaia to the senators he declared that it was a province dear to him through the association of kindred studies; while he often replied to Greek envoys in the senate in a set speech (*Claud.* 42.1 [Rolfe, LCL]).

This statement emphasized the linguistic division in the empire. One expected Latin to dominate in the West because the seat of government was there. As a result, Latin eventually became the vehicle of administrative and legal communication. However, in the East, Greek was the common language. Robert Gundry made the following observation:

Latin was the legal language of the Roman Empire but was used mainly in the West, though even there Greek was widely used. In the East, generally speaking, Greek predominated.[10]

Fitzmyer also observed that Latin, particularly in first-century CE Palestine, was used primarily by Romans who occupied the land "for more or less official purposes."[11] Such a restricted use of Latin is probably to be expected since Rome was more interested in absorbing cultures than in replacing them with their own. In Palestine, therefore, inscriptions connected to the Roman government, the administration, and the military were written primarily in Latin.

---

10. Gundry, *Survey*, 46.
11. Fitzmyer, *Wandering Aramean*, 30.

Herod the Great rebuilt Caesarea Maritima between 22 and 9 BCE to honor the Roman emperor Augustus. According to the Roman historian Tacitus, the town of Caesarea became the seat of the Roman government: "Antioch is the capitol of Syria, Caesarea of Judea" (*Iudaeae caput est, Hist. 2.78* [Moore, LCL]). An incomplete inscription from one of the buildings in Caesarea partially preserves the name of a Roman colony established by Vespasian:

[COLONIAE] PRIMAE FL(aviae) AVG(vstae) [Caesareae?]
[CLEO]PATRA MATER EIVS HOC F(ieri) I(vssit)[12]

Additionally, Italian archaeologists in 1961 discovered the famous Pilate inscription (26–36 CE) while working on a theater at Caesarea. Interestingly, the stone bearing the inscription was partially intact and was turned upside down and reused as a step during a renovation of the theater in the fourth century CE. Since the stone had been reused, archaeologists are not certain about its original location and usage. However, the inscription does indicate that a structure had once been erected in honor of the emperor Tiberius:

[TI(berio) CAES(are) AVG(vsto) V CO(n)]S(vie) TIBERIEVM
[. . . PO]ONTIVS PILATVS
[. . . PRAEF]ectvs ivda[ea]E

The name Pontius Pilate appears in line 2. The inscription also identifies Pilate as the *praefectus* of Judea, a post he served until he was recalled to Rome in the year of 36 CE. The discovery of the Pilate inscription is important for two reasons. First, although the name Pontius Pilate can be found in several ancient literary sources, the stone inscription represents the only nonliterary historical documentation. Second, the inscription affirms the biblical record of Pilate's governorship during the first century CE.[13] Luke provides a literary time marker in his gospel where he begins a narration about the ministry of John the Baptist that relates to the governorship of Pilate:

Ἐν ἔτει δὲ πεντεκαιδεκάτῳ τῆς ἡγεμονίας Τιβερίου Καίσαρος, ἡγεμονεύοντος *Ποντίου Πιλάτου τῆς Ἰουδαίας,* καὶ τετρααρχοῦντος τῆς Γαλιλαίας Ἡρῴδου, Φιλίππου δὲ τοῦ ἀδελφοῦ αὐτοῦ τετρααρχοῦντος τῆς Ἰτουραίας καὶ Τραχωνίτιδος χώρας, καὶ Λυσανίου τῆς Ἀβιληνῆς τετρααρχοῦντος . . . (Luke 3:1).

Now in the fifteenth year of the reign of Tiberias Caesar, when *Pontius Pilate* was governor *of Judea,* and Herod was tetrarch

12. Fitzmyer, "Languages of Palestine," 505.
13. Fant and Reddish, *Lost Treasures,* 311–15.

of Galilee, and Philip his brother was tetrarch of the region of Ituraea and Trachonitis, and Lysanias was tetrarch of Abilene.

The historical presence of Pilate in Judea during the first half of the first century CE is attested to by both biblical and nonbiblical documents and illustrates the official role Latin played in the Roman administration.

The restricted use of Latin is also supported by Josephus. He recorded a decree passed by the Senate and Julius Caesar concerning one Hyrcanus and the Jewish nation:

> Gaius Julius Caesar, Imperator and Pontifex Maximus, Dictator for the second time, to the magistrates, council and people of Sidon, greeting. If you are in good health, it is well; I also and the army are in good health. I am sending you a copy of the decree, inscribed on a tablet, concerning Hyracanus, son of Alexander, the high priest and ethnarch of the Jews, in order that it may be deposited among your public records. It is my wish that this be set up on a tablet of bronze in both Greek and Latin (*Ant.* 14.10.2 [Marcus, LCL]).

The directive by Julius Caesar to have the decree inscribed in both Greek and Latin illustrates an effort to accommodate the people in their language as well as to establish the authority of the directive by using the administrative language of Rome.

Another related inscription that reveals the administrative use of Latin was found in Corinth. One of the most imposing structures of antiquity in the city of Corinth was the theater. It was used for both theatrical entertainment and political or civic purposes.[14] It was built in the fifth century BCE and seated about fourteen thousand spectators. The Romans rebuilt the theater after 44 CE and then made more repairs after the earthquake in 77 CE. A sixty-two-square-foot area was paved with stone near the northeast corner of the theater. During excavations in April of 1929, archaeologists discovered a piece of a slab that contained an inscription written in Latin. Two other pieces were also discovered in 1928 and 1947. The inscription bears the name of Erastus, the treasurer of the city of Corinth:

Erastvs-Pro-Aedilit[at]e S-P-Stravit

The full version is "Erastus pro aedilitate sua pecunia stravit," which translates as "Erastus in return for his *aedileship* laid (the pavement) at his own expense."[15] The office of *aediles* was the only office in Roman colonies to

14. McRay, *Archaeology*, 331.
15. Ibid.

which officials were regularly elected.[16] While writing from Corinth, the Apostle Paul included greetings from Erastus to the Christians in Rome:

> ἀσπάζεται ὑμᾶς Γάϊος ὁ ξένος μου καὶ ὅλης τῆς ἐκκλησίας. ἀσπάζεται ὑμᾶς Ἔραστος ὁ οἰκονόμος τῆς πόλεως καὶ Κούαρτος ὁ ἀδελφός (Romans 16:23).

> Gaius, my host, greets you and the whole church. Erastus, the city treasurer, greets you and Quartus, the brother.

John McRay makes the following observation about the adaption of Roman ways by the Greek city of Corinth:

> The extent to which the rebuilt Greek city of Corinth adopted Roman ways after colonization is indicated by the predominance of Latin inscriptions. Of 104 inscriptions dating from colonization in 44 B.C. to the reign of Hadrian in the early second century, 101 are in Latin and only three in Greek. Yet the Romanization may have been in the administrative and official, rather than the everyday, spheres. Paul wrote to the church there in Greek. By the reign of Hadrian Greek had reestablished itself once again as the official language.[17]

Though the Erastus inscription is located in a city outside of Palestine, it nonetheless demonstrates that Latin served as the communication medium throughout the Roman Empire both in the East and the West.

Papyrus fragments, dating in the period between the two Jewish revolts (66–135 CE),[18] were discovered in the caves of Murabbaʿt. Although these fragments are small in number (about four or five), the Mur 158 appears to have been an official Roman document and preserves a Roman name on line 6: *C. Iulius R[?]*.[19]

The above inscriptions, historical attestations, and papyrus fragments, though not abundant, do provide a context for understanding how Latin was used in the Roman Empire and especially in the land of Palestine.

Hebrew: The Sacred Language

Hebrew is associated with a family of Semitic languages that are broadly classified into three primary groups: East Semitic (Akkadian), Northwest

---

16. Gill, "Erastus the Aedile," 293–302.

17. McRay, *Archaeology*, 333.

18. Koester, *History, Culture, and Religion*, 302–8.

19. Benoit et al., *Texte*, 270; also see Benoit et al., *Planches*, §158.

Semitic (Eblaic, Ugaritic, Hebrew, Phoenician, and Aramaic), and Southwest
Semitic (Arabic).[20] The term *Semitic* is derived from Shem, one of Noah's
three sons from whom the majority of people who spoke these languages
descended (Gen 9:18; 10:21–31).[21] The majority of the OT was written in
Hebrew. Only a small portion was composed in Aramaic, the language of
Israel's oppressors during the exilic period.[22]

These ancient Semitic languages trace back as far as the third to second
millennium BCE. The earliest reference to spoken Hebrew is found in the
biblical narrative in which Jacob and Laban made a covenant between them
to do each other no harm:

ועתה לכה נכרתה ברית אני ואתה והיה לעד ביני וביניך:
ויקח יעקב אבן וירימה מצבה:
ויאמר יעקב לאחיו לקטו אבנים ויקחו אבנים ויעשו־גל ויאכלו שם על־הגל:
ויקרא־לו לבן יגר שהדותא ויעקב קרא לו גלעד:

(Gen 31:44–47)

> Now come, let us make a covenant between you and let it become
> a witness between you and me. So Jacob took a stone and set it
> up as a pillar. And Jacob said to his kinsmen, "Gather stones." So
> they took stones and made a heap and they ate there by the heap.
> Now Laban called it Jegar-Sahadutha, but Jacob called it Galeed.

The text indicates that the disputing parties erected a heap of stones to
serve as a witness between them and their descendants. Interestingly, Laban
calls the place יגר שהדותא, which is Aramaic,[23] but Jacob calls it by a Hebrew
name—גלעד.[24] The two designations conform to the linguistic differences
between the Jews and their Semitic neighbors.

Later in Jewish history, the Assyrian king sent Rabshakeh to strongly
encourage Hezekiah, king of Judah, to surrender in order to prevent the city
of Jerusalem from being violently overtaken. Hezekiah's representatives—
Eliakim, Shebnah, and Joah—made the following request of Rabshakeh in
2 Kgs 18:26:

ויאמר אליקים בן־חלקיהו ושבנה ויואח אל־רב־שקה דבר־נא
אל־עבדיך ארמית כי שמעים אנחנו ואל־תדבר עמנו יהודית
באזני העם אשר על־החמה:

---

20. Liverani, "Semites," 392.

21. McFall, "Hebrew Language," 658.

22. Jer 10:11; Dan 2:4–7; Ezra 4:8–6:18; 7:12–26.

23. "The Heap of Witness." Holladay, *Hebrew and Aramaic*, 127 and 349.

24. Galeed, which means "heap of stones." Ibid., 59 and 61.

Then Eliakim the son of Hilkiah, Shebnah and Joah, said to Rabshakeh, "Speak now to your servants in Aramaic, for we understand it; and do not speak to us in Judean in the hearing of the people who are on the wall."

The delegation from Hezekiah insisted that Rabshakeh speak to the people in ארמית ("Aramaic") and not in יהודי ("Judean"). The text emphasizes the difference between the languages of Assyria and of Judah and shows that the common language understood by the majority of the Jewish people during the preexilic period was Hebrew, not Aramaic. The captivity, however, caused a linguistic reversal among the Jews, and Aramaic rather than Hebrew was adopted as the common language. In fact, Nehemiah rebuked his postexilic countrymen for having lost the ability to speak Hebrew, the language of the Judeans (יהודית):

גם| בימים ההם ראיתי את־היהודים השיבו נשים[אשדודיות] (אשדדיות)
עמוניות [עמניות] מואביות:
ובניהם חצי מדבר אשדודית ואינם מכירים לדבר יהודית וכלשון עם ועם:

(Neh 13:23–24)

Moreover, in those days, I saw that the Jews had married women from Ashdod, Ammon, and Moab. As to the children, half spoke Ashdod, and none of them was able to speak Judean, but the language of his own people.

Even if Nehemiah's assessment was an exaggeration, it is clear that he was deeply concerned that the Jews had disconnected from their linguistic heritage (יהודית). If the Jews were losing the ability to speak Hebrew, it stands to reason that the ability to write in Hebrew was rarer.

The biblical evidence suggests that the linguistic vacuum among the Jews was filled by Aramaic. The written Aramaic Targums that began to be composed in 200 CE had a much earlier oral antecedent. After Nehemiah had led a successful campaign to rebuild the wall around Jerusalem that had been destroyed by the Babylonians, the people assembled to hear Ezra and the priests read from the book of the law of Moses. As Ezra read while standing at a wooden podium above the people, the Levites interpreted the reading for the people:

ויקראו בספר בתורת האלהים מפרש ושום שכל ויבינו במקרא:

(Neh 8:8)

They read from the law of God, translating so as to give the sense, so that they understood the reading.

The Hebrew term פרש is equivalent to the Aramaic term of the same root. Both terms mean to explain precisely, to divide into sections, or to translate.[25] A similar use of פרש is found in the narrative of Ezra 4. Israel's enemies had sent a letter written and translated into Aramaic to Artaxerxes requesting an official decree to halt the rebuilding of the temple:

רחום בעל־טעם ושמשי ספרא כתבו
אגרה חדה על־ירושלם לארתחששתא מלכא כנמא:

(Ezra 4:8)

Rehum the commander and Shemshai the scribe wrote a letter against Jerusalem to the king, Artaxerxes, as follows. . . .

Artaxerxes responded and composed a document to be delivered to the Jews. The document began with the following words:

נשתונא די שלחתון עלינא מפרש קרי קדמי:

(Ezra 4:18)

The document which you sent to us has been translated and read before us.

In the above narratives, פרש describes the acts of both translation and explanation.[26] The greater emphasis, however, relates to each narrative's revelation of the linguistic division among the Jews. That Aramaic had become the common language among the Jews during the Second Temple period is certain since the Jews were unfamiliar with Hebrew and therefore needed Ezra and the Levites to translate the reading into Aramaic. It is also noteworthy that the educated class or priests appear to have been familiar enough with Hebrew to be able to read and translate it into another language.

Archer states that the development of the Aramaic Targums was primarily precipitated by the linguistic departure of Jews from their Hebrew heritage:

During the Babylonian exile, the Jewish people began to forsake their ancestral Hebrew more and more for the Aramaic tongue, which had become the international language for diplomacy and commerce and the principal medium of communication between the Persian government and its subjects after the

25. See "פרש" in Hess, *New International Dictionary*, 700. See also Holladay, *Hebrew and Aramaic*, 299.

26. Bowman states that פרש "is a technical term referring to extempore translation by a scribe" and that the term "is used for translation from Hebrew to Aramaic." Bowman, "Ezra," 604; Bowman, "Aramaeans," 65–90.

establishment of the Persian empire. As Jewish congregations became more uncertain of their Hebrew (although Hebrew never ceased to be studied and spoken by the learned class in Palestine right up to the second century A.D.), it became necessary for an interpreter to repeat to them in Aramaic the message which had just been read in the synagogue service from their Hebrew Bible.[27]

Additionally, the above observation also points to two significant developments that pertain to the function of Hebrew in Jewish life. First, the preservation of ancestral Hebrew became the work of the educated or priestly class. Second, the educated or priestly class was found mainly in and around Jerusalem in the land of Palestine because the Jewish temple was located there. Hebrew therefore most likely survived extinction because of the efforts of a committed class of educated Jews.

In addition to the Hebrew preserved by the OT, the discovery of the DSS produced over nine hundred ancient scrolls compiled between the second century BCE and 68 CE. Of those scrolls, five hundred and fifty were written in Hebrew.[28] Elisha Qimron wrote concerning the type of Hebrew used:

> Broadly speaking, the language of the Qumran sectarian literature is similar (especially in phraseology and syntax) to the language of those biblical books that were written in the post exilic period.[29]

Qimron's observation reveals a close tie between the Hebrew of the biblical text and the scrolls of the Qumran community. The difference in style between the former or classical Hebrew (Pentateuch and Former Prophets) and the latter Hebrew (Ezra, Nehemiah, Esther) portions of the OT is minimal. The Hebrew of the Qumran scrolls has been linked to the later Hebrew of the OT and therefore is essentially the same:

> The Hebrew of scripture, though far from uniform, is essentially a single language. In the oldest poetry, archaic forms, known from Ugarit, endure. Certain post-exilic materials differ from earlier texts. The bulk of the Hebrew Bible, later than Exodus 15 and earlier than Esther, presents a single if changing grammar.[30]

---

27. Archer, *Survey*, 45.

28. Hoerth and McRay, *Bible Archaeology*, 155.

29. Qimron and Strugnell, *Qumran Cave 4.5*, 108. See also Abegg, "Hebrew Language," 463.

30. Ibid., 459. The former writings are often referred to as Classical Biblical Hebrew

Despite the similarities among the Hebrew scrolls, there are linguistic variations in some of the scrolls that have been identified with a later development of Hebrew referred to as Mishnaic Hebrew. Jewish rabbis adopted this
style of Hebrew in their writings, of which the Mishnah (ca. 200 CE) is the
best example.[31]

One of the finds among the Qumran scrolls was the *Copper Scroll*
(3Q15), which was found by archaeologists in Cave 3 during excavations in
1952. It lists sixty-four places where treasures estimated to amount to sixty-
five tons of silver and twenty-six tons of gold were hidden.[32] This scroll
has been attributed to the temple priests who hid these treasures from the
Roman armies (ca. 70 CE).[33] The dissimilarity of this scroll when compared
to the other Hebrew scrolls has caused some scholars to believe that Hebrew
may represent the language used within the vicinity of Jerusalem during the
first century CE.[34]

Another important discovery was the *Halakhic Letter* (4Q394). The
title that has been attributed to the scroll is *Misqat Ma'ase Ha-Torah* ("Some
Precepts of the Torah"). It is also written in Mishnaic Hebrew. The title was
derived from the statement made in the conclusion of the letter indicating
that its purpose was to reveal the way of righteousness by declaring what
was right and good before God:

> We have also written to you concerning (27) some of the obser-
> vances of the Law (*miqsat ma'ase ha-Torah*), which we think are
> beneficial to you and your people. For [we have noticed] that
> (28) prudence and knowledge of the Law are with you.

> Understand all these (matters) and ask Him to straighten (29)
> your counsel and put you far away from thoughts of evil and the
> counsel of Belial. (30) Consequently, you will rejoice at the end
> of time when you discover that some of our sayings are true.
> (31) And it will be reckoned for you as righteousness when you

---

(CBH) and the latter writings as Late Biblical Hebrew (LBH); See Waltke and O'Connor,
Introduction, 15.

31. Abegg, "Hebrew Language," 460.

32. Some scholars believe the amount is grossly exaggerated or perhaps even a
deception. See Vermes, *Dead Sea Scrolls*, 308–9.

33. Ferguson cautions that the discovery of this scroll "was enough to turn scholars into treasure hunters. The work may have had nothing to do with the Qumran
community" (*Backgrounds*, 472).

34. Abegg, "Hebrew Language," 460.

perform what is right and good before Him, for your own good (32) and for that of Israel.[35]

Millard states that the letter's Mishnaic style of Hebrew "may be closer to the Hebrew actually spoken in the sect and, perhaps, by other Jews."[36]

Both the *Copper Scroll* and the *Halakhic Letter* appear to be linked to a special class of Jews who were driven to preserve and maintain their ancestral Hebrew heritage. At no other place during the first century was such a desire demonstrated more than in the vicinity of Jerusalem where the Jewish seat of government and the temple were located. Abegg makes the following observation concerning the aforementioned scrolls:

> [W]hen taken together the *Copper Scroll* and 4QMMT suggest that during the last couple of centuries B.C. and the first century A.D., LBH had begun the transition to the MH of the later rabbinic period. The Qumran sectarians, as is evidenced by the LBH-nature of the vast majority of the Hebrew scrolls and the presence of the MH characteristics in 4QMMT, may have practiced a form of *diglossia*, an upper language (LBH) for formal occasions and writing, and a lower language (with characteristics of MH) that was spoken in everyday life. The inhabitants of Judea and Jerusalem very likely spoke a Hebrew very similar to MH.[37]

Without the discovery of the DSS not much would be known about the state of Hebrew during the first century in Palestine. It may be difficult to speculate without reservation that only pockets of Palestinian Jews spoke Hebrew—primarily Jews within the vicinity of Jerusalem—but the extant evidence supports that speculation.[38]

---

35. Vermes, *Dead Sea Scrolls*, 228; see also Ferguson, *Backgrounds*, 473.

36. Millard, *Reading and Writing*, 119.

37. Abegg, "Hebrew Language," 461. Fitzmyer notes that the "late Hadrian script" of some of the scrolls "may be regarded as first-century compositions" ("Languages of Palestine," 529).

38. Fitzmyer, "Languages of Palestine," 531. Abegg states that "the evidence reviewed suggests that the language among the Jews in Jerusalem and Judea in the early first century A.D. was Hebrew." The evidence in fact may demonstrate a more restrictive use of Hebrew. The primary class of Hebrew speakers would be the Jewish priests, scribes, and other religious leaders in Jerusalem ("Hebrew Language," 462).

Aramaic: A Declining Language

The widespread distribution of Aramaic in the land of Palestine came after the fall of the northern kingdom of Israel (ca. 722 BCE) when Assyria repopulated the regions of Samaria and Galilee with Aramaic speakers (2 Kgs 17:24). Although the southern kingdom of Judah held off an Assyrian invasion in 701 BCE (2 Kgs 18–19; Isa 36:11–12), the new world power of Babylon toppled Jerusalem in 586 BCE and led the Jews away into exile. Aramaic continued as the imperial language of the Persian Empire (ca. 538–332 BCE). The penetration of three Aramaic-speaking world powers into the land of Palestine ensured that Aramaic became "the most widely spoken language in Syria and Palestine, and, presumably, among the Jews, with the possible exception of the Jews of Judea"[39] who would have maintained the sacred language of Hebrew. Consequently, Aramaic, along with Greek and Hebrew, was one of the three most commonly used languages in first-century Palestine.[40]

The impact of Aramaic upon the Jews is most notably found in the OT. As was discussed earlier concerning the covenant formed between Laban and Jacob, two Aramaic words are found—יגר שהדותא. Jeremiah's proclamation against Israel's idolatry contains one verse written in Aramaic (Jer 10:11), presumably because he condemns the gods of the nations:[41]

כדנה תאמרון להום אלהיא די־שמיא

וארקא לא עבדו יאבדו מארעא ומן־תחות שמיא אלה:

And thus you shall say to them, "The gods who did not make the heavens and the earth will perish from under these heavens."

Two Aramaic portions are also found in the book of Ezra containing correspondence between the enemies of the Jews and the Persian King Darius and a correspondence from Artaxerxes to Ezra (Ezra 4:8–6:18; 7:12–26). Additionally, the central portion of Daniel is written in Aramaic (Dan 2:4b–7:28). The portions found in Ezra and Daniel are actually referred to

39. Wise, "Languages of Palestine," 437.

40. Buth, "Aramaic Language," 86. It is my contention, however, that Greek actually emerged as the dominant language commonly used by the first century CE. Millard states that "it was in the Exile in Babylonia that the Jews took up Aramaic as their language of everyday life" (Reading and Writing, 86).

41. This verse appears to be carefully structured so as to emphasize the destiny of idols. Because of the Aramaic, it has been suggested that this passage represents a later insertion. However, the impact of Jeremiah's proclamation appears to be amplified by writing in the language of Israel's captors. See Ash, Jeremiah and Lamentations, 114.

as ארמית (Ezra 4:7; Dan 2:4). It is important to note that the aforementioned texts are in Aramaic because of the period in which they were composed:

> [T]here seems to be little doubt that the Aramaic of the OT must be placed in the 5th or 4th cents., with a possible deviation of a half-century on either side, in other words, between 550 and 250 B.C., probably around 400 or the time of Ezra.[42]

Additionally, since many Jews were losing the ability to read and understand Hebrew, it became prudent to communicate the teachings of the OT in Aramaic.[43] Since Hebrew had to be translated into Aramaic orally during the days of Ezra and Nehemiah (Neh 8:1–8) for the postexilic generation, written translations (i.e., Targums) of the OT would naturally have followed. Aramaic Targums were first made for the Torah and then for the rest of the OT, although Greek eclipsed Aramaic by the first century CE.[44] Wise states that the Aramaic Targums may preserve the actual verbal speech of the Jews most notably during the period after the exile and to some degree up to the period of the Bar Kokhba revolts.[45]

Only a few Aramaic Targums of the OT were found among the DSS. Two Aramaic translations of the biblical text were discovered in cave 4 in 1977 CE. The first discovery (4Q156/4QtgLev) was comprised of two fragments that contained eight verses found in Lev 16:12–15 and 16:18–21.[46] The literalness of the translation, which connects it closely to the MT, is out of character for the Targums since they are not generally "viewed as strictly literal translations in the modern sense."[47] The fragments have been dated to the end of the second century BCE.[48] The second discovery

---

42. Lasor, "Aramaic," 232.

43. Young states that "the Targums were designed to communicate the message of the text to people, and the translator (meturgeman) sometimes injected stories, Jewish Haggadic teachings, or Halakic stipulations into his interpretation of the Hebrew text . . . The Targums were indeed an actualization of the Bible, and they often elucidate the ancient Jewish understandings of particular texts" ("Targum," 728).

44. Greek's eclipse of Aramaic was not abrupt but a gradual process during the Hellenistic period. Lasor, "Aramaic," 229. The emerging dominance of the Greek language will be addressed in the next section.

45. Wise, "Language of Palestine," 438.

46. Buth, "Aramaic," 91. There seems to be some uncertainty as to whether these fragments represent a Targum "as opposed to a portion from some quite different liturgical work which happened to quote Leviticus" (see Wise, "Languages of Palestine," 438).

47. Ibid., 728.

48. For a catalogue of discoveries and translations of the Aramaic texts, see Fitzmyer and Harrington, *Palestinian Aramaic*.

(4Q157/4QtgJob) was an Aramaic translation of Job, containing Job 3:5 and 4:16—5:4. Like the Leviticus fragments mentioned above, this translation is also more literal in its style, lacking explanatory interpretations commonly characteristic of Targums. Additionally, a third Aramaic translation was found (11Q10/11QtgJob) in Cave 11 in 1956 CE. This translation, which was also of the OT book of Job, contains a lengthier section (Job 17—42) than the Job fragment found in Cave 4. The scroll dates from the mid-first century CE. In regard to the character of this scroll, Randall Buth makes the following observation:

> The dialect of Aramaic represented in this Qumran text is of a literary type that includes a few features that faintly hint as the East, far from Judea. The same features give it a slightly old, formal style. A general audience would appear to be in view, for example, Jews, in the Eastern Diaspora as much as in Judea.[49]

Based upon the evidence above, the following observations are in order: (1) The limited number of Aramaic Targums of the biblical text (at least beyond Job) may indicate that the Qumran community preferred Hebrew as their access to Scripture; (2) the Targums found at Qumran demonstrate that Aramaic may not have been as commonly used among the Jewish synagogues in the first century as is widely thought;[50] and (3) outside of Jerusalem, where Hebrew was not as common, Aramaic served as the natural choice for communication. The purpose of the Aramaic Targums prior to the first century CE, therefore, was to help Jews understand the Hebrew Scriptures:

> The most plausible explanation for the function of Aramaic targums, if such did exist in Jesus' day, is as interpretive devices. Having heard the Hebrew of the Scriptures read aloud, the audience would be informed of its meaning and application in Aramaic. Hebrew was not used because of the desire to avoid confusion between the words of the text and its interpretation.[51]

Aramaic seems to have been less prominent by the time of the first century CE since "Greek was clearly the language of choice in order to disseminate a message as widely as possible."[52]

---

49. Buth, "Aramaic," 92

50. Even Fitzmyer admits that in regard to his thesis the most commonly used language in Palestine during the time of Jesus was Aramaic and that "much of the material used as evidence . . . is not derived from the first century" ("Languages of Palestine," 518 n. 62).

51. Wise, "Languages of Palestine," 438.

52. Ferguson, *Backgrounds*, 135—36.

Further evidence that has bearing on Aramaic's presence during the first century CE is the discovery of a collection of papyri deposited in caves during the Second Jewish Revolt at Murabba'at. Although most of these documents date after 70 CE and on into the second century, they likely represent older customs that probably date within the early part of the first century CE. One particular find, however, was an Aramaic contract for a loan (Mur 18) that dates from Nero's reign in about 56 CE:

1. [the ye]ar two of the Emperor Nero [ ],

2. At Siwaya, Absalom, son of Hannin, from Siwaya, has declared

3. In my presence that there is on account with me, me Zechariah, Son of Yohanan, son of H . . [ ],

4. Living at Cheaslon, the sum of twe[nt]y zuzin. The sum I am to rep[ay)

5. b[y . . . But if]I have not paid (?) by this

6. time, I will reimburse you with (interest of) a fifth and will settle in en[tirety],

7. even if this is the Year of Release. And if I do not do so, indem[nity]

8. for you (will be) from my possessions, and whatever I acquire (will be) at your disposal.

9. [Zech]ariah, son of Yohan[an, f]or himself.

10. Joseph, so[n of], [wro]te (this), witness.

11. Jonathan, son of John, witness.

12. Joseph, so[n of J]udan, [J]udan, witness [Hebrew word].[53]

This discovery is significant for two reasons. First, the contract date places the document during the period of the early Christian church. Second, the document represents a common item that indicates that Aramaic was likely in use in everyday affairs during the first century CE. However, the mere presence of Aramaic in the first century CE does not mean that it remained the dominant language. Rather, I will demonstrate in the next section that when compared to Greek, Aramaic is less dominant. Lasor states the matter plainly: "With the spread of Hellenism, including the deliberate attempt to extend the usage of the Greek language, Aramaic all but vanished."[54]

The best evidence of Aramaic's impact upon first-century society in general and upon the Jews in particular is found in the GNT. The particular

53. Translation from Fitzmyer and Harrington, *Palestinian Aramaic*, 137–39.

54. Although Lasor continues to say that Aramaic survived in three areas—Arabia, Palestine, and Mesopotamia—Aramaic was on the decline and eventually faded as a dominant force, being absorbed by other dialects like Syriac ("Aramaic," 231).

kind of influence of Aramaic is often couched as a Semitic influence or "Semitism" that may be found in the GNT. Since Hebrew and Aramaic are closely related, a Semitism found in the GNT is defined as Greek elements of style, structure, grammar, vocabulary, or idiom that appear to conform more to Aramaic or Hebrew usage than to Greek.[55] A Semitic influence can be detected by the style or form in which a NT writer chose to communicate a thought. For example, Rabbi Hillel's (ca. 60 BCE–20 CE)[56] interpretive principle of *qal wā-ḥômer* ("light and heavy")[57] refers to an inference drawn from a minor premise to a weightier one. In other words, what applies in a lesser situation will most certainly apply in a greater one. This particular style of argumentation was prevalent in Jesus' teachings and represents a Hebraic rhetorical style that is often reproduced in the GNT.

Two examples from the Gospel of Matthew demonstrate the Semitic rhetorical style of Hillel's method of argumentation. First, according to Matt 12:1–8, the Pharisees accused Jesus' disciples of doing "what was not lawful on the Sabbath" when they were picking the heads of grain while passing through grain fields. Jesus responded and described how David because of hunger once ate the consecrated bread that only priests were allowed to eat. Jesus also reminded them that priests in the temple broke the Sabbath and were innocent. Jesus said that "someone greater than the temple is here" and that the "Son of Man is Lord of the Sabbath" (v. 8). The argumentation that Jesus followed coincided with Rabbi Hillel's rhetorical style: If the Pharisees excused David's actions because of special circumstances (and for being king!) and the priests were excused because of the nature of their work (a light or lesser case), *how much more* would the actions of Jesus—the King, Priest, and Lord—together with those of his disciples be justified, appropriate, and lawful (a heavy or weightier case)?

Second, according to Matt 12:9–14, Jesus entered a synagogue when a man with a withered hand was also there. Some asked Jesus whether it was lawful to heal on the Sabbath. Jesus asked them if they would rescue a sheep if it had fallen into a pit on the Sabbath. The implication is that no one would think twice about pulling a sheep out of a pit even on the Sabbath. Would it not be proper, therefore, to help a human being in need on the Sabbath? Again, the Hillel model was followed: Since it is lawful to help or to do

55. Wilcox, "Semitic Influence," 1094.

56. Wyatt, "Hillel," 716. See also Ellis, *Old Testament*, 87–90.

57. The Hebrew word *qal* means "light, agile, quick" (Holladay, *Hebrew and Aramaic*, 318) and is adopted by Hebrew grammarians as the representation of the simplest Hebrew verbal form—third, masculine, singular—before prefixes and suffixes are added or internal changes are made to the word (see Weingreen, *Grammar*, 100). The Hebrew term *homer* refers to a measurement—"heaps" (Holladay, *Hebrew and Aramaic*, 109).

good in respect to an animal (a light or lesser case), *how much more* would it be proper and "lawful to do good on the Sabbath" (v. 12), particularly when a human being is involved (a heavy or weightier case)?

Hillel's principle of inference *a fortiori* is also illustrated in several passages in the book of Hebrews. In Heb 2:2–5, the writer argues that if every transgression received a just recompense under the Law (a light or lesser case), *how much more* penalty would there be for those who neglect so great a salvation (a heavy or weightier case)? The core argument follows the same form in Heb 9:13–14. The writer poses the question that if the sacrifices under the Law sanctified the flesh of those who had been defiled (a light or lesser case), *how much more* will the blood of Christ cleanse the conscience from dead works to serve the living God (a heavy or weightier case)? Finally, in Heb 10:28–30, the writer makes another argument in classical Hillel style: If one who sets aside the law of Moses died without mercy on the testimony of two or three witnesses (a light or lesser case), *how much more* severe punishment will there be for one who has trampled underfoot the Son of God (a heavy or weightier case)?

Although one may argue that the above examples represent a Hebrew influence upon the NT, it should be kept in mind that the Christian movement began within a Semitic context and that the writers of the NT had Semitic backgrounds. This was also true of Rabbi Hillel whose rabbinical writings have been preserved in a few relics of first-century CE Aramaic compositions.[58]

Several Aramaic words,[59] expressions,[60] and names[61] are also found in the GNT. Some references to Aramaic are from the book of Acts where Paul speaks to his countrymen in a Semitic dialect:

> ἐπιτρέψαντος δὲ αὐτοῦ ὁ Παῦλος ἑστὼς ἐπὶ τῶν ἀναβαθμῶν κατέσεισεν τῇ χειρὶ τῷ λαῷ. πολλῆς δὲ σιγῆς γενομένης προσεφώνησεν τῇ Ἑβραΐδι διαλέκτῳ λέγων ... (Acts 21:40, emphasis mine).

> And when he had given him permission, Paul while standing on the stairs, motioned to the people with his hands; and when

---

58. Some of the brief sayings of Hillel are found in the tractate "Sayings of the Fathers." See Millard, *Reading and Writing*, 91.

59. βάτους (*bath*—a liquid measure, Luke 16:6); μνᾶς (*mina*—a monetary unit, Luke 19:24); κορβανᾶν (*corban*—a dedication gift, Matt 27:6).

60. ταλιθα κουμ (*talitha cum*—"Little girl, arise!" Mark 5:41); Εφφαθα (*ephphatha*—"Be opened!" Mark 7:34); μαράνα θά (*marana tha*—"O Lord come!" 1 Cor 16:22).

61. Κηφᾶς (*Cephas*—Peter's Aramaic surname, John 1:42); Βαρναβᾶς (*Barnabas*, Acts 4:36); Ταβιθά (*Tabitha*, Acts 9:36, 40).

it became quiet, he began to speak in the *Hebrew tongue* saying
. . . .

ἀκούσαντες δὲ ὅτι τῇ Ἐβραΐδι διαλέκτῳ προσεφώνει αὐτοῖς, μᾶλλον παρέσχον ἡσυχίαν. καὶ φησίν . . . (Acts 22:2, emphasis mine).

And hearing that he was speaking to them in the *Hebrew tongue*, they became quieter. And he said . . . .

Interestingly, Paul stated in his defense before King Agrippa that Jesus spoke to him in a Semitic language while he was travelling on the road to Damascus:

πάντων τε καταπεσόντων ἡμῶν εἰς τὴν γῆν ἤκουσα φωνὴν λέγουσαν πρός με τῇ Ἐβραΐδι διαλέκτῳ·Σαοὺλ Σαούλ, τί με διώκεις; σκληρόν σοι πρὸς κέντρα λακτίζειν (Acts 26:14, emphasis mine).

Now when we all fell to the ground, I heard a voice saying to me in the *Hebrew tongue*, "Saul, Saul, why are you persecuting me? It is hard for you to kick against the goads."

In each reference above, the Greek term τῇ Ἐβραΐδι is translated as the "Hebrew tongue" ("dialect" NASB, 2005). Bruce states that in regard to the NT references to the Hebrew language, "Aramaic appears to be meant" since in most instances, especially among Jews in Jerusalem, Aramaic was the vernacular.[62] In reference to Acts 26:14, the vocative, Σαοὺλ Σαούλ, is obviously a Semitism; otherwise the vocative would be Σαῦλε Σαῦλε.[63] In fact, Dalman proposes the following Aramaic reconstruction: *Shāūl, Shāūl, mā att rādephinni.*[64] The presence of such Semitisms in the GNT indicates that Aramaic has influenced its composition in many ways.

There is no question, based upon the evidence presented, that Aramaic was the mother tongue of both Jesus and the disciples. One would therefore expect the GNT to have in many respects a Semitic flair. However, the evidence is not conclusive that Aramaic was as widely used in the first century CE as it had been during the postexilic period. Lasor's words of caution concerning studies of the Aramaic backgrounds of the NT seem most appropriate: "The entire subject needs very careful restudy, and theories of

---

62. Rev 9:11 and 16:16 are exceptions. See Bruce, *Acts*, 413. Aramaic was often inaccurately called "Hebrew." See Macgregor, *Acts*, 288; Danker, "Ἐβραΐς," 270.

63. See Acts 9:4 and 22:7.

64. Dalman, *Jesus—Jeshua*, 18.

Aramaic backgrounds to the Gospels, etc., must not be allowed to distort this study."[65]

Greek: The Common Language

Isocrates (436–338 BCE) is considered the father of Hellenism. He was an Athenian orator who sought to extol the refinement of speech as a sign of education and therefore defined a true Greek as one by education and not by birth:

> [W]hether men have been liberally educated from their earliest years is not to be determined by their courage or their wealth or such advantages but is made manifest most of all by their speech, and that this has proved itself to be the surest sign of culture in every one of us, and that those who are skilled in speech are not only men of power in their own cities but are also held in honour in other states. And so far has our city [Athens] distanced the rest of mankind in thought and speech that her pupils have become the teachers of the rest of the world; and she has brought it about that the name "Hellenes" suggests no longer a race but an intelligence, and the title "Hellenes" is applied rather to those who share our culture than to those who share a common blood (*Paneg.* 49–50 [Norlin, LCL]).

There is a certain prophetic irony in the words of Isocrates. During the Hellenistic expansion (332–167 BCE) initiated by Alexander the Great, Greeks were indeed identified more by their culture than by their birth.

Hellenism generally refers to the ancient Greek language and culture. In contrast to the Romans who absorbed the cultures and religion of conquered states, the Greeks wanted to spread Greek ideals and culture to the world. Hellenistic indoctrination was promoted passionately by Alexander the Great and began to accelerate after his death in 323 BCE. "Alexander ushered in the Hellenistic Age," wrote Everett Ferguson, "but the ingredients of that age were already there. He accelerated the pace of change."[66]

When the Jews went into exile, Greek influence had already made advances into Babylonian culture. A Greek band seems to have provided the musical entertainment at the dedication of Nebuchadnezzar's golden image. The announcement was made to everyone that when they heard the sound of music, they were to worship the image:

---

65. Lasor, "Aramaic," 233.

66. Ferguson, *Backgrounds*, 21.

וכרוזא קרא בחיל לכון אמרין עממﬞיא אמיא ולשניא:
בעדנא די־תשמעון קל קרנא משרוקיתא (קיתרוס) [קתרוס]
סבכא פסנתרין סומפניה וכל זני זמרא תפלון ותסגדון לצלם
דהבא די הקים נבוכדנצר מלכא:

> Then the herald loudly proclaimed: "To you the command is
> given, O peoples, nations and men of every language, that at
> the moment you hear the sound of the horn, flute, lyre, trigon,
> psaltery, bagpipe and all kinds of music, you are to fall down and
> worship the gold image that Nebuchadnezzar the king has set
> up" (Dan 3:4–5; cf. vv. 7, 10 and 15).

Behind the Aramaic words identifying the various instruments mentioned
above are Greek loanwords.[67] Such evidence along with the bilingual ostracon from Khirbet el-Kôm (see chapter 1) argues favorably that Greek
by the time of the fourth century BCE had already invaded Aramaic "even
for mundane concepts and matters for which perfectly good words already
existed in Aramaic."[68]

The monumental task of translating the Hebrew Scriptures that resulted in the LXX demonstrates the wide use of Greek by Jews outside as
well as inside Palestine. Interestingly, "Jerusalem was the place where Jewish
knowledge of the Greek language was concentrated," wrote Gerard Mussies, "and where it was taught."[69] It was truly a remarkable undertaking in
that it was the first attempt to translate the Hebrew Scriptures into another
language. The translators began in the third century BCE and appear to have
taken nearly a century to complete the task.

The catalyst for such a monumental production can be linked to the
conquests of Alexander the Great. The expansion of the Greek Empire broke
down international barriers as the world came under Hellenistic influence.

---

67. Four of the six instruments bear Greek names: קיתרוס (κίθαρις), סבכא (σαμβύκη),
פסנתרין (ψαλτήριον), סומפניה (συμφωνία).

68. Wise, "Languages of Palestine," 439. See also Mitchell and Joyce, "Musical
Instruments," 19–27. Fitzmyer is somewhat reluctant to accept the presence of these
loanwords as evidence of wide Greek influence upon Semitic languages. He states that
"part of the evidence that these words are foreign in the Aramaic text is the lack of the
distinctive Aramaic ending on them in contrast to the names of other instruments in
the same verse. These are the only words of certain Greek origin in Daniel; it is significant that they are the names of musical instruments and were probably borrowed with
the importation of the instruments themselves. Since they are isolated instances and
technical words, it is difficult to say to what extent they are a gauge of the influence of
Greek on the Palestinian Semitic languages" ("Languages of Palestine," 501).

69. Mussies, "Languages (Greek)," 196.

As Greek culture became more entrenched, people gradually absorbed its cultural peculiarities.

In the vast cosmopolitan city of Alexandria, many Jews believed that in order for Jewish faith to live on and be vibrant, a translation of their sacred Scriptures was of paramount importance since "by the early years of the Christian era we are told that there were almost a million Jews in Egypt, that two out of the five wards of Alexandria were known as Jewish districts, and that others were scattered throughout the remaining three wards."[70]

A translation of the Hebrew Scriptures served two purposes. First, a translation served as a safeguard to Jewish beliefs and religious understanding. Since the ability among Jews to read and to speak the native language of Hebrew was fading and since Greek was eclipsing Aramaic, it became obvious that Jewish faith needed to be preserved in the language of Greek. Second, having a translation in the language of the people facilitated worship and the educational needs of the synagogue. In addition, however, a third benefit arose. A Greek translation of the Hebrew Scriptures provided a practical means for a broader Gentile world to gain an introduction to Jewish faith and history.[71]

The origin of the LXX is enveloped in mystery. The most famous and most mysterious explanation of the origin of the LXX and of the acquiring of its abbreviation relates to an account in a letter written by Aristeas, an official who served in the court of King Ptolemy II Philadelphus of Egypt (285–246 BCE). F. F. Bruce made this statement about the heightened interest in literature during this period: "Ptolemy was renowned as a patron of literature and it was under him that the great library of Alexandria, one of the world's cultural wonders for 900 years, was inaugurated."[72] Supposedly the royal librarian at Alexandria, one Demetrius of Phalerum, convinced the king of the importance of preserving a copy of the Jewish law. In order for the Hebrew Scriptures to find their place in the great library, they had to be translated into Greek. After the king was persuaded, he dispatched a delegation to meet with Eleazer, the high priest, in Jerusalem. Aristeas, a member of the emerging delegation, requested that seventy-two elders (the number was more than likely rounded to seventy), six from each of the twelve tribes of Israel, be sent to Alexandria to undertake the translation. Eleazer agreed and sent to the king of Egypt seventy-two translators with the Hebrew Scriptures which were supposedly written in letters of gold. After an honorable reception, the seventy-two elders or translators were escorted

---

70. Bruce, *Books and Parchments*, 136.

71. Soderlund, "Septuagint," 401–2.

72. Bruce, *Books and Parchments*, 136.

to the island of Pharos. There, after intensive collaborating, the translators completed their monumental task. Initially, it was believed to be only the Law that was translated into the Greek. However, the legend grew over the years to include the entire translation of the complete Hebrew Scriptures. The new translation received the approval of the Jewish community and was then submitted to the king. A curse accompanied the new translation for anyone who dared to tamper with its contents by adding to, subtracting from, or otherwise altering the translation.

Allusions to the event described by Aristeas were made by such Jewish writers as Philo (*Mos.2* 2.8–7.44), Justin Martyr (*1 Apol.* 1.31), and Irenaeus (*Haer.* 3.21.2). Even Josephus paraphrased large portions of it and accepted the account as factual:

> Alexander reigned twelve years, and after him Ptolemy Soter forty-one; then Philadelphus took over the royal power in Egypt and held it for thirty-nine years; and he had the Law translated and released from slavery some hundred and twenty thousand natives of Jerusalem who were slaves in Egypt, for the following reason. Demetrius of Phalerum, who was in charge of the kings' library, was anxious to collect, if he could, all the books in the inhabited world, and, if he heard of, or saw, any book worthy of study, he would buy it; and so he endeavoured to meet the wishes of the king, for he was very much devoted to the art of book-collecting. Now, when Ptolemy once asked him how many tens of thousands of books he had already gathered together, he replied that the present number was about two hundred thousand but that within a short time he would assemble some five hundred thousand. He added that he had been informed that among the Jews also there were many works on their law, which were worthy of study and of a place in the kings' library, but, being written in the script and language of this people, they would be no small trouble to have translated into the Greek tongue. For, he said, though their script seemed to be similar to the peculiar Syrian (Aramaic) writing, and their language to sound like the other, it was, as it happened, of a distinct type. There was, however, nothing, he said, to prevent them from having these books translated and having the writings of this people also in their library, for he had abundant resources from which to meet the expense. And so the king, deciding that Demetrius had given him excellent advice as to how to realize his ambition of obtaining a large number of books, wrote to the high priest of the Jews that this might be done. Now a certain Aristaeus . . . (*Ant.* 12.11–17 [Marcus, LCL]).

Josephus described in great detail the honor bestowed upon the translators after they had completed the translation of the Torah:

> The king, then, having received these books from the hands of Demetrius, did obeisance to them and ordered that great care should be taken of the books in order that they might remain intact; he also invited the translators to come to him frequently from Judea, for this would be profitable for them both on account of the honour to be received from him and the gifts they would gain. At this time, he said, it was only right to send them home, but, if they came to him of their own will, they would obtain all that their wisdom deserved to obtain and his own generosity was able to provide. For the time being, therefore, he sent them home, giving each of them three very fine garments, two talents of gold, a small wine-cup worth a talent, and the covering for a banquet-table. Now these gifts he ha\gave them to keep for themselves, but to the high priest Eleazar he sent by them ten couches with feet of silver and the furnishings belonging to them and a small wine-cup worth thirty talents, and, in addition to these, ten garments, a purple robe, a very handsome crown and a hundred pieces of fine-linen weave, as well as shallow bowls and cups and libation-bowls and two golden mixing-bowls to be dedicated to God. He also requested of him by letter that, if any of these men wished to come to him, he should permit them to do so, for he highly valued the society of those possessed of learning, and took pleasure in using his wealth for the benefit of such persons. These, then, were the things done by Ptolemy Philadelphus in appreciation and honour of the Jews (*Ant.* 12.114–118 [Marcus, LCL]).

Although many ancient writers accepted the letter from Aristeas as being an accurate account of the origin of the LXX, modern scholarship (since the sixteenth century) has disputed the account because of historical inaccuracies, internal contradictions, and exaggerations over time. R. W. Klein discussed the situation:

> Later, as this story was retold in the early church, it got "better and better." According to Justin Martyr, the translation included the whole Old Testament. Later in the second century Irenaeus reports that the translators worked in isolation but came up with identical results, thanks to the inspiration of God. Finally, Epiphanius of Salamis (314–403) pushed the isolation idea to the limit. He had the translators do everything in pairs, even

going by thirty-six boats each night to dine with the king. When the thirty-six independent translations were read before the king, they were found to be completely identical.[73]

Nothing is known about Aristeas except that he was a devout Jew and an ardent defender of Jewish faith. Despite the letter's legendary components, Mussies makes the following pertinent observation:

> Although this story is certainly etiological fiction pretending to be history, the presuppositions on which it rests cannot be too wild, and the most central presupposition is of course, that Jerusalem priests knew Greek.[74]

The fact that priests in Jerusalem were skilled enough in Greek to translate the Hebrew Scriptures reveals that the Jews of Judea were not isolated from the broader linguistic transformation occurring throughout the Roman Empire.[75]

Although it may be difficult to establish the exact date when the LXX was completed, it nevertheless seems evident that all three parts of the Hebrew Scriptures were available in Greek by the end of the second century BCE. According to the prologue of the Greek translation of Sirach (Ecclesiasticus), the grandson of Joshua ben Sira went to Egypt in 132 BCE and made a translation of the original Hebrew version that was written by his grandfather between 190 and 175 BCE. The prologue contains a qualifying statement about the accuracy of the translation and compares it to the similar difficulties found in the LXX:

> You are urged therefore to read with good will and attention, and to be indulgent in cases where, despite our diligent labor in translating, we may seem to have rendered some phrases imperfectly. For what was originally expressed in Hebrew does not have exactly the same sense when translated into another language. Not only this work, but even the law itself, the prophecies, and the rest of the books differ not a little as originally expressed.[76]

---

73. Klein, *Textual Criticism*, 1–2.

74. Mussies, "Languages (Greek)," 196. Mussies also notes that Greek was very much central in Jerusalem among the educated class prior to the first century CE. See Mussies, "Greek in Palestine," 1054–55. See also Soderlund, "Septuagint," 404.

75. Lieberman, *Greek in Jewish Palestine*, 15–90.

76. Caird, "Ben Sira," 21–22.

Ferguson states that "Sirach continued the conservative religious views of the Old Testament but was aware of and tried to meet the challenges of Hellenism."[77]

Perhaps the most fascinating phenomenon concerning the LXX was the fact that a translation that was meant to serve as a Jewish witness to their faith and life was taken over by Christians of the first century CE.

> It is interesting that a work which the Jewish people originally esteemed so highly should eventually be rejected and condemned by them. This drastic change came about at least partly because the Septuagint increasingly became a sacred book for Christians, who used it to propagate Christian teaching. One example of a passage that supports the Christian teaching is Isaiah 7:14, where the word παρθένος (parthenos) is sometimes translated "virgin." It was used by Christians as strong evidence of their views about the virgin birth of Jesus (Matt. 1:23). Also, as the scribes began to accept the authoritative, standardized text of the Masorectic Text, the Septuagint, which was not based upon this text, was necessarily condemned.[78]

The wider circulation of the LXX made it the ideal translation for most of the NT writers.[79] The LXX was the Bible of the early church as is obvious from the many citations of NT letters. It also became the translation used by the early church fathers as they formulated their doctrinal beliefs to provide proof texts to refute what they believed were false doctrines and challenges to the purity of the gospel. As the church grew, the LXX was employed as a valuable missionary tool. As copies of Scriptures were made, it became the practice that such were made not from the Hebrew but from the LXX.

In addition to the LXX, it appears that Greek penetrated the more conservative circles of Judaism during the Maccabean revolt (168–166 BCE). The Jewish book of *Jubilees* (ca. 150 BCE) is a rewriting of Gen 1—Exod 19. About fifteen copies of the book were discovered among the DSS.[80] The

77. Ferguson, *Backgrounds*, 445.

78. Wegner, *Journey*, 195.

79. Swete states that "every part of the N.T. affords evidence of a knowledge of the LXX., and that a great majority of the passages cited from the O.T. are in general agreement with the Greek version . . . the LXX is the principal source from which the writers of the N.T. derived their O. T. quotations" (*Introduction to the Old Testament*, 392). See also Porter, "Septuagint/Greek Old Testament," 1104–5.

80. Two were found in Cave 2 (2Q19–20), one in Cave 3 (3Q5), eight or nine in Cave 4 (4Q176 frags. 19–21; 4Q216, 4Q218, 4Q219, 4Q220, 4Q221, 4Q222 and 4Q223–224), and one in Cave 11 (4Q12). See VanderKam, "Jubilees," 601; also VanderKam and Milik, "Jubilees," 1–140.

author of the book of *Jubilees* wrote in Hebrew yet relied heavily upon the Greek language and ideas, specifically Greek geographic literature that required an advanced understanding. Wise makes the following observation:

> Since the author of *Jubilees* would certainly not have been among those Jews most enthusiastic for Greek ways, one must assume that in those circles the knowledge of Greek was generally at least as profound as was his.[81]

Not only does one find Greek ideas couched in Hebrew disseminated among the Jews, but Greek epigraphy is found also among Palestinian Jewish authors who began to compose in Greek. For example, a deputy of Judas Maccabeus named Eupolemus wrote a work entitled *Concerning the Kings of Judea* (ca. 158 BCE) of which only fragments have been preserved by later Greek authors.[82] Carl Holladay observes that these fragments demonstrate an advanced proficiency in Greek:

> The fragments reflect use of both the LXX and MT, thus suggesting a bilingual author. The form of his syntax and use of language suggest that Hebrew or Aramaic was his first, Greek his second language. Nevertheless, he is skilled in the use of the latter and the fragments reflect knowledge, and perhaps direct use, of Greek sources, such as Ctesias and Herodotus.[83]

Additionally, 2 Maccabees (100 BCE),[84] 1 Esdras (150 BCE),[85] and the additions to the book of Esther (114 BCE) were all composed in Greek, the latter being translated in Jerusalem, the city of Jewish identity. If Aramaic (or Hebrew) was not fading as the common language among the Jews, one wonders why there existed such an accelerated movement toward Greek during this period of Jewish nationalism.

---

81. Wise, "Languages of Palestine," 439.

82. Eupolemus was a member of the priestly family Accos and was sent by Judas Maccabeus to Rome as an ambassador (1 Macc 8:17; 2 Macc 4:11; Josephus, *J.W.* 12.10.6 §415–16). A few fragments of the history of Eupolemus have survived in the form of quotations in later Greek writers such as Eusebius (*Praep. Evang.* 9.26.1 §519; 9.30–34.18 §538–43; 9.34.20 §545; 9.39.1–5 §548).

83. Holladay, "Eupolemus," 671.

84. Jason of Cyrene is the author of 2 Maccabees. Ferguson notes that he was "a Jewish historian well-schooled in Hellenistic rhetoric" (*Backgrounds*, 447).

85. First Esdras (also referred to as Greek Ezra) covers the history of Israel from about 621 BCE to the reading of the law by Ezra after the captives returned to their homeland. See Myers, *I and II Esdras*. Steward states that although the Semitic original is lost, "the Greek offers a polished, idiomatic version" ("Esdras," 143).

The hellenization of Palestine after the death of Alexander the Great continued under the Seleucid kings (312–95 BCE) by establishing Greek cities and settlements like Pella, Dion, and Philoteria. Even the region referred to as the Decapolis was notably a Greek designation. Additionally, older towns like Acco, Rabbat-Ammon, and Beth-shan were renamed Ptolemais, Philadelphia, and Scythopolis respectively. The tradition of the Seleucid kings was further advanced under the reign of the Herods. Fortresses and towns like Caesarea Maritima, Sebaste, Antipatris, Phasaelis, and Antonia at Jerusalem were transformed into Hellenistic centers under Herod the Great (37–4 BCE). Herod the Great's heirs founded also such cities as Caesarea Philippi, Tiberias, and Bethsaida. Julias Fitzmyer admits that the Hellenistic transformation of Palestine prior to the first century served to advance the primacy of Greek throughout the countryside:

> These Hellenistic cities dotted the countryside of Palestine for several centuries prior to the first Christian century and were clearly centers from which the Greek language spread to less formally Hellenistic towns, such as Jerusalem, Jericho, or Nazareth. As in the case of the Roman occupiers of the land, the new language was undoubtedly used at first in official texts, decrees, and inscriptions, and from such use it spread to the indigenous populations.[86]

In fact, Greek had made such inroads into the East that by the first century CE the inhabitants of Phoenicia were called Greek:

> ἡ δὲ γυνὴ ἦν Ἑλληνίς, Συροφοινίκισσα τῷ γένει·καὶ ἠρώτα αὐτὸν ἵνα τὸ δαιμόνιον ἐκβάλῃ ἐκ τῆς θυγατρὸς αὐτῆς (Mark 7:26).

> Now the woman was a Greek, of the Syrophoenician race. And she kept asking Him to cast the demon out of her daughter.

To identity the woman as a Ἑλληνίς was to describe her culture, not her race. The culture division is made even more apparent in Paul's letters when he speaks of people as primarily being Jew or Greek:

> Οὐ γὰρ ἐπαισχύνομαι τὸ εὐαγγέλιον, δύναμις γὰρ θεοῦ ἐστιν εἰς σωτηρίαν παντὶ τῷ πιστεύοντι, Ἰουδαίῳ τε πρῶτον καὶ Ἕλληνι (Rom 1:16).

> For I am not ashamed of the gospel, for it is the power of God for salvation to everyone who believes, to the Jew first and also to the Greek.

86. Fitzmyer, "Languages of Palestine," 508.

οὐκ ἔνι Ἰουδαῖος οὐδὲ Ἕλλην, οὐκ ἔνι δοῦλος οὐδὲ ἐλεύθερος, οὐκ ἔνι ἄρσεν καὶ θῆλυ· πάντες γὰρ ὑμεῖς εἷς ἐστε ἐν Χριστῷ Ἰησοῦ (Gal 3:28).

There is neither Jew nor Greek, there is neither slave nor free man, there is neither male nor female; for you are all one in Christ Jesus.

ὅπου οὐκ ἔνι Ἕλλην καὶ Ἰουδαῖος, περιτομὴ καὶ ἀκροβυστία, βάρβαρος, Σκύθης, δοῦλος, ἐλεύθερος, ἀλλὰ [τὰ] πάντα καὶ ἐν πᾶσιν Χριστός (Col 3:11).

[I]n which there is no distinction between Greek and Jew, circumcised and uncircumcised, barbarian, Scythian, slave and freeman, but Christ is all, and in all.

It is clear that the hellenization of the land of Palestine occurred over many centuries and even reached deep within Jewish frontiers.[87]

Naturally it is of some significance that for some time and almost continuously the country had been governed by rulers who themselves shared in this civilization, who often deliberately propagated it and consequently also the use of Greek as ordinary language.[88]

Consequently, by the first century CE, Greek had become the common language and as such provided a unifying means of communication across cultural and linguistic boundaries not previously possible.[89] Ferguson makes the following observation:

Although Palestine was multilingual in the first century—Greek, various Aramaic dialects, Hebrew, and some Latin—Greek was

87. The Jewish Sanhedrin stands as a linguistic symbol of the impact of Greek upon the very heart of Judaism, an institution that derived its very name from the Greek word συνέδριον. See Argyle, "Greek among the Jews," 87.

88. Sevenster, "Do You Know Greek?," 97. See also Koester, History, Culture, and Religion, 104.

89. Pearson, "Alexander the Great," 22. Ferguson enumerates ten silent but salient features of hellenization that transformed the culture: (1) The movement of Greeks abroad; (2) the accelerated pace of conquest by Greek culture; (3) the emergence of a one-world economy; (4) the spread of the Greek language; (5) a body of ideas universally accepted; (6) the call for a higher level of education; (7) the spread of Greek religious ideas; (8) the emergence of philosophy as a way of life; (9) the Greek polis forming the framework of society; and (10) the increase in stature of the individual. "It is hard to imagine Christianity," wrote Ferguson, "succeeding in any other environment than that which resulted from the conquests of Alexander the Great" (Backgrounds, 14–15).

clearly the language of choice in order to disseminate a message
as widely as possible.[90]

Therefore, it stands to reason that the means chosen by early Christians to
communicate the gospel was naturally Greek. Despite the hypothesis that
Aramaic or Hebrew sources may lie behind some early Christian documents, the fact of the matter is that the entire NT was written in Greek,
a dialect that has been coined as *koinē,* meaning a common or everyday
dialect of the language.[91] This is significant for several reasons. First, it
demonstrates that Jewish authors of the NT were competent enough in the
Greek language to communicate their message to both Jews and Gentiles.[92]
Second, the use of Greek by the Jewish authors presupposes that their readers were skilled enough in the language to comprehend their message.[93] Finally, the absence of any Aramaic documents of the NT or documents that
were considered sources for the NT suggests that Greek had become in the
first century CE the common language not only of Palestine but also of the
Roman Empire.[94]

---

90. Ferguson, *Backgrounds,* 136.

91. Mussies, "Greek as the Vehicle," 356–69.

92. Argyle wrote that "there is greater readiness now than there was formerly to
admit that Jesus and his disciples, all of whom were Galileans (Acts ii.7), were bilingual,
speaking Greek as well as Aramaic . . ." ("Greek Among the Jews," 89).

93. Since the turn of the twentieth century CE, 2 Peter has long been held as a
pseudonymous work of the second century CE and therefore does not represent an
authentic Greek document written in the first century by the apostle Peter. For a summary of the various positions, see Mayor, *Jude and 2 Peter,* cxxiv; Kruger, "2 Peter," 645;
Bauckham, "2 Peter and the Apocalypse of Peter," 303; Carson and Moo, *Introduction,*
664; Michaels, "Peter," 815. I find, however, that the acceptance of 2 Peter's canonical
status by the church of the fourth century is an argument more for its authenticity
than against it. The resilience of 2 Peter, despite its difficult canonical journey, found
its place in Scripture. Second Peter's credibility is further underscored by prevailing
over its competition of pseudo-Petrine literature. Therefore, the document represents
an authentic Greek document of the first century CE.

94. Koester states, "All books of the New Testament were originally written in
Greek; not a single early Christian Greek writing can be shown to have been translated
from Hebrew or Aramaic" (*History, Culture, and Religion,* 111–12). Fitzmyer argues
that the absence of Aramaic originals of the Gospels can be explained by the fact that
they are the "immediate products of a non-Palestinian Christian tradition" and thus
composed outside of Palestine ("Did Jesus Speak Greek?," 259). The argument, however, does not take into consideration the Palestinian background of the NT authors.

THE HELLENISTIC CHARACTER OF GALILEE

The region of Galilee played a central role in the prophetic oracles of Isaiah. The prophet Isaiah[95] told the nation of Judah that they were to experience a difficult future because of their unfaithfulness to Yahweh:

ועבר בה נקשה ורעב והיה כי־ירעב והתקצף וקלל במלכו ובאלהיו ופנה למעלה:
ואל־ארץ יביט והנה צרה וחשכה מעוף צוקה ואפלה מנדח:

(Isa 8:21–22)

> They will pass through the land hard-pressed and famished, and
> it will turn out that when they are hungry, they will be enraged
> and curse their king and their God as they face upward. Then
> they will look to the earth, and behold, distress and darkness, the
> gloom of anguish; and they will be driven away into darkness.

However, Isaiah spoke also of an undisclosed time when God will restore Israel to her previous glory:

כי לא מועף לאשר מוצק לה כעת הראשון הקל ארצה זבלון
וארצה נפתלי והאחרון הכביד דרך הים עבר הירדן גליל הגוים:
העם ההלכים בחשך ראו אור גדול ישבי בארץ צלמות אור נגה עליהם:

(Isa 8:23—9:1)

> But there will be no more gloom for her who was in anguish;
> in earlier times He treated the land of Zebulun and the land of
> Naphtali with contempt, but later on He shall make it glorious,
> by the way of the sea, on the other side of Jordan, Galilee of the
> Gentiles.
>   The people who walk in darkness
>   Will see a great light;
>   Those who live in a dark land,
>   The light will shine on them (Isa 9:1–2).

These passages relate to a desperate time during the reign of Ahaz (735–716 BCE).[96] God sent Isaiah to encourage Ahaz. Four important signs were given to Ahaz to remind him not to fear but to trust in God. The signs centered on the names of three children (Shear-Jashub, Immanuel, and Maher-Shalal-Hash-Baz) and on the prophetic message of Isaiah (8:16–20). Since Ahaz proved to be faithless, Isaiah offered hope for the people who will suffer the

---

95. The book of Isaiah addresses three different historical settings: 739–701 BCE (chs. 1–39), 605–539 BCE (chs. 40–55), and 530–400 BCE (chs. 56–66). See Oswalt, *Isaiah*, 4.

96. Caldecott and Schultz, "Ahaz," 76–78.

consequences of the sins of Ahaz. Although the people will endure distress, darkness, gloom, and anguish, Isaiah spoke of a day when the people who were in darkness will see a great light (9:1–2). Their gladness will increase as their miserable situation improves (9:3–5). A new king will be crowned and he will be a faithful king. His very name symbolizes the character of his reign—Wonderful Counselor, Mighty God, Eternal Father, Prince of Peace (9:6–7).[97]

Matthew reported that after John the Baptist was taken into custody by the Jews, Jesus entered Galilee and began his ministry in Capernaum, located in the region of Zebulun and Naphtali (Matt 4:12–13). Matthew indicated that such actions by Jesus confirmed the messianic character of his ministry prophesied by Isaiah (4:14–16) and that Jesus began his preaching ministry at this point (4:17). Matthew, therefore, presented Jesus as the "Light" to the people who were dwelling in darkness (cf. John 1:6–9).

Matthew saw in Jesus a case involving a fulfillment of prophecy. The light that appeared in the original context in Isaiah's prophecy was probably a reference to the faith of Hezekiah (716–687 BCE)[98] who stood as the polar opposite in character to Ahaz. In fact, Isaiah drew a sharp contrast between the reactions of these two kings toward similar crises (Isa 7 and 36–37). Although a large amount of prophetic material separated the two narrative events, both kings served as object lessons. King Ahaz, of course, reacted inappropriately and consequently was a poor example. King Hezekiah, however, reacted appropriately and served as a positive role model for those who encountered threatening circumstances. Jesus, in Matthew's application, was the ultimate example of a faithful leader.

The region of enlightenment described by Isaiah was "Galilee of the Gentiles." This area was significant because Jesus and his twelve disciples were Galileans. J. N. Sevenster described the land of Palestine in the first century as "an island in the sea of Hellenistic powers."[99] Consequently, Jesus and his disciples were likely inundated by the Hellenistic culture that surrounded them and impacted small towns like Nazareth and the villages that dotted the landscape around the Sea of Galilee. Interestingly, Steven D. Fraade notes that both Hebrew and Aramaic were widely used in study and in worship among the Jews in Palestine since the culture of the day was bilingual. Parenthetically, however, he also admits that these religious

97. For a historical overview of Isaiah's proclamation see Willis, *Isaiah*, 147–87; Hayes and Irvine, *Isaiah*, 118–84; Motyer, *Isaiah*, 80–105; Oswalt, *Isaiah*, 192–248.

98. Schultz, "Hezekiah," 703–5.

99. Sevenster, *Do You Know Greek?*, 96.

activities were "of course" conducted in Greek.[100] Fraade appears to be over-reaching since his parenthetic statement about Greek mitigates his assertion regarding Aramaic and Hebrew. Eric M. Meyers offers the following description of the cultural landscape of the region of Galilee:

> Lower Galilee in light of recent archaeology was less isolated than Upper Galilee and presumably less conservative. It was more Greek-speaking—a judgment based on epigraphy—and more Hellenized; i.e., it exhibited more aspects of Graeco-Roman urbanization as judged from archaeological data, and was less rural, based on the obvious role and influence of Sepphoris and Tiberias on the local economies.[101]

Although many towns were located in Galilee, there were at least four principal cities that were connected in a significant way to Jesus and his apostles. Two of the cities played a key role in the ministry of Jesus. He lived and grew to adulthood in Nazareth (Matt 2:23), and his ministry began in Capernaum (4:12–17). The Gospel of John mentions briefly the city of Tiberias (John 6:23). The city of Sepphoris is not mentioned at all in the NT. However, one must not infer from this lack of biblical witness that these two cities were insignificant to the times in which Jesus and his disciples lived.[102] Sepphoris and Tiberias, as well as other key Hellenistic cities in Galilee and in Decapolis, were instrumental in the dissemination of Greek throughout Galilee. These cities were also located near Nazareth and surely impacted its inhabitants in major ways. Sepphoris was only a few miles northwest of Nazareth, and Tiberias was on the Sea of Galilee south of Capernaum. A closer look at the city of Nazareth, the city of Capernaum, the cities in Galilee and in Decapolis, the city of Tiberias, and the city of Sepphoris will provide insight into the Hellenistic character of Galilee.

The City of Nazareth

Matthew recorded the narrow escape of Joseph and Mary from Herod's plot to have their baby, Jesus, killed. Joseph and his family fled to Egypt for

---

100. Fraade, "Rabinic Views," 253–88.

101. Meyers, "Jesus and His Galilean Context," 63.

102. Meyers postulates that the remarkable silence in the NT may indicate that Jesus intentionally restricted his activities in the cities of Sepphoris and Tiberias in order to "avoid a clash with Antipas, the authorities, or some of the upper class citizens who might have been uncomfortable with his message" (cf. Mark 6:17–29). Meyers, "Jesus and His Galilean Context," 64.

protection (Matt 2:13–18). After the death of Herod, the family returned to the land of Palestine and made its home in Nazareth (2:19–23).

Matthew saw in these events a fulfillment of OT prophecy. Isaiah spoke of a stump (remnant) that will survive God's judgment and from that stump a branch will arise (11:1). This branch or stem, Isaiah proclaimed, will be the perfect ruler (11:2–5), and the people under his reign will enjoy peaceful days (11:6–10). The Hebrew term for branch is נֵצֶר (nēṭṣar). Consequently, in order to identify Jesus with the branch of Isaiah's prophecy, Matthew may have constructed a wordplay in order to make a typological connection with Jesus and his family dwelling in Nazareth:[103]

> καὶ ἐλθὼν κατῴκησεν εἰς πόλιν λεγομένην Ναζαρέτ·ὅπως
> πληρωθῇ τὸ ῥηθὲν διὰ τῶν προφητῶν ὅτι Ναζωραῖος κληθήσεται
> (Matt 2:23, emphasis mine)

> And they came and lived in a city called *Nazareth*. This was to fulfill what was spoken through the prophets, "He shall be called a *Nazarene*."

Although Matthew does not identify any particular prophet, he seems to be making a general application to this event. Jesus also began his ministry in Nazareth and enraged many people who heard him speak in the synagogue, so much so that they drove him out of the city and led him to the edge of a hill to cast him down (Luke 4:14–30).

Although Nazareth was a prominent place in the life of Jesus, it was an obscure agricultural village located in southern Galilee in the hill country north of the great Plain of Esdraelon.[104] The city sat about twelve hundred feet above sea level, covered an area of approximately one hundred by four hundred yards, and contained between one hundred and eight hundred homes.[105] The city's obscurity is further accentuated by the fact that neither the OT, Josephus, nor the Jewish Talmud refers to Nazareth.[106]

---

103. Wallace, "Nazarene," 500. The term נצר also occurs in Isa 14:19; 60:21; and Dan 11:7. The term is derived from the verb "to grow green" and so refers to "a sapling" and often stands as a metaphor for a family tree. See Motyer, *Isaiah*, 122. Walker states that the term "is the same root that gives us the place name Nazareth, although the city is not mentioned in the OT. This word may be in the background of Matt 2:23." See "נצר" in Walker, *New International Dictionary*, 148.

104. Mounce, "Nazareth," 500. See also Albright and Foxwell, "'Nazareth' and 'Nazoraean,'" 397–401. Nazareth's seeming unimportance may be indicated by Nathanael's remark in John's gospel: ἐκ Ναζαρὲτ δύναταί τι ἀγαθὸν εἶναι; ("Can any good thing come out of Nazareth?" John 1:46).

105. Anonymous, "Resurrecting Nazareth," 16.

106. *NIV Archeological Study Bible*, "Nazareth," 1623; McRay, *Archaeology*, 157. See also Pfann et al., "Surveys and Excavations," 19–21.

The importance of Nazareth is not necessarily found in the archaeo-logical discoveries in the town itself, even though recent excavations have uncovered a floor of a synagogue dating in the third century beneath the floor of the Church of the Annunciation, perhaps with a first-century foun-dation beneath it.[107] Rather, Nazareth is important because of its close prox-imity to many Hellenistic centers like Dora, Ptolemais, Caesarea, Tiberias, and Sepphoris.[108]

The City of Capernaum

Capernaum, a seaport town located on the north shore of the Sea of Galilee, became the operational headquarters of Jesus' ministry (Luke 4:16, 29–31; Matt 4:13). The city was the home of Peter and Andrew (Mark 1:29). Mat-thew, the tax collector, probably lived at Capernaum since the "harbor and nearby roads made Capernaum an important location for collecting taxes" (see Mark 2:1, 13–14; Matt 9:1, 9; 10:3).[109] Because of Capernaum's location, this seaport town served as a vital hub for traders, travelers, and anglers.

Capernaum is identified as the site Tell Hum (Kfar Tanhum in the Talmud)[110] and is certainly one of the most important sites to both Jews and Christians.[111] Excavations at Capernaum have determined that the limestone remains of an ancient synagogue date within the Byzantine pe-riod (third-sixth centuries CE). Ten thousand coins that were also excavated beneath the limestone floor show that the prayer hall dates to the fourth century CE.[112] Attached to the east wall of the main structure is an adjoining room from the fifth century CE. As interesting as those finds are, there is one that is more captivating: basalt stone walls that are four feet thick from a more primitive synagogue.[113] The analysis of pottery found beneath the basalt cobblestone floor shows that this earlier structure is from the first

---

107. Bagatti, *The Church*, 126.

108. Kuhrt and Sherwin-White, *Hellenism in the East*, 357.

109. Hoerth and McRay, *Bible Archaeology*, 160.

110. There is some dispute about the location of Capernaum since Joseph seems to equate the city with Tabgha Springs which is located west of Tell Hum (*J.W.* 3.10.8 §516–21). See McRay, *Archaeology*, 164.

111. Ibid., 162.

112. Hoerth and McRay, *Bible Archaeology*, 161.

113. Strange and Shanks state that "the Capernaum synagogue is the most impres-sive synagogue unearthed in all of ancient Galilee" ("Synagogue Where Jesus Preached," 26).

century CE and may be the very synagogue that Jesus, Peter, and Andrew attended (Luke 4:33, 38).[114]

Another interesting discovery in Capernaum about one hundred feet from the synagogue was the basalt wall remains of a one-storied first-century house. The roof would have been made of wooden branches much like the roof that was dug out in order for the paralytic to be lowered and placed before Jesus (Mark 2:4). A structure that was built over the house in later centuries seems to have served as a chapel and now marks the place as Peter's house. Inscriptions that date from the third to the fourth century CE were written predominantly in Greek on the plastered walls of the house.[115]

Capernaum seems to have been a multicultural city with a thriving and prosperous population. John Laughlin describes first-century CE Capernaum:

> New evidence indicates that Romans indeed lived in Capernaum in the first century A.D. Moreover, far from being a poor, isolated village, Capernaum, the center of Jesus' Galilean ministry, was quite prosperous and was apparently home to gentiles as well as Jews.[116]

Jesus and his disciples apparently were comfortable living amidst the diversification.

The Cities in Galilee and in the Decapolis

Many cities in Galilee and Decapolis were proud of their Greek connections and character. Richard Horsley stated that such sites "boasted most of the typical Hellenistic-Roman urban institutions that made a city a *polis*: courts, theater, palace, colonnaded streets, city walls, markets, archives, bank, amphitheater, aqueduct, stadium."[117] For example, Dor (Dora) was a pagan Greek city located fourteen miles south of Haifa on the Carmel coast west of Nazareth.[118] Excavations have revealed three strata of a city built on an orthogonal plan. Residential buildings, shops, and workshops butted up to the city wall. Among many of the public buildings discovered were some large Hellenistic temples.

---

114. Hoerth and McRay, *Bible Archaeology*, 161.

115. Strange and Shanks, "House Where Jesus Stayed," 88–90.

116. Laughlin, "Capernaum," 55.

117. Horsley, *Archaeology*, 44. See also Overman, "First Urban Christians," 16–68.

118. Ortiz, "Archaeology," 102.

Ptolemais (Acco) was located on a broad plain at the northern end of the Haifa Bay. Excavations of the city have revealed an extensive system of fortified walls and towers, a well-designed city plan, and residential quarters containing spacious areas and numerous ovens for cooking, all of which are characteristics of Hellenistic cities. One particular find was a small public building dedicated to Zeus Sotē on behalf of King Antiochus VII Sidetes.[119]

Caesarea Maritima (Strato's Tower) is another coastal city located on the northwest corner of the Sharon plain. Josephus describes Herod's construction projects in Caesarea Maritima as follows:

> Herod also built a theatre of stone in the city, and on the south side of the harbor, farther back, an amphitheatre large enough to hold a great crowd of people and conveniently situated for a view of the sea (*Ant.* 15.9.6 §341 [Thackeray, LCL]).

> The rest of the buildings—amphitheatre, theatre, public places— were constructed in a style worthy of the name which the city bore. He further instituted quinquennial games, likewise named after Caesar, and inaugurated them himself, in the hundred and ninety-second Olympiad, offering prizes of the highest value; at these games not the victors only, but also those who obtained second and third places participated in the royal bounty (*J.W.* 1.21.8 §415 [Marcus, LCL]).

The above features in Herod's construction projects in Caesarea Maritima reveal a strong Hellenistic influence. J. N. Sevenster provides a summary of the rapid increase of Hellenistic towns under the Herodians:

> Herod the Great transformed the ancient Straton's Tower into a modernized, Hellenistic Caesarea and founded such new towns as Antipatris (Acts 23:31) and Phasaelis to the north of Jericho. Under his rule the process of Hellenisation spread inland as far as Sebaste, the ancient Samaria. Macedonians had settled in this town as early as the time of Alexander the Great. Herod, who named the town in honour of emperor Augustus Sebaste, brought it new prosperity. It was he who had it peopled with veterans, and in the heart of Palestine there was created a town that was peopled mainly by non-Jews, where Greek undoubt- edly was the colloquial language.[120]

119. Ibid., 103.

120. Sevenster, *Do You Know Greek?*, 97.

Herod also built gymnasiums, walls, porticoes, temples, marketplaces, and baths in other cities like Damascus, Ptolemais, Byblus, Berytus, Tyre, Sidon, Laodicea, and Ascalon (See Josephus, *J.W.* 1.21.11 §422).

Archaeological excavations have also produced pottery, vessels, amphorae handles with seal impressions, coins, paved walkways, and buildings characteristic of Hellenistic settlements in upper Galilee in Philoteria, Tel Anafa, Tel Dan, and Banias and in the Decapolis at Pella, Abila, Gerasa, and Gadara.[121]

The Greek term *Decapolis* means "Ten Towns" and refers to a group of Hellenistic cities east of the Jordan and Lake Tiberias. These cities have been variously identified as Abila, Canata, Dius, Gadara, Gerasa, Hippos, Pella, Philadelphia, Scythopolis, and Capitolias. As a result of these cities, Hellenistic influences were felt even in the rural areas throughout Galilee and Decapolis in the first century CE. Jean-Paul Rey-Coquais stated that the ten cities "boasted of being cities of Greek culture, institutions, and origin," and they were united because of their Hellenistic culture.[122]

The City of Tiberias

Herod Antipas founded the city of Tiberias around 20 CE with the intention of its becoming his new capital. It was named in honor of Tiberius Caesar and interestingly bears a Greek version of the emperor's name. The city was located on the southwestern shore of the Sea of Galilee, two miles south of Magdala. The city of Hammath, a mile away, was apparently combined with Tiberias sometime in the first century to form one city and was well known for its hot springs.[123]

According to Josephus, many tombs were moved from the site of Tiberias to make room for the city. Because of this, Antipas needed to coerce people to populate the city and remain there. He did this by inviting foreigners and the poor, building good houses at his own expense, granting land, and granting freedom to many slaves. Josephus described the actions of Antipas in the following way:

> The tetrarch Herod, inasmuch as he had gained a high place among the friends of Tiberius, had a city built, named after him Tiberias, which he established in the best region of Galilee on Lake Gennesaritis. There is a hot spring not far from it in a

121. Ibid., 107; see also Harrison, "Hellenization," 54–65, and Stern, "Persia and Greece," 432–45.

122. Rey-Coquais, "Decapolis," 117–19.

123. McRay, *Archaeology*, 178.

village called Ammathus. The new settlers were a promiscuous rabble, no small contingent being Galilean, with such as were drafted from territory subject to him and brought forcibly to the new foundation. Some of these were magistrates. Herod accepted as participants even poor men who were brought in to join the others from any and all places of origin. It was a question whether some were even free beyond cavil. These latter he often and in large bodies liberated and benefited (imposing the condition that they should not quit the city), by equipping houses at his own expense and adding new gifts of land. For he knew that this settlement was contrary to the law and tradition of the Jews because Tiberias was built on the site of tombs that had been obliterated, of which there were many there (*Ant.*18.2.3 §36–38 [Feldman, LCL]).

Archaeologists have not uncovered much at Tiberias that relates to the first century CE.[124] Nonetheless, a paved road and gate complex from the founding of the city have been uncovered, and there is evidence that two round towers stood south of the gate mimicking patterns of Hellenistic settlements.[125]

Although little has been found relating to the first century CE, in 1990 CE a promising find was discovered. While working on Mount Berenice to the west of the city, excavators noticed three large basalt stones protruding from the slope. Preliminary excavations uncovered a portion of a large amphitheater.[126] It was not until 2009, however, that substantial excavations began. These excavations uncovered a Roman amphitheater dating to the first century CE. The enormous theater with a seating capacity of approximately seven thousand affirms the Hellenistic nature of Tiberias in the first century CE and the grand scale of the building projects sponsored by Antipas.[127]

124. The site was excavated in the 1950s by Bezalel Rabani, but his findings are unpublished. See Shurkin, "Tiberias," 12.

125. McRay, *Archaeology*, 178. A coin from Tiberias minted during the reign of Trajan attests to the hot springs at Hammath. The coin shows Hygieia, the goddess of healing, on a rock from which water is flowing. She is holding a serpent (a sign of healing), which she feeds from a bowl. See Dvorjetski, "Healing Waters," 20 and 26. A ten-year excavation effort is currently underway at Tiberias, initially headed by Yizhar Hirschfeld of Hebrew University and Katharina Galor of Brown University (Shurkin, "Tiberias," 12).

126. Hirschfeld, "Excavations at Tiberias," 170.

127. There is some debate as to whether the amphitheater was a part of the original construction project. See Ashkenazi, "Amphitheatre."

The City of Sepphoris

Sepphoris has gained significant scholarly attention over the last thirty years as a large Hellenistic center located just a few miles from Jesus' hometown.[128] Because of its nearness to Nazareth, Jesus and his disciples could not escape the shadow of its influence. In fact, Joseph and Jesus may have found work in Sepphoris during the time of the ambitious building programs of Antipas. Accordingly, Richard A. Batey suggests that "Jesus lived in a Galilean culture much more urban and sophisticated than previously believed."[129]

The city of Sepphoris was strategically located along an important Galilean passageway approximately three miles north of Nazareth.[130] The Mediterranean Sea was eighteen miles to the west, and the Sea of Galilee was eighteen miles to the east of the city. Sepphoris sat about three hundred feet above the adjoining valley below.[131] The city was an administrative center as early as the Hellenistic period. Both the Persians and the Hasmoneans stationed garrisons there presumably because it was an ideal location for a fortress. Richard Horsley noted that "since the Seleucid administration of Galilee had been based there, one would therefore presume that Sepphoris was a Greek-speaking Hellenistic town when the Hasmoneans took it over."[132] Although the Hasmoneans were not unsympathetic to Jewish sensibilities, the "regime was otherwise characterized by increasing Hellenistic influence, particularly under Alexander Janneus."[133] The population of Sepphoris was about eighteen thousand in the first century.[134] Because the city was near Nazareth, Jesus may have passed through the city on multiple occasions

---

128. Archaeological excavations have continued on the site of Sepphoris for nearly a century. These excavations have been conducted by the University of Michigan, Hebrew University, Duke University, and the University of South Florida. The most recent excavators at Sepphoris have been Richard Batey and James Strange from the University of South Florida and Ehud Netzer and Eric Meyers from Hebrew University and Duke University. See Waterman et al., *Preliminary Report*; Meyers and Strange, "Galilee," 7–18; Meyers et al., "Meiron," 1–24; Tsuk, "Aqueducts," 101–8; Meyers et al., "Sepphoris," 4–19.

129. Batey, *Jesus and the Forgotten City*, 28.

130. Chancey and Meyers, "Sepphoris," 21.

131. Meyers et al., *Sepphoris*, 3.

132. Horsley, *Archaeology*, 48.

133. Ibid.

134. Meyers, "Jesus and His Galilean Context," 58. Batey, however, argues for a population closer to thirty thousand (*Jesus and the Forgotten City*, 70). Horsley puts the population at less than ten thousand (*Archaeology*, 45).

since "one logical route from Nazareth to Cana of Galilee ran through Sepphoris."[135]

According to Josephus, Herod the Great moved to conquer Sepphoris while his brother subdued Idumea. When the guards who were stationed there had fled, he captured the city without much effort:

> While the Romans were thus living on the fat of the land, at rest from arms, Herod, never idle, occupied Idumaea with two thousand foot and four hundred horse, which he sent thither under his brother Joseph, to prevent any insurrection in favour of Antigonus. His own care was the removal of his mother and other relations, whom he had rescued from Masada, to Samaria; having safely installed them there, he set out to reduce the remaining strong holds of Galilee and to expel the garrisons of Antigonus. He pushed on to Sepphoris through a very heavy snowstorm and took possession of the city without a contest, the garrison having fled before his assault. Here, provisions being abundant, he refreshed his troops, sorely tried by the tempest, and then started on a campaign against the cave-dwelling brigands ... (*J.W.* 1.16.1–2 §303–304 [Henderson, LCL]; see also *Ant.* 14.15.4 §413–416).

After the death of Herod the Great in 4 BCE, Judas, son of Ezekias, led a rebellion at Sepphoris that caused Rome to recapture and burn the city and enslave its citizens:

> Then there was Judas, the son of the brigand chief Ezekias, who had been a man of great power and had been captured by Herod only with great difficulty. This Judas got together a large number of desperate men at Sepphoris in Galilee and there made an assault on the royal palace, and having seized all the arms that were stored there, he armed every single one of his men and made off with all the property that had been seized there. He became an object of terror to all men by plundering those he came across in his desire for great possessions and his ambition for royal rank, a prize that he expected to obtain not through the practice of virtue but through excessive ill-treatment of others (*Ant.* 17.10.5 §271 [Marcus, LCL]).

> When, therefore, his whole army had assembled in Ptolemais, Varus turned over part of it to his son and to one of his friends, and sent them out to fight against the Galilaeans who inhabit the region adjoining Ptolemais. His son attacked all who opposed

---

135. Strange, "Sepphoris," 1091.

him and routed them, and after capturing Sepphoris, he re-
duced its inhabitants to slavery and burnt the city (*Ant.* 17.10.9
§288–289 [Marcus, LCL]).

When Herod's son Antipas secured his inheritance, he immediately
rebuilt Sepphoris and made "it to be the ornament of all Galilee" (*Ant.*
18.2.1 §27 [Feldman, LCL]) by making it the capital of Galilee and his royal
residence.[136] This reference may have referred more to its fortifications than
to its beauty since Josephus described Sepphoris as an important Galilean
stronghold and called it "the strongest city in Galilee" (*J.W.* 2.18.11 §510–11
[Thackeray, LCL]).[137] Sepphoris remained the administrative capital of
Galilee until about 20 CE when Antipas built Tiberias for that purpose. The
administration, however, returned to Sepphoris in 61 CE. During the Jewish
War, Sepphoris was Rome's ally.[138]

A theater at Sepphoris measuring 156 feet wide with a seating capacity
of four thousand sat on the southern slope of the city. It was initially excavated in 1931 CE by Leroy Watermann from the University of Michigan.[139]
Batey and Strange, based upon pottery found at its foundation, argue for a
date during the reign of Antipas (4 BCE to 39 CE).[140] This would place the
existence of the theater in the time of Jesus. It is possible, therefore, that
Jesus' use of the Greek term ὑποκριταί ("hypocrites") in his teachings may
have been derived from the plays performed at nearby Sepphoris.[141] Batey
makes the following observation:

> The presence of several theaters in the areas where Jesus trav-
> eled offered opportunities for him and his audience to become
> acquainted with actors and the stage. The recurring image of
> the actor in Jesus' teachings suggests a person who pretends
> or plays a role. The actor provides a vivid comparison with the

136. Batey, "Sepphoris Theater," 111.

137. Meyers, "Roman Sepphoris," 323.

138. Ibid., 23. The city's pro-Roman stance did not dissuade rabbis from establishing academies in Sepphoris and eventually compiling the Mishnah in the early third
century. See Horsley, *Archaeology*, 62.

139. Watermann dated the building of the theater to the time of either Herod the
Great or Antipas. Albright, however, suggested a date in the second century CE. McRay,
Archaeology, 176.

140. Batey, "Sepphoris," 60–61; Batey, "Sepphoris Theater," 111. Working from the
same pottery finds, however, Meyers dates the theater to somewhere between 50 CE
and 120 CE with a preference for a late first-century date. See McRay, *Archaeology*, 176.
For Antipas, see Hoehner, "Herod," 694–96.

141. Batey, "Sepphoris," 60–61 (sidebar); See also Batey, "Jesus and the Theatre,"
563–74, and Meyers, "Jesus and His Galilean Context," 64.

religious showman whose affected piety has become a public performance. Jesus primarily censures the religious establishment who substitute outward form for inner faith. But, the criticism applies to all whose religious lives are devoid of genuine commitment to God's sovereignty or "the kingdom of heaven."[142]

Additionally, since Antipas built his royal residence and ruled as a Roman client king or tetrarch at Sepphoris, the seat of government provided Jesus an opportunity on numerous occasions to use the imagery of a king in his teachings. Batey continues his observations as follows:

> The Herodian family constructed a number of opulent palaces at strategic locations. Herod the Great built palaces in Jerusalem and Jericho, as well as in the fortresses at Masada, Herodium, and Machaerus. Antipas also erected royal palaces at both Sepphoris and Tiberias. The luxury and ostentation of the Herodian court were legendary and no expense was spared to keep alive its conspicuous affluence.[143]

Many of Jesus' parables drew from the familiar behavior and attitudes of those who were in positions of power and authority (e.g., Matt 17:24–27; 18:1–5, 23–35; 20:20–28; 22:1–3, 11–14; Luke 14:25–33 and 19:12–27). Jesus was surely affected in many ways by the cultural and political activities at Sepphoris. His disciples, the Jewish inhabitants in Galilee, and those who dwelled within the city proper were likewise unable to escape its influence.

The Hellenistic characteristics of the architecture in Sepphoris are evident by its paved colonnaded streets, water installations, a bathhouse, public structures, and multistoried buildings. However, archaeologists seem to have uncovered evidence of a large Jewish population also in Sepphoris. The major evidence of Jewish presence is the discovery of nearly thirty ritual baths or *mikva'ot* that have been found in the city. These ritual baths, designed to be used in Jewish purification, have been dated from the first and second centuries CE to the mid-fourth century CE.[144] Scholars debate whether these were truly *mikva'ot* or merely regular baths. Hanan Eshel argued that the pools were not *mikva'ot* when compared to *mikva'ot* found elsewhere. He described the pools at Sepphoris as small, having no division on the steps, no nearby holding tank (*otzer*), and no nearby bathtubs where normal bathing could have occurred.[145] Eric Meyers, however, countered

142. Batey, *Jesus and the Forgotten City,* 100–101.

143. Ibid., 120.

144. Meyers et al., *Sepphoris,* 28–29.

145. Hanan, "Pools of Sepphoris," 43–45.

Eshel's arguments by noting that the pools were characteristically *mikva'ot* in size, were similar to those discovered elsewhere, which did not have step divisions or holding tanks and were not far from public baths.[146] Ronny Reich agreed with Meyers and noted that the presence of the *mikva'ot* in Sepphoris served as confirmation of a large Jewish population in the first century CE.[147]

Additionally, coins that appeared at Sepphoris in 66 CE suggest a sympathetic attitude toward Jews. They bore the legendary inscription *eirenopolis* ("city of peace"). An inscription honoring Emperor Nero was located on one side of the coin. The reverse side had the image of two cornucopias intersected by a staff (common symbols on first-century Jewish coins). Mark Chancey and Eric Meyers note that the coin does not bear the image of the emperor or pagan deities in deference to Jewish sensibilities.[148] Later coins from the time of Trajan (98–117 CE) bear the image of the emperor as well as common Jewish symbols such as the laurel wreath, palm tree, caduceus, and ears of grain. During the reign of Antoninus Pius (138–161 CE), coins from Sepphoris displayed images of temples and pagan gods as well as the pagan name of the city, Diocaesarea (in honor of Caesar and Zeus).[149] The evolutionary development of these coins may suggest a gradual shift among the ruling class to an attitude of indifference toward the Jewish population or perhaps may indicate the gradual assimilation of Jews into the city's pagan culture.

Additional finds of interest that relate to later periods in its history have been excavated at Sepphoris. These include the *decamus* (main road) dated to the first half of the second century CE, a monumental building of the second century CE, and a temple that was abandoned in the fourth

---

146. Meyers, "Yes, They Are," 46–49.

147. Reich, "Ritual Baths," 50–55. Meyers believes that the following factors serve as inferential evidence of a thriving Jewish culture in Sepphoris: (1) Josephus does not mention Gentiles or Gentile institutions (temples or gymnasiums) in connection with Sepphoris; (2) from the "thousands upon thousands" of bone fragments found, there is a striking lack of pig bones which may suggest a population interested in keeping Jewish dietary laws; (3) in light of the fact that Jews preferred stone vessels because they were not subject to ritual purity, it is significant that 114 stone vessels have been found in the residential area; (4) coins minted during the Great Revolt did not contain images of the emperor or pagan deities which were common on coins of this period issued by cities on the Palestinian coast and of the Decapolis; and (5) although his father promoted a pagan ethos, Antipas generally respected Jewish religious sensibilities and was careful not to offend the Jewish religious elements in Galilee (*Jesus and His Galilean Context*, 60).

148. Chancey and Meyers, "Sepphoris," 24.

149. Meyers et al., *Sepphoris*, 12–13.

century CE.[150] These archaeological discoveries indicate that by the second century CE Sepphoris was a burgeoning Hellenistic center. Meyers offers the following summary concerning Sepphoris:

> Hence, the archaeology and history of Sepphoris strongly support a case for Sepphoris in the time of Jesus being overwhelmingly Jewish in population, traditional in orientation toward language and common religious practice, urban in character but still not a city of the magnitude of one of the gentile cities, connected to the other towns and villages of Galilee by trade and the new requirements of an expanding population base, somewhat aristocratic because of its priestly component, retainer class and pro-Roman posture during the Great War, and perhaps an uncongenial but not unfamiliar place for Jesus as he went about Galilee preaching and teaching the new gospel.[151]

The inferential evidence that Meyers offers to substantiate his argument does not take into account the overwhelmingly Hellenistic character of the city's origins and its architectural character. Although there may have been a large Jewish population in Sepphoris (if one can draw such a conclusion based upon the number of *mikva'ot* that have been discovered), the character of the city was Hellenistic—"a melting pot of Greek language and culture for a very long time."[152] Although Meyers argues for a more substantial Jewish population at Sepphoris, he offers an interesting synopsis:

> The fact that Sepphoris was at the same time an important center of rabbinic learning, however, leads us to conclude that the mixture of Hebrew, Greek, and Aramaic was symbiotic. Nevertheless, the cosmopolitan world of the Roman city was never too far removed from the village or town of the Galilean peasant, who, for better or for worse—and it would seem for worse much of the time—was dependent on these centers for their economic well-being and growth, supplies, and services.[153]

---

150. Weiss, "Sepphoris," 99, 103. The most famous find at Sepphoris is a Roman villa housing a fabulous mosaic floor that was part of its *triclinia*. The central portion of the mosaic presents the Dionysos myth. The mosaic also contains a stunning portrait of a woman that has become known as the "Mona Lisa of the Galilee." The mosaic has been moved to the Israel Museum. Unfortunately the Roman villa and mosaic date to the first half of the third century CE and therefore shed no light on the NT period. See Meyers et al., *Sepphoris*, 38–59.

151. Meyers, *Jesus and His Galilean Context*, 64.

152. Meyers, "Roman Sepphoris," 330.

153. Ibid.

SUMMARY

The purpose of this chapter is to establish the fact that Greek was the most common means of communication among Romans and Jews in the first century CE. The architectural landscape of the eastern half of the Roman Empire was familiar to both Jews and Christians in the first century. G. R. Stanton offers the following characteristics of Hellenistic centers:

> [A]n open space surrounded by shops and public buildings (the *agora*), a council house (*bouleuterion*), a ceremonial headquarters (*prytaneion*), a theater such as the great one at Ephesus, a range of temples and (under Roman influence) baths.[154]

Paul's use of athletic imagery indicates that he was also familiar with the gymnasium as well as the athletic festivals that typified Greco-Roman culture (e.g., 1 Cor 9:24–26).

Despite the fact that many Jews, if not most, were bilingual (and likely trilingual), my analysis of the linguistic diversity in Palestine reveals that Greek was the default language for the purpose of broader communication, especially in the region of Galilee where Hellenistic influences abounded. Based upon the literary and archaeological data, Sevenster offers a fitting conclusion:

> [F]or a long time and at close quarters, the centre of the Jewish country was surrounded by regions that were strongly influenced by Hellenism, and this is manifested by the wide use of the Greek language. And the inhabitants of the Jewish country cannot but have come into regular contact with regions only a short distance away. This must have greatly stimulated the use of Greek as common language. Hence much Greek was spoken in the immediate vicinity of the heart of the Jewish land, also by the Jews who lived there.[155]

---

154. Stanton, "Hellenism," 472.
155. Sevenster, *Do You Know Greek?*, 114.

CHAPTER 3

The Linguistic Proficiency in Greek of Some of the Primary Disciples of Jesus

GREEK CULTURE AND IDEAS rapidly penetrated Palestine after the Hellenistic expansion started by Alexander the Great. Although there was a volcanic reaction to Greek influence during the Maccabean period, Greek culture nevertheless had already taken hold by the time of Jesus. Greek architecture, literature, and language permeated the countryside as well as larger cities like Sepphoris, Caesarea Maritima, Tiberias, and Jerusalem. G. R. Stanton provides an appraisal of the linguistic diversity in the first century CE:

> We may conclude that by the time of Jesus areas such as Galilee and Judea were trilingual, with Aramaic the language used for many day-to-day activities, Mishnaic Hebrew used for religious worship and learned discussion and Greek the normal language for commerce, trade and administration.[1]

Interestingly, the issue of whether Jesus spoke Greek remains a controversial one despite the fact that there is no evidence against it. As I have already shown, the evidence thus far seems to confirm the strong probability that Jesus did in fact speak Greek. I can also safely assume that both Jesus and his disciples were fluent in Greek because the cultural landscape of the times demanded such fluency. The knowledge that Greek was the common language and that the cultural character of Palestine (especially in Galilee) was primarily Greek provides two major pieces of supporting evidence. Additionally, this chapter will investigate the linguistic background of the apostles,

1. Stanton, "Hellenism," 464.

the half brothers of Jesus, and three key second-generational messengers that represent some of Jesus' primary disciples in order to determine the degree of proficiency in the Greek language that they had in the first century CE.

THE DISCIPLES OF JESUS

What Is the Meaning of μαθητής?

The most commonly used term to designate the followers of Jesus is μαθητής ("disciple"). In a general sense μαθητής refers to a person who "binds himself to someone else in order to acquire his practical and theoretical knowledge."[2] According to the Gospel of Matthew, the objective of Jesus' Great Commission was to make disciples of all nations (Matt 28:19).

In the Greek-speaking world μαθητής described a learner, an adherent, or a pupil. Each of these ideas depicts one who is devoted to his teacher or master.[3] Rabbinical scribes among the Jews listed God's divine will for them in three simple goals. The *Mishnah* records these in the following tractate:

> Moses received Torah at Sinai and handed it on to Joshua, Joshua to elders, and elders to prophets. And prophets handed it on to the men of the great assembly. They said three things: "Be prudent in judgment. Raise up many disciples. Make a fence for the Torah" (*m. Avot* 1:1).[4]

Josephus records an interesting situation in which the ruler and high priest of the Jews, John Hyrcanus I (63–40 BCE),[5] was referred to as a disciple of the religious movement of the Pharisees:

> As for Hyrcanus, the envy of the Jews was aroused against him by his own successes and those of his sons; particularly hostile to him were the Pharisees, who are one of the Jewish schools, as we have related above. And so great is their influence with the masses that even when they speak against a king or high priest, they immediately gain credence. Hyrcanus too was a disciple of theirs, and was greatly loved by them. And once he invited them to a feast and entertained them hospitably, and when he saw that they were having a very good time, he began by saying that they knew he wished to be righteous and in everything he did

2. Müller, "Disciple," 484.

3. Wilkins, "Disciples," 182.

4. Neusner, *Mishnah*, 679.

5. Hoehner, "Hasmoneans," 625.

tried to please God and them—for the Pharisees profess such beliefs; at the same time he begged them, if they observed him doing anything wrong or straying from the right path, to lead him back to it and correct him. But they testified to his being altogether virtuous, and he was delighted with their praise (*Ant.* 13.10.5 §288–290 [Marcus, LCL]).

Unfortunately, the rise of Hyrcanus in power and popularity began to create a rift between him and the Pharisees. Although the Pharisees were somewhat ambivalent toward the political success of the Hasmonian leaders, they "felt that the high priesthood had become worldly by hellenization and secularization."[6] Josephus captures the discontent that some had toward Hyrcanus as he continues the narration of the aforementioned event:

However, one of the guests, named Eleazar, who had an evil nature and took pleasure in dissension, said, "Since you have asked to be told the truth, if you wish to be righteous, give up the high-priesthood and be content with governing the people" (*Ant.* 13.10.5 §291–292 [Marcus, LCL]).

In addition to the many references to the disciples of Jesus, the NT refers to disciples of other recognized leaders, teachers, or movements. Jesus' broader fellowship with tax collectors and sinners disturbed the more exclusive tendencies of the scribes and Pharisees. Jesus also appeared to violate the ritualistic traditions of many of the Jews by not fasting. The Gospel of Mark records one of the many confrontations between Jesus and the Jews as follows:

Καὶ ἦσαν οἱ μαθηταὶ Ἰωάννου καὶ οἱ Φαρισαῖοι νηστεύοντες. καὶ ἔρχονται καὶ λέγουσιν αὐτῷ· διὰ τί οἱ μαθηταὶ Ἰωάννου καὶ οἱ μαθηταὶ τῶν Φαρισαίων νηστεύουσιν, οἱ δὲ σοὶ μαθηταὶ οὐ νηστεύουσιν; (Mark 2:18; cf. Matt 22:15–16).

While the disciples of John and the Pharisees were fasting, they came and said to him, "Why do the disciples of John and the disciples of the Pharisees fast but your disciples do not fast?"

From the above text, two religious movements are identified as the disciples of John (the Baptist) and the disciples of the Pharisees. The former represents a movement calling for a radical departure from the status quo of Jewish society. The latter refers to adherents to a conservative Jewish movement or possibly to a particular rabbinical school.[7]

---

6. Ibid., 624.

7. Wilkins, "Disciples," 176. See also Wyatt, "Pharisees," 827.

During a hostile interrogation of a blind man, presumably healed by Jesus (John 9:1–11, 13–14), the Pharisees angrily dismissed the blind man's claims:

ἀπεκρίθη αὐτοῖς· εἶπον ὑμῖν ἤδη καὶ οὐκ ἠκούσατε·τί πάλιν θέλετε ἀκούειν; μὴ καὶ ὑμεῖς θέλετε αὐτοῦ μαθηταὶ γενέσθαι; καὶ ἐλοιδόρησαν αὐτὸν καὶ εἶπον· σὺ μαθητὴς εἶ ἐκείνου, ἡμεῖς δὲ τοῦ Μωϋσέως ἐσμὲν μαθηταί (John 9:27–28).

He answered them and said, "I told you already and you did not listen; why do you want to listen again? You do not want to become his disciples also, do you?" They reviled him and said, "You are his disciple, but we are disciples of Moses."

Interestingly, the Pharisees referred to themselves as disciples of Moses, a designation that "focused on their privileged position as those to whom God had revealed himself through Moses."[8] They also disparagingly identified the blind man as a disciple of Jesus.

A few observations from the preceding discussion will help to clarify the practical meaning of μαθητής. First, there seems to be various degrees of commitment shown by a μαθητής. Hyrcanus, for example, though identified as a disciple of the Pharisees, did not necessarily adhere strictly to the movement and perhaps was more of an institutional pupil than a passionate follower. Second, the general goal of a μαθητής seems to be more egocentric in self-identification in that the ultimate purpose was to become the master and thereby obtain the recognition and authority inherent in the role. For instance, the Pharisees who sat in "the chair of Moses" (Matt 23:2) thought of themselves as "ordained guardians and interpreters of the Mosaic law."[9] Finally, μαθητής seems to convey the idea of a specific human relationship that is established with a leader, teacher, or movement. There were a number of movements available to an aspiring young disciple that ranged from the ascetic to the more hedonistic in character.

Jesus in a very distinctive way redefined the meaning and image of a μαθητής. Jesus gathered a circle of disciples around him and apparently adopted the familiar Jewish role of a rabbi. He was often addressed by those of his inner circle and by people outside as ῥαββί ("Rabbi," Mark 9:5, 11:21; John 1:38, 3:2, 4:31). However, Jesus went beyond the traditional role of a ῥαββί and radically altered the typical disciple/master relationship. D. Müller lists a number of ways in which μαθητής was transformed by Jesus. Three

8. Wilkins, "Disciples," 177.
9. Garland, "Moses' Seat," 425.

of the more significant ways relate to the response, the goal, and the reach of discipleship.[10]

First, disciples among both Jewish and Greek circles typically made a voluntary decision to join a particular religious movement, school, or leader. The emphasis, however, in following Jesus was not upon one's voluntary choice from among many options currently available as much as it was upon a compelling and decisive call from Jesus to follow him forthrightly. The Gospel of Matthew provides an example of this radical demand by Jesus in the following text:

> καὶ λέγει αὐτοῖς· δεῦτε ὀπίσω μου, καὶ ποιήσω ὑμᾶς ἁλιεῖς ἀνθρώπων. οἱ δὲ εὐθέως ἀφέντες τὰ δίκτυα ἠκολούθησαν αὐτῷ. καὶ προβὰς ἐκεῖθεν εἶδεν ἄλλους δύο ἀδελφούς, Ἰάκωβον τὸν τοῦ Ζεβεδαίου καὶ Ἰωάννην τὸν ἀδελφὸν αὐτοῦ, ἐν τῷ πλοίῳ μετὰ Ζεβεδαίου τοῦ πατρὸς αὐτῶν καταρτίζοντας τὰ δίκτυα αὐτῶν, καὶ ἐκάλεσεν αὐτούς. οἱ δὲ εὐθέως ἀφέντες τὸ πλοῖον καὶ τὸν πατέρα αὐτῶν ἠκολούθησαν αὐτῷ (Matt 4:19–22).

> And he said to them, "Follow me and I will make you fishers of men." They immediately left their nets and followed him. And while leaving from there he saw two others, James the son of Zebedee and John his brother, in the boat with their father Zebedee, mending their nets; and he called them. Immediately they left the boat and their father and followed him.

The above passage illustrates the departure from a self-initiated decision to become a disciple. Jesus, as the leader, takes the initiative and chooses his disciples (John 15:16). The anticipated response involves a belief in his identity (John 2:11, 6:68–69), obedience to his call (Mark 1:18, 20), and a complete surrender of one's life to his cause (Luke 14:25–28; Matt 19:23–30).[11]

Second, the normal goal of any disciple was that he would ultimately become like his master or would eventually obtain the role of master himself. In contrast, the learning relationship that one establishes with Jesus is not something one outgrows. A disciple is unconditionally bound to Jesus and is to follow behind him. The Greek term ἀκολουθέω ("to follow") means to move behind someone and is used often as a technical term to describe the relationship of a disciple to his master and "of the reckless abandonment of the former way of life."[12] During his Galilean ministry, Jesus passed by a tax booth and called Levi the son of Alphaeus who was sitting there to

---

10. Müller, "Disciple," 488–89.

11. Wilkins, "Discipleship," 187.

12. Danker, "ἀκολουθέω," 36. See also France, *Mark*, 132.

follow him, and ἀναστὰς ἠκολούθησεν αὐτῷ ("he got up and followed him," Mark 2:14). Consequently, to follow Jesus is to "accept the renunciatory lot of wandering about with him."[13]

Third, Jesus elicited disciples from a broad spectrum of society, breaking social taboos and crossing traditional social barriers. Those whom he chose as disciples were not normally associated with the Jewish educational or religious institutions. The disciples that Jesus summoned to follow him were frequently categorized as "tax-collectors and sinners" (Luke 15:1–2). Consequently, the inner circle of disciples that Jesus selected included individuals who were tax collectors (Mark 2:14), fishermen (Mark 1:16–20), and revolutionaries (Luke 6:15; Acts 1:13). Jesus' actions were consistent with the inclusive nature of his mission and, as Eduard Schweizer observed, extremely radical for his time:

> The very fact that Jesus calls people to follow him, and that he does this with consequence that they leave boat and toll-office and family, denotes a quite astonishing knowledge of his mission. . . . This holds good to an even great extent of the breaking through all barriers as in the case of Levi. Grace becomes an event in such calling.[14]

Who Are οἱ μαθηταί?

The Gospels indicate that οἱ μαθηταί ("the disciples") of Jesus encompassed a very large group of people (Luke 6:17; John 6:66).[15] Many of these disciples came from the communities in which Jesus ministered (primarily in Galilee) and included, in addition to those mentioned earlier, women (Luke 8:1–3), Joseph of Arimathea (John 19:38), and possibly a Pharisee named Nicodemus (John 19:39).

The wider group of disciples on occasions received special commissions of service, as demonstrated by the seventy who were sent to cities throughout Palestine to preach (Luke 10:1–24). Other disciples seemed to be loosely attached to Jesus, especially when his teachings did not conform to their expectations. The Gospel of John describes some disciples who had difficulty accepting certain things that Jesus taught and ultimately departed from him. The following text illustrates such a departure after Jesus spoke of eternal life in terms of eating his flesh and drinking his blood:

13. Müller, "Disciple," 488. See also Bornkamm, *Jesus*, 146.

14. Schweizer, *Lordship*, 13–14.

15. Meye, "Disciple," 947–48.

Πολλοὶ οὖν ἀκούσαντες ἐκ τῶν μαθητῶν αὐτοῦ εἶπαν·σκληρός ἐστιν ὁ λόγος οὗτος·τίς δύναται αὐτοῦ ἀκούειν; εἰδὼς δὲ ὁ Ἰησοῦς ἐν ἑαυτῷ ὅτι γογγύζουσιν περὶ τούτου οἱ μαθηταὶ αὐτοῦ εἶπεν αὐτοῖς·τοῦτο ὑμᾶς σκανδαλίζει; ἐὰν οὖν θεωρῆτε τὸν υἱὸν τοῦ ἀνθρώπου ἀναβαίνοντα ὅπου ἦν τὸ πρότερον; τὸ πνεῦμά ἐστιν τὸ ζῳοποιοῦν, ἡ σὰρξ οὐκ ὠφελεῖ οὐδέν·τὰ ῥήματα ἃ ἐγὼ λελάληκα ὑμῖν πνεῦμά ἐστιν καὶ ζωή ἐστιν. ἀλλ᾽ εἰσὶν ἐξ ὑμῶν τινες οἳ οὐ πιστεύουσιν. ᾔδει γὰρ ἐξ ἀρχῆς ὁ Ἰησοῦς τίνες εἰσὶν οἱ μὴ πιστεύοντες καὶ τίς ἐστιν ὁ παραδώσων αὐτόν. καὶ ἔλεγεν·διὰ τοῦτο εἴρηκα ὑμῖν ὅτι οὐδεὶς δύναται ἐλθεῖν πρός με ἐὰν μὴ ᾖ δεδομένον αὐτῷ ἐκ τοῦ πατρός. Ἐκ τούτου πολλοὶ [ἐκ] τῶν μαθητῶν αὐτοῦ ἀπῆλθον εἰς τὰ ὀπίσω καὶ οὐκέτι μετ᾽ αὐτοῦ περιεπάτουν (John 6:60–66).

Many of his disciples, therefore, when they heard this said, "This is a difficult statement. Who is able to accept it?" But Jesus aware that his disciples grumbled at this said to them, "Does this cause you to stumble? If you see the Son of Man ascending to where He was before, what then? The Spirit is the One who gives life, the flesh profits nothing. The word which I have spoken to you is spirit and is life; but there are some among you who do not believe." Jesus knew from the beginning the ones who were not believing and who the one that would betray him was. And he was saying, "Because of this I have spoken to you that no one is able to come to me unless it has been granted by the Father." Because of this statement, many of his disciples went away and withdrew and no longer were walking with him.

Although the above disciples had once made some conscious decision to join the movement, the level of their commitment did not rise to the level of Jesus' expectations. The objective of Jesus was to make disciples. By his teaching, preaching, and ministry Jesus inspired faith in him among people, and many of those very people surrendered themselves to obey him, to serve him as Lord, and to become his disciples (Matt 8:18–21, 17:14–15).

Who Are οἱ ἀπόστολοι?

From among this larger number of disciples Jesus selected a smaller band of emissaries whom he designated as ἀπόστολοι ("apostles").[16] The Gospel of Luke in particular records the formation of this special group of disciples:

16. Technically, the Greek term ἀπόστολος refers to one who has received a commission and thereby has been authorized by the sender as a representative or ambassador. Although twelve disciples were called ἀπόστολοι, the term had a broader generic

Ἐγένετο δὲ ἐν ταῖς ἡμέραις ταύταις ἐξελθεῖν αὐτὸν εἰς τὸ ὄρος προσεύξασθαι, καὶ ἦν διανυκτερεύων ἐν τῇ προσευχῇ τοῦ θεοῦ. καὶ ὅτε ἐγένετο ἡμέρα, οσεφώνησεν τοὺς μαθητὰς αὐτοῦ, καὶ ἐκλεξάμενος ἀπ᾽ αὐτῶν δώδεκα, οὓς καὶ ἀποστόλους ὠνόμασεν·Σίμωνα ὃν καὶ ὠνόμασεν Πέτρον, καὶ Ἀνδρέαν τὸν ἀδελφὸν αὐτοῦ, καὶ Ἰάκωβον καὶ Ἰωάννην καὶ Φίλιππον καὶ Βαρθολομαῖον καὶ Μαθθαῖον καὶ Θωμᾶν καὶ Ἰάκωβον Ἀλφαίου καὶ Σίμωνα τὸν καλούμενον ζηλωτὴν καὶ Ἰούδαν Ἰακώβου καὶ Ἰούδαν Ἰσκαριώθ, ὃς ἐγένετο προδότης (Luke 6:12–16).

Now it happened during these days that he went away to the mountain to pray and he spent the entire night in prayer to God. And when day came, he called his disciples and selected twelve from among them whom he also named apostles: Simon whom he also named Peter, Andrew his brother, James, John, Philip, Bartholomew, Matthew, Thomas, James the son of Alphaeus, Simon the one called the Zealot, Judas the son of James, and Judas Iscariot who became a betrayer.

Although twelve were chosen to be apostles, they also continued to remain, in a broader sense of the term, disciples (Matt 10:1). Further, the Gospel of Mark describes the mandates of the apostolic mission in the following text:

Καὶ ἀναβαίνει εἰς τὸ ὄρος καὶ προσκαλεῖται οὓς ἤθελεν αὐτός, καὶ ἀπῆλθον πρὸς αὐτόν. καὶ ἐποίησεν δώδεκα [οὓς καὶ ἀποστόλους ὠνόμασεν][17] ἵνα ὦσιν μετ᾽ αὐτοῦ καὶ ἵνα ἀποστέλλῃ αὐτοὺς κηρύσσειν (Mark 3:13–14).

And he went up on the mountain and called those whom he himself wanted. And they came to him; and he appointed twelve [whom also he named apostles] so that they would be with him and so he could send them to preach.

The two ἵνα clauses indicate that there were two apostolic mandates: to share in the ministry of Jesus as fellow travelers with him and to become an extension of his ministry in the act of preaching for him.[18]

application in describing other disciples who apparently possessed commissioned authority (1 Cor 15:5; Gal 1:15; Acts 14:4, 14; Heb 13:1). See Danker, "ἀπόστολος," 122; Robinson, "Apostle," 192–95.

17. Many scholars consider the phrase in question to be a harmonization to Luke although a number of important manuscript witnesses support it (e.g., ℵ, B, θ, *f*[13], syh, mg, and Coptic). See France, *Mark*, 157. Although Metzger and the UBS committee felt that the phrase was an interpolation of Luke 6:13, they retained it in the text within brackets because the external evidence for its inclusion was stronger than the evidence for its exclusion. See Metzger, *Textual Commentary*, 69.

18. Ibid., 160; see Wallace, *Greek Grammar*, 472; Kruse, "Apostle," 31; Agnew,

Jesus worked closely with the twelve apostles in order to teach, to train, and to mentor them. There is one interesting question that has yet to be raised: Why did Jesus choose these specific individuals? The answer to this question will require an analysis of the background of each member of the apostolate in order to uncover any clues that may provide some kind of connection that they may have had with Jesus and with each other.

Although the NT unanimously testifies to the existence of a core group of disciples called "the apostles" in the restricted sense of the term, there are only four separate lists in the NT that contain their names. Table 3.1 is drawn from the lists contained in the Synoptic Gospels and the book of Acts:

Table 3.1. Comparative list of the apostles

Matt 10:2–4	Mark 3:14–19	Luke 6:13–16	Acts 1:13
Τῶν δὲ δώδεκα ἀποστόλων τὰ ὀνόματά ἐστιν ταῦτα·πρῶτος Σίμων ὁ λεγόμενος *Πέτρος* καὶ *Ἀνδρέας* ὁ ἀδελφὸς αὐτοῦ, καὶ *Ἰάκωβος* ὁ τοῦ Ζεβεδαίου καὶ *Ἰωάννης* ὁ ἀδελφὸς αὐτοῦ, *Φίλιππος* καὶ *Βαρθολομαῖος*, *Θωμᾶς* καὶ *Μαθθαῖος* ὁ τελώνης, *Ἰάκωβος* ὁ τοῦ Ἀλφαίου καὶ *Θαδδαῖος*, *Σίμων* ὁ Καναναῖος καὶ *Ἰούδας* ὁ Ἰσκαριώτης ὁ καὶ παραδοὺς αὐτόν.	καὶ ἐποίησεν δώδεκα [οὓς καὶ ἀποστόλους ὠνόμασεν] ἵνα ὦσιν μετ᾽ αὐτοῦ καὶ ἵνα ἀποστέλλῃ αὐτοὺς κηρύσσειν καὶ ἔχειν ἐξουσίαν ἐκβάλλειν τὰ δαιμόνια [καὶ ἐποίησεν τοὺς δώδεκα,] καὶ ἐπέθηκεν ὄνομα τῷ Σίμωνι *Πέτρον*,καὶ *Ἰάκωβον* τὸν τοῦ Ζεβεδαίου καὶ *Ἰωάννην* τὸν ἀδελφὸν τοῦ *Ἰακώβου* καὶ ἐπέθηκεν αὐτοῖς ὀνόμα[τα] βοανηργές, ὅ ἐστιν υἱοὶ βροντῆς·καὶ *Ἀνδρέαν* καὶ *Φίλιππον* καὶ *Βαρθολομαῖον* καὶ *Μαθθαῖον* καὶ *Θωμᾶν* καὶ *Ἰάκωβον*τὸν τοῦ Ἀλφαίου καὶ *Θαδδαῖον* καὶ *Σίμωνα* τὸν Καναναῖον καὶ *Ἰούδαν*Ἰσκαριώθ, ὃς καὶ παρέδωκεν αὐτόν.	καὶ ὅτε ἐγένετο ἡμέρα, προσεφώνησεν τοὺς μαθητὰς αὐτοῦ, καὶ ἐκλεξάμενος ἀπ᾽ αὐτῶν δώδεκα, οὓς καὶ ἀποστόλους ὠνόμασεν·Σίμωνα ὃν καὶ ὠνόμασεν *Πέτρον* καὶ *Ἀνδρέαν* τὸν ἀδελφὸν αὐτοῦ, καὶ *Ἰάκωβον* καὶ *Ἰωάννην* καὶ *Φίλιππον*καὶ *Βαρθολομαῖον* καὶ *Μαθθαῖον*καὶ *Θωμᾶν* καὶ *Ἰάκωβον* Ἀλφαίου καὶ *Σίμωνα*τὸν καλούμενον ζηλωτὴν καὶ *Ἰούδαν* Ἰακώβου καὶ *Ἰούδαν* Ἰσκαριώθ, ὃς ἐγένετο προδότης.	καὶ ὅτε εἰσῆλθον, εἰς τὸ ὑπερῷον ἀνέβησαν οὗ ἦσαν καταμένοντες, ὅ τε *Πέτρος* καὶ *Ἰωάννης* καὶ *Ἰάκωβος* καὶ *Ἀνδρέας*, *Φίλιππος* καὶ *Θωμᾶς*, *Βαρθολομαῖος* καὶ *Μαθθαῖος*,*Ἰάκωβος* Ἀλφαίου καὶ *Σίμων* ὁ ζηλωτὴς καὶ *Ἰούδας*Ἰακώβου. οὗτοι πάντες ἦσαν προσκαρτεροῦντες ὁμοθυμαδὸν τῇ προσευχῇ σὺν γυναιξὶν καὶ Μαριὰμ τῇ μητρὶ τοῦ Ἰησοῦ καὶ τοῖς ἀδελφοῖς αὐτοῦ.

Source: Table is based upon Aland, *Synopsis*, 90–92 (emphasis mine).

When the four lists are compared to each other a number of peculiarities are found. First, the Table 3.1 calls attention to the fact that Jesus

"Apostolos," 49–53; Herron, "Apostolate," 101–31.

selected a special group of twelve disciples to be his ambassadors. In several places in the Gospel of Mark they are simply referred to as όι δώδεκα ("the twelve," Mark 3:16, 6:7, 9:35, 10:32, 11:11, 14:10, 17, 20, 43). Second, in every list Peter is first. The consistent placement of Peter's name when compared to the varied way in which the others are listed may indicate the leading role that he had among the others. For instance, the Gospel of Matthew refers to Peter as πρῶτος ("first") and places emphasis on Peter's confession and the authority that Jesus gave him although the same authority was also given to the other apostles (Matt 16:13–19, 18:18).[19] Third, in the lists found in the Synoptic Gospels, Judas Iscariot is last in sequence and falls completely off the list found in the book of Acts. Judas Iscariot's betrayal and suicide opened the door for a new apostle named Μαθθίαν ("Matthias") to be selected and to join the rank of apostles (Acts 1:15–26). Fourth, there seems to be an intentional grouping of the apostles into smaller units. Peter, Andrew, James, and John form one distinctive group. Additionally, Peter, James, and John form a special inner circle during exceptional situations (Mark 5:37, 9:2, 13:3). Fifth, there are a few apparent discrepancies about the names of the twelve apostles. In the Gospel of Luke and in Acts, the list has Ἰούδαν Ἰακώβου ("Judas of James") in place of Θαδδαῖος ("Thaddeus"). Since the lists of the twelve clearly point to their unique role, it seems reasonable to expect that their identities became widely known. This suggests that the variations of names are not references to different people but that some among them were probably known by or called by different names. Therefore, Judas of James is likely the same person as Thaddeus, who is also the one referred to as Ιούδας, οὐχ ὁ Ἰσκαριώτης ("Judas, not Iscariot") in John 14:22.[20]

Additionally, a limited but helpful amount of information about the relationships, the personalities, and the cultural backgrounds of the apostles can be obtained from the chart above. References throughout the remainder of the NT provide more biographical material about some of the apostles.

19. Because no other number sequencing is used in the list, it seems probable that πρῶτος "is not meant to indicate the position of Simon in the list [. . .] but to single him out as the most *prominent* of the twelve." See Danker, πρῶτος, 894; see also Nolland, *Matthew*, 411. Though Peter appears to be recognized as a particularly important leader, his role may be more aptly described by the principle of *primus inter pares* ("first ones among equals") rather than assigning him some official rank above the others listed (cf. 1 Pet 5:1). See Strauch, *Eldership*, 45–47; Wilkins, "Disciples," 179.

20. Wilkins, "Disciples," 177–81.

Simon Peter and Andrew

Συμεών ("Symeon") was Peter's original Jewish name (Acts 15:14; 2 Pet 1:1) before Jesus changed it (John 1:42) to Κηφᾶς ("Cephas"), which was rendered in Greek as Πέτρος ("Peter"). His father's name was Ἰωάννης ("John," Matt 16:17) and Andrew was his brother. According to the Gospel of John, Andrew introduced Peter to Jesus. Their home was located in the Jewish village of Bethsaida[21] in the region of Galilee where they engaged in the fishing trade.[22] Ralph P. Martin notes that although the local character of the city was Jewish, "it was also cosmopolitan."[23] Additionally, Gustaf Dalman notes that the cosmopolitan character of Bethsaida broadened the linguistic abilities of the Jews who lived there: "Anyone brought up in Bethsaida would not only have understood Greek, but would also have been polished by intercourse with foreigners and have had some Greek culture."[24] Interestingly, the name Σίμων ("Simon") appears to be a hellenized adaptation of Συμεών ("Symeon") and the name Ἀνδρέας ("Andrew") is Greek. Oscar Cullman makes the following observation:

> The Gospels use the Greek name Simon. This did not originate, as has been supposed, by rendering into Greek the Hebrew name. It is rather 'native Greek' and is already attested by Aristophanes. It is probable that the original Hebrew name Symeon was later replaced by the Greek name of similar sound. However, it does not seem to me at all impossible that Peter, like his brother Andrew, had been given a Greek name from the outset, especially since this is true of Philip, who according to John 1:44

21. Although the location is uncertain, Bethsaida in Galilee has been identified with el-Araj on the western side of the Jordan. This location fits the geographical narrative in the gospels (Mark 6:45–53; Matt 14:34; Luke 9:10). See McRay, *Archaeology*, 169–70. MacDonald argues that the background information concerning Peter and Andrew in the Gospel of John contradicts the Synoptic Gospels. For instance, Mark appears to indicate that Andrew's home was in Capernaum (1:16–18) as opposed to Bethsaida (John 1:49). See MacDonald, "Andrew," 242. However, France notes that the reference in Mark is more likely to Jesus' home in Capernaum where Peter, Andrew, James, and John had their temporary headquarters during the Galilean ministry; France, *Mark*, 107.

22. Interestingly, a fishing boat was found in January of 1986, buried in the mud on the northern shore of the Sea of Galilee, less than four miles from Capernaum where Jesus began his ministry. The boat has been dated from the first century BCE to the end of the first century CE. See Wachsmann et al., "Kinneret Boat," 243; Batey, *Jesus and the Forgotten City*, 144.

23. Martin, "Peter," 803.

24. Dalman, *Sacred Sites and Ways*, 165.

comes from the same place, Bethsaida, and still more since Hellenistic influence is attested precisely for this region.[25]

Semitic names during the first century CE often took on Hellenistic characteristics in four different ways. First, Semitic names were often appended with ος as in the case of Ἰάκωβος ("James") and Ἄγαβος ("Agabus") unless the person of reference was a significant OT figure like Ἀβραάμ ("Abraham"), Δαυίδ ("David"), or Ἰακώβ (Jacob) and therefore remained unaltered. Second, if a name terminated with a vowel, a ς was attached to the end of it in the nominative, Ἰησοῦς ("Jesus") being the most notable example. Third, Semitic names that ended in ה‏ָ and ‏ָו were changed to an ας ending and declined according to the first declension: Ἰούδας, Ἰούδα, Ἰούδᾳ, Ἰούδαν, Ἰούδα ("Judas"). Finally, names were grecized by substituting Greek names that sounded similar to the original Semitic ones. This action best describes how Συμεών became Σίμων.[26] David Garland makes the following observation about the presence of both Semitic and Greek names found in the same apostolic list: "The Greek names (Philip, Andrew) reveal how Hellenized Palestine had become, and they are striking beside the names of Jewish patriarchs and Maccabean military heroes (Simon, Jacob [James])."[27] The Hellenistic characteristics as they relate to Peter and Andrew may hint at their bilingual background that could only arise from a predominantly Greek culture.

Additionally, according to the book of Acts, many who heard Peter and the rest of the apostles speak on the day of Pentecost recognized the peculiarity in their dialect and connected them to Galilee (Acts 2:7; see also Mark 14:70 and Matt 26:73). F. F. Bruce notes that "these Galileans appeared for the moment to share among them a command of most of the tongues spoken throughout the known world," albeit with a certain Galilean quality.[28] Since neither Aramaic nor Greek was a strange language to the apostles, the reference to Galilee must have been a comment about their peculiar dialect of Aramaic or recognition of their Galilean Greek. Since a multitude of Greek-speaking Jews travelled to Jerusalem (cf. Acts 6:1–7), the fact may very well be that Greek was the language which was widely spoken. "If Peter had been speaking Aramaic," wrote G. R. Selby, "most of his audience would have been baffled."[29]

---

25. Cullman, *Peter*, 19.

26. Blass and Debrunner, *Greek Grammar*, 29–30 §53.

27. Garland, *Luke*, 274.

28. Bruce, *Acts*, 54. Bruce notes that the apostles were comfortable speaking both Aramaic and Greek.

29. Selby, *Jesus*, 95.

Peter would later come to realize that his Hellenistic background would serve him well because the apostolic mission compelled him to preach to Gentiles.[30] For example, a Roman centurion, Cornelius, from Caesarea Maritima once invited Peter to come to speak to him and his household. Although Caesarea was the center of Roman rule and contained Herod's temple, palace, and theater, many Jews also lived and worshipped there.[31] As a Godfearer, Cornelius already sympathized with the religious beliefs and practices of the Jews (Acts 10:22). Despite the fact that he was a good and honorable man, Cornelius bore the label of being an unclean foreigner (Acts 10:28). According to the text below, Peter went to Cornelius because of a divine directive and preached the gospel of Jesus to him:

> ἔφη τε πρὸς αὐτούς· ὑμεῖς ἐπίστασθε ὡς ἀθέμιτόν ἐστιν ἀνδρὶ Ἰουδαίῳ κολλᾶσθαι ἢ προσέρχεσθαι ἀλλοφύλῳ· κἀμοὶ ὁ θεὸς ἔδειξεν μηδένα κοινὸν ἢ ἀκάθαρτον λέγειν ἄνθρωπον διὸ καὶ ἀναντιρρήτως ἦλθον μεταπεμφθείς. πυνθάνομαι οὖν τίνι λόγῳ μετεπέμψασθέ με; (Acts 10:28–29).

> And he said to them, "You know how unlawful it is for a Jewish man to associate with or to visit a foreigner. God has shown to me that I should not call any man unholy or unclean. This is why I came without objection when I was summoned. Now I ask for what reason you have sent for me."

The Greek term ἀλλοφύλῳ ("foreigner") is commonly used in the LXX as a reference to the Philistines.[32] It is also the term selected by Josephus when paraphrasing the notice that was placed in the temple of Jerusalem forbidding Gentiles from entering the inner courts. Josephus provides the following details:

> Proceeding across this towards the second court of the temple, one found it surrounded by a stone balustrade, three cubits high and of exquisite workmanship; in this at regular intervals stood slabs giving warning, some in Greek, others in Latin characters, of the law of purification, to wit that no foreigner [ἀλλόφυλον]

---

30. Although the penetration into Gentile territory was ultimately taken over by the Apostle Paul, Luke nevertheless portrays Peter as the initial bridge over which Christianity expanded to include Gentiles. The seeds of the Gentile mission were first planted by Jesus when he ministered in the Decapolis (Mark 5:1–20). See Dunn, *Unity and Diversity*, 385; Bruce, *Acts*, 209.

31. Hoerth and McRay, *Bible Archaeology*, 172–76.

32. The majority of the references are found in the books of Judges, 1 Samuel, and 2 Samuel.

was permitted to enter the holy place, for so the second enclosure
of the temple was called (*J. W.* 5.4.2 §193–94 [Thackeray, LCL]).

Despite the obvious cultural differences between Peter and Cornelius, the
Greek language was the one common bond between them.[33] Bruce argues
that since the Greek translation of Scripture was read in many Jewish synagogues, Gentiles became conversant in its ritualistic practices.[34] Unless Peter communicated through an interpreter, he probably spoke to Cornelius
and his household in Greek and also heard them respond by praising God
in Greek (Acts 10:46).[35]

James and John

James and John, along with their father Zebedee, were fishing partners
with Peter and Andrew in Bethsaida (Luke 5:10). Zebedee might have been
among the more prosperous families since he was able to employ workers in addition to the help he received from family members in the fishing
trade (cf. Mark 1:20; Luke 5:10; John 18:15).[36] The call of James and John to
discipleship is described in the following way:

> καὶ προβὰς ἐκεῖθεν εἶδεν ἄλλους δύο ἀδελφούς, Ἰάκωβον τὸν
> τοῦ Ζεβεδαίου καὶ Ἰωάννην τὸν ἀδελφὸν αὐτοῦ, ἐν τῷ πλοίῳ
> μετὰ Ζεβεδαίου τοῦ πατρὸς αὐτῶν καταρτίζοντας τὰ δίκτυα
> αὐτῶν, καὶ ἐκάλεσεν αὐτούς. οἱ δὲ εὐθέως ἀφέντες τὸ πλοῖον
> καὶ τὸν πατέρα αὐτῶν ἠκολούθησαν αὐτῷ (Matt 4:21–22).

> And going on from there he saw two other brothers, James the
> son of Zebedee and John his brother, in the boat with their father
> Zebedee, mending their nets; and he called them. Immediately,
> they left the boat and their father and followed him.

The above account reveals that Peter, Andrew, James, and John shared the
same trade as fishermen. The two pairs of brothers were probably more than

---

33. Sevenster states that "there lived in the capital of Judea many Jews, who had the
same civic rights as all the other inhabitants and who therefore could likewise participate in the municipal administration. They undoubtedly spoke Greek in their frequent
intercourse with each other." Sevenster, *Do You Know Greek?*, 105.

34. Bruce, *Acts*, 203.

35. Bruce admits that "Peter may have spoken Greek" but takes the position that
in all likelihood he employed a translator. However, it is not unrealistic to expect Peter
to communicate with Cornelius in Greek, especially since he was adept at using the
language. See ibid., 213; Selby, *Jesus*, 96–97.

36. Davids, "Rich and Poor," 702.

mere acquaintances. Additional information found in the Synoptic Gospels indicates that Jesus had a special relationship with the sons of Zebedee. Several factors seem to affirm this special bond. First, according to the apostolic list in Mark, Jesus called James and John by a unique nickname:

> [. . .] καὶ Ἰάκωβον τὸν τοῦ Ζεβεδαίου καὶ Ἰωάννην τὸν ἀδελφὸν τοῦ Ἰακώβου καὶ ἐπέθηκεν[37] αὐτοῖς ὀνόμα[τα] βοανηργές, ὅ ἐστιν υἱοὶ βροντῆς (Mark 3:17).

> [. . .] and James the son of Zebedee and John the brother of James and He gave them the name Boanerges which means, "Sons of Thunder."

Jesus evidently had enough familiarity with James and John for him to apply a fitting appellation consistent with their aggressive temperament (Mark 3:17; cf. 9:38–41). The descriptive tag, βοανηργές, is likely a Semitic expression that would have naturally derived from a shared native language spoken within tight familial circles.[38]

Second, John has been traditionally identified as the disciple ὃν ἠγάπα ὁ Ἰησοῦς ("whom Jesus loved"; John 13:23, 19:26–27, 20:2, 21:7, 20, 24). Church fathers, as early as the second century CE, have identified John the apostle as the author of the Fourth Gospel. For instance, Irenaeus (second century CE)[39] made the following remark concerning John the apostle: "Afterwards, John, the disciple of the Lord, who also had leaned upon His breast, did himself publish a Gospel during his residence at Ephesus in Asia" (*Haer.* 3.1.1 [W. H. Rambaut, *ANF*]). Additionally, in a couple of passages, Eusebius (third-fourth centuries CE) cites letters written by Polycrates (second century CE)[40] that specifically mention John as the beloved disciple of Jesus:

37. The Greek term ἐπιτίθημι signifies an act of bestowing upon someone a name that characterizes his personality or attributes. See Danker, "ἐπιτίθημι," 384.

38. It is difficult to identify the linguistic origin of the word βοανηργές. It has been typically understood as having an Aramaic origin; however, there is some doubt because the etymology of "βοαν" is not easily determined. Normally, the Aramaic בר ("son") is employed to denote male familial relationships. Contrary to Dalman, the term may have derived from the Hebrew רגש בני ("sons of commotion" or "sons of wrath" depending upon the diacritical marks). The translation in the text is βροντῆς ("thunder"). Mark's use of υἱοί ("son") almost certainly implies a Semitic origin of the term. See Dalman, *Jesus—Jeshua*, 12; Danker, "βοανηργές," 179–80; France, *Mark*, 161–62. However, Buth argues that although the term might be Semitic in origin, it was likely grecized by a copyist and therefore the Hebrew construct בני ("sons of") was altered in transliteration to βοάω which means "to shout" or "cry out" (cf. Mark 1:3 and 15:34). The wordplay corresponds to the loudness associated with thunder. See Buth, "Mark 3:17 ΒΟΝΕΡΓΕΣ," 29–33.

39. See González, *Christianity*, 68.

40. Online: http://www.earlychristianwritings.com/polycrates.html.

> And there is also John, who leaned on the Lord's breast, who
> was a priest wearing the mitre, and martyr and teacher, and he
> sleeps at Ephesus [. . .] Moreover, there is also John, who lay on
> the Lord's breast, who was a priest wearing the breastplate, and
> a martyr, and teacher. He sleeps at Ephesus (*Hist. eccl.* 3.31.3;
> 5.24.2–3 [Lake, LCL]).

This external evidence strongly corroborates the traditional belief regarding the close ties between John and Jesus.

Third, the bold request by the mother of James and John suggests that she and Jesus shared some unique relationship; otherwise, the request seems odd at best and obtuse at worst (Matt 20:20–21; cf. Mark 10:35–45). Finally, while on the cross, Jesus entrusted the care of his mother to John. These factors are hardly coincidental. What is the underlying relationship between Jesus and John? Table 3.2 shows the parallels in the Gospels of Matthew, Mark, Luke, and John of the women who were present at Jesus' crucifixion:

Table 3.2. The women at the crucifixion

Matt 27:55–56	Mark 15:40–41	Luke 23:49	John 19:25–27
Ἦσαν δὲ ἐκεῖ γυναῖκες πολλαὶ ἀπὸ μακρόθεν θεωροῦσαι, αἵτινες ἠκολούθησαν τῷ Ἰησοῦ ἀπὸ τῆς Γαλιλαίας διακονοῦσαι αὐτῷ· ἐν αἷς ἦν Μαρία ἡ Μαγδαληνὴ καὶ Μαρία ἡ τοῦ Ἰακώβου καὶ Ἰωσὴφ μήτηρ καὶ ἡ μήτηρ τῶν υἱῶν Ζεβεδαίου.	Ἦσαν δὲ καὶ γυναῖκες ἀπὸ μακρόθεν θεωροῦσαι, ἐν αἷς καὶ Μαρία ἡ Μαγδαληνὴ καὶ Μαρία ἡ Ἰακώβου τοῦ μικροῦ καὶ Ἰωσῆτος μήτηρ καὶ Σαλώμη, αἳ ὅτε ἦν ἐν τῇ Γαλιλαίᾳ ἠκολούθουν αὐτῷ καὶ διηκόνουν αὐτῷ, καὶ ἄλλαι πολλαὶ αἱ συναναβᾶσαι αὐτῷ εἰς Ἱεροσόλυμα.	Εἱστήκεισαν δὲ πάντες οἱ γνωστοὶ αὐτῷ ἀπὸ μακρόθεν καὶ γυναῖκες αἱ συνακολουθοῦσαι αὐτῷ ἀπὸ τῆς Γαλιλαίας ὁρῶσαι ταῦτα.	Εἱστήκεισαν δὲ παρὰ τῷ σταυρῷ τοῦ Ἰησοῦ ἡ μήτηρ αὐτοῦ καὶ ἡ ἀδελφὴ τῆς μητρὸς αὐτοῦ, Μαρία ἡ τοῦ Κλωπᾶ καὶ Μαρία ἡ Μαγδαληνή. Ἰησοῦς οὖν ἰδὼν τὴν μητέρα καὶ τὸν μαθητὴν παρεστῶτα ὃν ἠγάπα, λέγει τῇ μητρί· γύναι, ἴδε ὁ υἱός σου. εἶτα λέγει τῷ μαθητῇ· ἴδε ἡ μήτηρ σου. καὶ ἀπ᾽ ἐκείνης τῆς ὥρας ἔλαβεν ὁ μαθητὴς αὐτὴν εἰς τὰ ἴδια.

Source: The chart is based on Aland, *Synopsis*, 322 (emphasis mine).

According to Table 3.2, there were many women from the region of Galilee who observed the crucifixion. Since they were singled out in the text, the following women appear to have some degree of importance in the narrative:

Matt 27:56	Mark 15:40	John 19:25
Μαρία ἡ Μαγδαληνὴ ("Mary Magdalene")	Μαρία ἡ Μαγδαληνὴ ("Mary Magdalene")	Μαρία ἡ Μαγδαληνὴ ("Mary Magdalene")
Μαρία ἡ τοῦ Ἰακώβου καὶ Ἰωσὴφ μήτηρ ("Mary, the mother of James and Joseph")	Μαρία ἡ Ἰακώβου τοῦ μικροῦ καὶ Ἰωσῆτος μήτηρ ("Mary, the mother of James the Less and Joses")	Μαρία ἡ τοῦ Κλωπᾶ ("Mary, the wife of Clopas")
ἡ μήτηρ τῶν υἱῶν Ζεβεδαίου ("the mother of the sons of Zebedee")	Σαλώμη ("Salome")	ἡ ἀδελφὴ τῆς μητρὸς αὐτοῦ ("the sister of his mother")
(Mary, the mother of Jesus, not mentioned)	(Mary, the mother of Jesus, not mentioned)	ἡ μήτηρ αὐτοῦ ("His [Jesus'] mother [Mary]")

A fuller picture develops when the three different accounts are placed side by side. In each account, three women are identified who appear to be linked together. Mary Magdalene and another Mary are found in all three lists. Although there are different peculiarities in each reference to the other Mary (mother of James and Joses, mother of James the Less, and wife of Clopas), it seems reasonable to conclude that each reference to this Mary is to the same woman. What relationship then does the mother of Zebedee's sons have with Jesus? The following reconstruction may help explain the mystery:[41]

1. A woman named Salome was a bystander at the crucifixion of Jesus (Mark 15:40).[42]

2. The mother of the sons of Zebedee was one of the onlookers (Matt 27:56).

3. Salome may have been the name of John's mother (John 19:25).

4. Salome was probably the sister of Mary, the mother of Jesus.

5. If so, Jesus and the sons of Zebedee may have been first cousins and Salome may have been Jesus' aunt.

The above scenario reveals a rational motivation behind the bold request of Jesus by the mother of James and John to place her two sons (Jesus' first cousins) on his right hand and left hand in the kingdom (Matt 20:20–21). Because of their kindred relationship, Mary felt comfortable asserting

41. Collins, "John (Disciple)," 883; Morris, "John," 1107.

42. Hagner states that Matthew seems to be identifying Salome for his readers. Hagner, "James," 617. Harris, however, is more cautious and states that "it is not certain whether the sister of Jesus' mother in Jn. 19:25 is this Salome or Mary the wife of Clopas" (ibid., 958).

herself before Jesus. This may also explain the actions of Jesus while his mother and John stood watching him on the cross:

Ἰησοῦς οὖν ἰδὼν τὴν μητέρα καὶ τὸν μαθητὴν παρεστῶτα ὃν ἠγάπα, λέγει τῇ μητρί·γύναι, ἴδε ὁ υἱός σου. εἶτα λέγει τῷ μαθητῇ·ἴδε ἡ μήτηρ σου. καὶ ἀπ᾽ ἐκείνης τῆς ὥρας ἔλαβεν ὁ μαθητὴς αὐτὴν εἰς τὰ ἴδια (John 19:26–27).

Now when Jesus saw his mother and the disciple whom he loved standing nearby, he said to his mother, "Woman, behold your son." Then he said to the disciple, "Behold your mother." And from that hour, the disciple took her into his own family.

The family relationship provides the background in which to understand why Jesus enjoined John to care for his mother after his death. John, the disciple whom *he loved* and his *first cousin*, would be the natural choice to assume the responsibility of his mother's care. Mary would live under the loving supervision of supporting family members.

Philip and Bartholomew

Φίλιππος ("Philip") is a Greek name. He is closely linked with Andrew (John 6:5–9, 12:22) and is also from Bethsaida. Philip introduced Ναθαναήλ ("Nathanael") to Jesus (John 1:45–46) as Andrew introduced his brother Peter. Nathanael is a Jewish name that means "God has given"[43] and may also be identified as the same person as Βαρθολομαῖος ("Bartholomew") in the apostolic list. Since Bartholomew is probably a patronymic meaning "son of Tolmai," it seems best to understand it as a surname for Nathanael.[44] If Nathanael and Bartholomew were the same person, then his home was Cana of Galilee (John 21:2), also located in the same region as Peter, Andrew, and Philip.[45]

43. Gordon, "Nathanael," 491.

44. Bock, *Luke*, 544; Hendriksen, *Luke*, 329; Marshall, *Luke*, 239. Plummer offers four reasons for identifying Nathanael as Bartholomew: (1) The patronymic is not a full name; (2) John mentions Nathanael and the Synoptic Gospels refer to Bartholomew; (3) the apostolic lists in the Synoptic Gospels group Philip and Bartholomew together; and (4) Nathanael is listed among the apostles in John 21:2. Plummer, *Luke*, 173. Wilkins is not convinced that Bartholomew is necessarily a patronymic since the name "is normally expressed in the lists by the Greek genitive, not by the Aramaic *bar*." Wilkins, "Bartholomew," 615.

45. The village of Cana has been connected to a number of sites but the most probable site is eight miles NE of Nazareth and identified as Khirbeth Qânā. See Mounce, "Cana," 585. Cana was strategically located on the Roman road and served as an important hub for travelers to Ptolemais (Acco) on the Mediterranean shore and to Magdala

According to the Gospel of John, some Greeks once came to Jerusalem for the Passover searching for Jesus. The following text describes what happened:

> Ἦσαν δὲ Ἕλληνές τινες ἐκ τῶν ἀναβαινόντων ἵνα προσκυνήσωσιν ἐν τῇ ἑορτῇ· οὗτοι οὖν προσῆλθον Φιλίππῳ τῷ ἀπὸ Βηθσαϊδὰ τῆς Γαλιλαίας καὶ ἠρώτων αὐτὸν λέγοντες· κύριε, θέλομεν τὸν Ἰησοῦν ἰδεῖν. ἔρχεται ὁ Φίλιππος καὶ λέγει τῷ Ἀνδρέᾳ, ἔρχεται Ἀνδρέας καὶ Φίλιππος καὶ λέγουσιν τῷ Ἰησοῦ (John 12:20–22).

> Now there were some Greeks among those going up to worship at the feast. These men came to Philip, who was from Bethsaida of Galilee, and asked him, "Sir, we desire to see Jesus." Philip came and told Andrew; Andrew and Philip came and told Jesus.

The Greek term Ἕλληνές refers to a Gentile who in this case had an expressed interest in the religion of the Jews. These individuals were normally God-fearing people like Cornelius (Acts 10:22) and the Greeks (Ἑλλήνων πλῆθος πολύ) who joined Paul and Silas in Thessalonica (Acts 17:4).[46] Since Philip and Andrew were the only apostles with Greek names and came from a predominantly Greek area (John 12:21), those who contacted them may have assumed that they spoke Greek and could represent their interests before Jesus.[47] C. M. Kerr makes the point below that Andrew was perfectly suited for ministry among the Gentiles:

> [Andrew] occupies a more prominent place in the Gospel of John than the Synoptics, and this is explicable at least in part in that Andrew was Greek both in language and sympathies [. . .], and that his subsequent labors were intimately connected with the people for whom John was immediately writing.[48]

The above statement certainly applies also to Philip. Like the previous disciples discussed above, the cultural background of both Andrew and Philip also equipped them with the linguistic and social skills to interact with Gentiles.

---

on the Sea of Galilee. Riesner, "Archaeology," 37. Josephus states that he was stationed in Cana for a period of time during the Galilean Jewish revolt against Rome (*Life* 16 §84–86).

46. Danker, "Ἕλλην," 318.

47. Garland, "Philip," 833; Watson, "Philip," 331.

48. Kerr, "Andrew," 122.

Thomas, James (son of Alphaeus), Thaddaeus, and Simon (the Zealot)

Not much is given in the NT about the backgrounds of Thomas, James (son of Alphaeus), Thaddaeus, and Simon (the Zealot) apart from the vicinity from which they were called to be apostles. The unifying factors between them were their Jewish descent and the Hellenistic culture that they shared in Galilee.

However, another example of the extent to which Greek culture affected the Jews is seen in the name Thomas. The Aramaic word תאומא means "twin" and became associated with the Greek name Θωμᾶς in regions like Galilee where Greek was spoken.[49] Three times in the Gospel of John Thomas is called Δίδυμος ("Didymus"), which also means "twin" (John 11:16, 20:24, 21:2) and was probably the name that Thomas was known by among those who spoke Greek.[50] The conflation of Hebrew and Greek words as found in the name of Thomas and the fact that many Jews possessed both a Semitic and a Greek name may illustrate a broad spectrum of Hellenistic assimilation. Additionally Thomas, along with Simon Peter and Nathanael, returned to Galilee, the region where his apostolic commission began, after the resurrection of Jesus (John 21:2).

Simon is called both Σίμων ὁ ζηλωτὴς ("Simon the Zealot," Acts 1:13) and Σίμων ὁ Καναναῖος ("Simon the Cananean," Matt 10:4 and Mark 3:18 KJV, ASV, RSV). The word Καναναῖος is actually a Greek transliteration of the Aramaic word קנאן, which means an "enthusiast" or "zealot" and probably describes Simon's former involvement in Jewish revolutionary movements.[51] W. J. Heard states that "the first century was one of the most violent epochs of Jewish history." Galilee was certainly the spawning ground of many violent revolutions in reaction to Roman control and Hellenistic encroachment.[52] Simon's revolutionary background certainly attests to his familiarity with the cultural diversity in Galilee, though in his case such diversity was not welcomed but strongly opposed.

49. Danker, "Θωμᾶς," 463; Blomberg, "Thomas," 841.

50. Danker, "Δίδυμος," 242; Collins, "Thomas," 528.

51. Danker, "Καναναῖος," 107; Dalman, *Jesus—Jeshua*, 12; Wilkins, "Disciples," 181.

52. For example, Menahem the Galilean was one of the principal leaders during the First Jewish Revolt (66–74 CE). See *J.W.* 2.17.8 §433–34; Heard, "Revolutionary Movements," 668; see also Kingdon, "Zealots" 60–75.

Matthew (the Tax Collector)

Ματθαῖον ("Matthew"), a simple Greek transliteration from the Hebrew term מתתיאל, means "Gift of God." The name occurs in all four lists of the apostles and only in one other additional passage in the NT. However, in the parallel accounts (Mark 2:14 and Luke 5:27–29), the name of the tax collector is Λευὶν τὸν τοῦ Ἁλφαίου ("Levi son of Alphaeus," Mark 2:14). Since some of the apostles noted above appear to have two names, one with two Semitic names (Συμεὼν Πέτρος [Κηφᾶς]) and another one with a Semitic name and a Greek name (Θωμᾶς Δίδυμος), it seems reasonable to conclude that Λευί (Mark 2:14) was simply another name for Matthew.[53] Otherwise, one would have to conclude that an unknown man has been inserted in the text.[54]

Matthew's call to follow Jesus, though brief in its description, contains crucial background information:

> Καὶ παράγων ὁ Ἰησοῦς ἐκεῖθεν εἶδεν ἄνθρωπον καθήμενον ἐπὶ τὸ τελώνιον, Ματθαῖον λεγόμενον, καὶ λέγει αὐτῷ· ἀκολούθει μοι. καὶ ἀναστὰς ἠκολούθησεν αὐτῷ (Matt 9:9)

> And as he went on from there, Jesus saw a man who was sitting in the tax collector's booth; his name was Matthew, and he said to him, "Follow me!" And standing up he followed him.

Matthew was employed as a τὸ τελώνιον ("tax collector"). Since Jesus had just returned from the country of the Gadarenes to his home in Capernaum (Matt 8:28, 9:1), Matthew's tax collection booth was probably stationed on one of the main roads near the entrance into Capernaum to collect dues on goods entering the kingdom of Herod Antipas.[55] The Romans stationed tax offices near city gates in order to collect tolls and duties. The office of tax collector was often offered by the Romans to the highest bidder. Consequently, Rome would receive their taxes a year in advance and the winning bidder would recoup expenses and profit from the commission on the tolls. Jewish tax collectors had the opportunity to become wealthy (Luke 19:1–10) but at the same time suffered the brunt of Jewish pejorative comments (Matt 5:46, 18:17; Mark 2:25; Luke 3:12, 7:29, 8:10–14, 15:1).[56] Matthew appears to

53. France, *Mark*, 131. That Levi and James might be brothers is a possibility but seems unlikely in view of the fact that the apostolic lists seem to group family members together (cf. Mark 1:16–20).

54. Ibid., 132. See also Hagner, "Matthew," 280.

55. Ibid.; Marshall, *Luke*, 219; See Dunn, *Jesus Remembered*, 318–19; Riesner, "Archaeology," 39.

56. Schmidt, "Taxes," 805.

have profited financially from his tax employment since he was able to host a large reception for Jesus in his home (Matt 9:10; Luke 5:29).

Matthew's occupation certainly brought him in contact with numerous people of various cultures and linguistic variety. As a tax collector, Matthew more than likely had to be fluent in Greek and proficient in Greek composition. Living in Capernaum of Galilee provided the environment to develop his linguistic skills.

Judas Iscariot and Matthias

Not much is known about the backgrounds of Judas Iscariot and Matthias. Ἰούδας Ἰσκαριώθ ("Judas Iscariot") was the son of Σίμωνος Ἰσκαριώτου ("Simon of Iscariot," John 6:71, 13:2, 26). His name is found in three basic forms in the NT: (1) the hellenized form Ἰούδας from the Hebrew name יהודה ("Judah," Matt 26:25, 47; 27:3; Mark 14:43; Luke 22:47–48), (2) the Semitic form of Ἰσκαριώθ added to the hellenized Ἰούδας (Mark 3:19; 14:10; Luke 6:16), and (3) the Greek form Ἰούδας ὁ Ἰσκαριώτης (Matt 10:4, 26:14; Luke 22:3; John 6:71, 12:4, 13:2, 26,14:22, 26).

Judas may have been the only apostle who was not originally from Galilee. The meaning of Iscariot has been explained as either referring to a region in Judea,[57] deriving from an Aramaic term that means "false one,"[58] originating from the Latin *sicarius*, which means "an assassin,"[59] or pointing to his occupation as a dyer.[60] The term "Iscariot," based upon the reference to the father of Judas, appears to refer to a region. Despite his seemingly Judean connection, Judas apparently possessed the ability to minister among Greek-speaking Galileans along with the other eleven apostles.

Μαθθίας ("Matthias") is derived from the Hebrew word מתתיהו, which means "Gift of God."[61] The apostles appointed Matthias to replace Judas (Acts 1:23–26). The implication of his appointment is that he had been a disciple of Jesus and had accompanied the apostles since the baptism of Jesus and his ascension. Matthias might have been numbered among the seventy disciples Jesus sent out to preach. If so, Jesus was undoubtedly confident that Matthias would be able to navigate through the Hellenistic countryside of Galilee without much difficulty.

---

57. Danker, "Ἰσκαριώθ," 480. Compare Josh 15:25; Jer 31:24 LXX (48:24 MT).

58. Ellis, *Luke*, 110; Marshall, *Luke*, 240.

59. Danker, "Ἰσκαριώθ," 480.

60. Ehrman, "Judas Iscariot," 572–73; Carson, *Matthew*, 239–40.

61. Scott, "Matthias," 288; Martin, "Matthias," 644.

THE BROTHERS OF JESUS

Upon Jesus' return from the region of Decapolis, he went to his home town, Nazareth. When the Sabbath came, Jesus attended the synagogue and astonished those present by his teaching. The assembled crowd expressed their amazement with the following offensive retort:

> οὐχ οὗτός ἐστιν ὁ τέκτων, ὁ υἱὸς τῆς Μαρίας καὶ ἀδελφὸς Ἰακώβου καὶ Ἰωσῆτος καὶ Ἰούδα καὶ Σίμωνος; καὶ οὐκ εἰσὶν αἱ ἀδελφαὶ αὐτοῦ ὧδε πρὸς ἡμᾶς; καὶ ἐσκανδαλίζοντο ἐν αὐτῷ (Mark 6:3; cf. Matt 13:55–56).
>
> Is not this the carpenter, the son of Mary, and brother of James and Joses and Judas and Simon? Are not His sisters here with us?

According to the passage above, Jesus had four brothers and at least two sisters.[62] Despite growing up with him, Jesus' siblings did not fully believe in his divinity (John 7:1–5). However, after the resurrection, the brothers of Jesus were numbered among the disciples who had gathered in an upper room in Jerusalem (Acts 1:14). Their presence, along with the apostles, revealed a change that had taken place in the way they viewed Jesus and understood their relationship to him. Eventually they would also become travelling missionaries (1 Cor 9:5).

Jude, the Brother of James

Two of Jesus' brothers stand out more prominently than the others. Ἰούδα ("Jude") is an abbreviated version of the grecized Ἰούδας ("Judas"). The letter that bears Jude's name contains the following self-identification:

> Ἰούδας Ἰησοῦ Χριστοῦ δοῦλος, ἀδελφὸς δὲ Ἰακώβου . . . (Jude 1:1).
>
> Jude, a slave of Jesus Christ, and brother of James. . . .

The description no doubt reveals Jude's spiritual relationship to Jesus and also seems to suggest that he was the younger brother of James. Scholars have been divided over the authenticity of the book of Jude. The assumption has been that since Jesus' relatives were Galilean peasants, Jude's writing skills could not have produced a composition in Greek of the quality found

---

62. Redditt provides a general summary of the various scholarly positions regarding how to understand the terms "brothers" and "sisters" as they relate to Jesus ("Judas," 1090). See also Brashler, "Jesus," 819–20.

in the book of Jude.[63] However, it has been shown that such an assumption is inaccurate. Jesus and his disciples were very capable of communicating in Greek and more than likely possessed the skills necessary to write in Greek. Paul L. Redditt notes in the passage below that Jude's linguistic skills would have developed as he travelled throughout Galilee preaching the gospel:

> The kind of skills he shows are the rhetorical skills which a Jewish preacher in Greek would need to acquire from familiarity with Jewish literature in Greek and from much listening to Jewish and Christian sermons. It is not easy to estimate how competent in Greek a Galilean Jew would have been, but in Jude's case, if his missionary career took him among Greek-speaking Jews, there seems no reason why he should not have acquired the degree of competence displayed in this letter.[64]

Even more convincing than the experience Jude gained in his use of Greek during his missionary travels was the training he received while growing up in a Hellenistic region of Palestine just a few miles from Sepphoris.

James, the Brother of Jesus

Ἰάκωβος ("James") is the most prominent brother of Jesus.[65] The resurrection of Jesus had a transforming impact upon James (1 Cor 15:7), for he

---

63. Bauckham notes that the high number of *hapax legomena* indicated an impressive command of the Greek language (*Jude, 2 Peter*, 6–7).

64. Redditt, "Jude," 1102. Additionally, Bauckham states that "despite the competence in Greek, the author's real intellectual background is in the literature of Palestinian Judaism" (*Jude, 2 Peter*, 7). What is interesting about Bauckham's observation is that he unwittingly acknowledges Jude's bilingual ability to engage the larger Hellenistic world.

65. There is a long history of debate about the relationship of James and the other children of Joseph to Jesus. Gillman summarizes the three dominant positions: (1) a literal interpretation that implies that Mary and Joseph had children after Jesus was born, (2) an apocryphal interpretation that suggests that Joseph had children from a previous marriage, or (3) a Semitic idiomatic interpretation that broadens the meaning of brothers to cousins. See Gillman, "James," 620. Moo argues that the corroborative evidence strongly suggests that James is both the brother of Jesus and the author of the epistle of James. First, there are linguistic similarities between the epistle of James and the speech of James at the Jerusalem meeting. Second, the circumstances of the epistle correlate with the issues that would have concerned James. Third, the epistle has primitive theological positions. See Moo, *James*, 10–11. Painter argues that the modern church tradition—Roman Catholics and the Reformation—gravitated to early Christian personalities like Peter or Paul. In order to promote certain theological positions, they sought to identify James as the son of Alphaeus ("James the less") instead of James, the brother of the Lord. "One of the aims of this book," Painter states, "is to show that

emerged as an influential leader in the early church (Acts 15:1–20). The Apostle Paul identified James as τὸν ἀδελφὸν τοῦ κυρίου ("the Lord's brother," Gal 1:19) and referred to him, Cephas, and John as οἱ στῦλοι ("pillars," Gal 2:9) in the early church. The epistle of James begins with a description similar to the one found in Jude's letter:

> Ἰάκωβος θεοῦ καὶ κυρίου Ἰησοῦ Χριστοῦ δοῦλος . . . (Jas 1:1).
> James, bond-servant of God and of Jesus Christ . . .

The epistle amplifies the theological shift in the perspective of James toward Jesus. James no longer entertained doubts about Jesus' divine nature but ostensibly affirmed it.[66] John Painter questions the authenticity of the epistle of James principally because he believes that James was faithful to the law of Moses and therefore was in conflict with the Christian message that asserted that believers were set free from the Mosaic law. Although James validated the Gentile mission, Painter argues that there remained a persistent division between the Jerusalem church and the mission to the nations.[67] Consequently, the commitment of James to Jewish laws and regulations would have prevented him from composing a letter that contained what he viewed as anti-Jewish themes in the epistle of James.[68] However, Douglas Moo argues below that the epistle of James represents a Hellenistic orientation in which James would have been well qualified as the author:

> But the key question is this: Could a person with this kind of torah-loyalty have written the letter we have before us? We think the clear answer to the question is yes. The letter, with its

---

the grounds for dismissively regarding James the brother of Jesus as 'less' are misguided and that it is necessary to recognize him as a towering figure in the earliest church." See Painter, *Just James*, 1, 324.

66. Davids observes that the reference to Ἰησοῦ Χριστοῦ is unusual, for the term "Christ" at the time the epistle was written was a name and no longer a title. "That use of the word would be surprising for a Jew who spent most of his time in Jerusalem where the titular use would have been meaningful. . . . Thus it is an indication that this verse stems from a Hellenistic Christian." Davids accepts the possibility that an editor has shaped verse one and thereby by implication rejects its authenticity. See Davids, *James*, 63. The assumption, however, that James was somehow incapable of expressing Hellenistic concepts belies his Galilean background despite the amount of time he may have spent in Jerusalem.

67. Painter, *Just James*, 27.

68. Ibid., 44–45. Painter tries to paint a picture of the early church as one embroiled in power struggles ("rivalry") to take over the Christian movement. Any conflict is the result of "a sinister undertone" as leaders compete for the top spot. A fair reading of the text demonstrates the opposite as the church faces challenges and resolves issues that threaten the gospel. His assertions about the conflict between James and Paul seem to be exaggerated. The gospel's original intent was to go into the entire world (Acts 1:8).

concern with the ethical dimensions of torah, stands squarely in a widespread tradition among Hellenistic-oriented Jews and reflected, in some ways, in the teaching of Jesus.[69]

The prominence of James in Jerusalem must not be viewed as a rejection of his Galilean upbringing.[70] In fact, his Hellenistic background provided both insight and sensitivity during the cultural battles between some Jewish Christians and Gentiles (Acts 15:19–21; cf. Gal 2:11–14).

THREE KEY MESSENGERS OF JESUS

Three additional disciples whose backgrounds also need to be analyzed are important to this study. John Mark, Luke, and Paul each played a significant role in disseminating the gospel message to the broader world. As second-generation disciples, each of these three men appears to have had an un-mitigated passion to be involved in the Gentile mission of the early church.

John Mark

John Mark appears by name for the first time in the book of Acts. Within the first few years of the church's existence, Herod had the apostle James, the brother of John, killed. Since the Jews approved of his actions, Herod also arrested the apostle Peter, probably intending to execute him after the Passover. The following passage describes the actions of the church on Peter's behalf:

> ὁ μὲν οὖν Πέτρος ἐτηρεῖτο ἐν τῇ φυλακῇ· προσευχὴ δὲ ἦν ἐκτενῶς γινομένη ὑπὸ τῆς ἐκκλησίας πρὸς τὸν θεὸν περὶ αὐτοῦ (Acts 12:5)

> So Peter was kept in the prison, but prayer was being made fervently on his behalf by the church to God.

Interestingly, Peter escaped imprisonment with the help of divine intervention (Acts 12:6–11) and found refuge in the house of Mary where the church had gathered to pray (12:12). Mary is identified as Μαρίας τῆς

---

69. Moo, *James*, 19–20.

70. Scholars like Painter play with the facts too loosely and often make assumptions based upon silence. Such "historical" reconstructions make for good fiction as efforts are made to analyze the moods, feelings, and hidden agendas of key members of the early church. Peter Davids provides a helpful chart that shows the various scholarly positions concerning the authorship of the epistle of James. See Davids, *James*, 4.

μητρὸς Ἰωάννου τοῦ ἐπικαλουμένου Μάρκου ("Mary, the mother of John who was called Mark," 12:12, 25; 15:37). Elsewhere, Mary's son, John, is known simply as Ἰωάννης ("John," Acts 13:5, 13) or Μᾶρκος ("Mark," Acts 15:39) or Μᾶρκος ὁ ἀνεψιὸς Βαρναβᾶ ("Mark the cousin of Barnabas," Col 4:10). Mark's dual name is consistent with the common practice employed within Hellenistic Judaism.[71] John Mark was very much involved in the church in Jerusalem. His mother's house possibly served as one of the many house churches in the city. Apparently, he also had a close association with the apostles of Jesus, especially with Peter, Paul, and Barnabas.

John Mark received his first exposure to missionary work under Paul's leadership, an experience that proved too difficult for Mark and an extreme disappointment to Paul (Acts 13:13, 15:37–38).[72] However, John Mark later regained the trust of his mentor and became a fellow worker with him (2 Tim 4:11; Phlm 24).

The missionary travels of John Mark also led him to Rome where he and Peter worked together (1 Pet 5:13). Early church tradition affirms the close relationship between John Mark and Peter. Clement of Alexandria (second century CE) linked the origin of the Gospel of Mark to the relationship that Mark and Peter shared. Eusebius recorded Clement's words in the following citation:

> [Clement] said that those Gospels were first written which include the genealogies, but that the Gospel according to Mark came into being in this matter: When Peter had publicly preached the word at Rome, and by the Spirit had proclaimed the Gospel, that those present, who were many, exhorted Mark, as one who had followed him for a long time and remembered what had been spoken, to make a record of what was said; and that he did this, and distributed the Gospel among those that asked him. And that when the matter came to Peter's knowledge he neither strongly forbade it nor urged it forward. But that John, last of all, conscious that the outward facts had been set forth in the Gospels, was urged on by his disciples, and, divinely moved by the Spirit, composed a spiritual Gospel. This is Clement's account (*Hist. eccl.* 6.14.5–7 [Oulton, LCL]).

Additionally, Eusebius also noted that Clement referred to Mark as Peter's follower:

---

71. Other examples are Ἰωσὴφ/Ἰοῦστος ("Joseph/Justus," Acts 1:23), Ἰησοῦς/Ἰοῦστος ("Jesus/Justus," Col 4:11), and Σαῦλος/Παῦλος ("Saul/Paul," Acts 13:9). See Jefford, "Mark, John," 557.

72. Martin, "Mark, John," 259.

> But a great light of religion shone on the minds of the hearers of Peter, so that they were not satisfied with a single hearing or with the unwritten teaching of the divine proclamation, but with every kind of exhortation besought Mark, whose Gospel is extant, seeing that he was Peter's follower, to leave them a written statement of the teaching given them verbally, nor did they cease until they had persuaded him, and so became the cause of the Scripture called the Gospel according to Mark. And they say that the Apostle, knowing by the revelation of the spirit to him what had been done, was pleased at their zeal, and ratified the scripture for study in the churches. Clement quotes the story in the sixth book of the *Hypotyposes*, and the bishop of Hierapolis, named Papias, confirms him. He also says that Peter mentions Mark in his first Epistle, and he composed this in Rome itself, which they say that he himself indicates, referring to the city metaphorically as Babylon, in the words, "the elect one in Babylon greets you, and Marcus my son" (*Hist. eccl.* 2.15.2 [Oulton, LCL]).

As indicated above, Papias (second century CE) was a bishop of Hierapolis in Phrygia.[73] His fragmentary writings have been preserved by later patristic writers. For example, Irenaeus (second century CE) indicated that Papias compiled four books, was a disciple of the apostle John, and was a companion of Polycarp (*Haer.* 5.33.4). Irenaeus also notes below that Mark was Peter's interpreter: "After their departure, Mark, the disciple and interpreter of Peter, did also hand down to us in writing what had been preached by Peter" (*Haer.* 3.1.1 [Rambaut, Ante-Nicene Fathers]). Eusebius preserved the following description of the relationship of John Mark and Peter:

> [W]e are now obliged to append to the words already quoted from him a tradition about the Mark who wrote the Gospel, which he expounds as follows. "And the Presbyter used to say this, 'Mark became Peter's interpreter and wrote accurately all that he remembered, not, indeed, in order, of the things said or done by the Lord. For he had not heard the Lord, nor had he followed him, but later on, as I said, followed Peter, who used to give teaching as necessity demanded but not making, as it were, an arrangement of the Lord's oracles, so that Mark did nothing wrong in thus writing down single points as he remembered them. For to one thing he gave attention, to leave out nothing of what he had heard and to make no false statements in them'" (*Hist. eccl.* 3.39.15 [Lake, LCL]).

---

73. Michaels, "Apostolic Fathers," 211.

The above citation is actually a quotation by Papias of another individual referred to as the Presbyter (or Elder).[74] What exactly does the reference mean that Mark served as Peter's interpreter? The term ἑρμηνευτής ("interpreter") refers to a person who helps others understand thoughts expressed in words and the verb ἑρμηνεύω means to explain or to translate.[75] Ralph Martin notes at least three substantive ways to understand the reference of Papias to Mark.[76] First, Mark acted as Peter's interpreter by translating Peter's Aramaic or Greek into a more acceptable form. This interpretation falsely assumes that Peter lacked the linguistic skills to communicate either in Aramaic or Greek. Second, Mark acted as a teacher and provided an instructional manual based upon the content of Peter's preaching. Third, Mark's role of interpreter simply implies that he published a gospel in which he recorded Peter's teachings.

If the words of Papias are authentic,[77] then a few general observations can be made about the Gospel of Mark. First, the Presbyter appears to be defending Mark's gospel against some who were making false claims about its trustworthiness.[78] The Presbyter says that Mark wrote accurately even though he had not necessarily presented an orderly account of Jesus' life. Second, it may be inferred that other gospel accounts were already circulating. Luke's prologue (1:1–4) to his gospel acknowledges many who had also produced works about Jesus' life and ministry. Third, Mark was not an eyewitness of Jesus and was not numbered among the original followers (apostles). However, Mark 14:51–52 describes the actions of some unknown young man who barely escaped capture by the soldiers who came to arrest Jesus. Some scholars view this episode as Mark's way of portraying himself in his gospel.[79] France sees it as an amplification of the fact that all disciples—known and unknown—fled.[80] The context, however, does not seem to lend itself to a figurative interpretation.[81] Fourth, Mark's account

74. France, *Mark*, 7–8; see also Turner, "Tradition," 260–63; Perumalil, "Papias and Irenaeus," 332–37.

75. Danker, "ἑρμηνευτής," 393.

76. Martin, "Mark, John," 260. See also Unnik, "Papias," 276–77. Additionally, Martin suggests that the purpose of the statement by Papias was to link Mark closely to an apostolic figure in order to refute Marcion's Gnostic use of Luke's gospel. Martin thinks that Mark has closer ties to Paul (*Mark*, 80–83).

77. More about the role of Papias and the patristic tradition regarding gospel origins will be addressed in chapter 4.

78. Harrison, *Introduction*, 182.

79. Guelich, "Mark," 514.

80. France, *Mark*, 595–97.

81. Cole, *Mark*, 224.

originated from what he learned or heard while in the company of Peter. Finally, Mark's gospel was trustworthy and without error.

Regardless of whether one or none of the above explanations presents the most accurate picture of Mark's role as Peter's interpreter, the fact remains that from a very early period, the early church fathers believed that Mark was the author of the gospel that bears his name. Additionally, France notes below that although the literary genre of Mark is consistent with similar biographies produced in the ancient Greco-Roman world, the message is distinctively different because the deity of Jesus undergirds the message:

> This means that Mark's book reflects not the distant evaluation of a scholarly admirer of Jesus but the subjective experience of one of those who shared most closely in the stirring and yet profoundly disturbing events of Jesus' public ministry and his confrontation with the Jerusalem establishment. And it reflects those experiences as they were passed on in the day-to-day teaching ministry, "as occasion required," of a living community of the followers of Jesus (within which Mark no doubt himself also followed Peter as a recognized teller of the stories of Jesus). It is, perhaps, this grounding in the active life of the church which gives much of the special flavor (and "feeling of otherness") to the "good news" as told by Mark.[82]

Everett F. Harrison notes several reasons why the Gospel of Mark may have originated from Rome.[83] First, Mark 15:21 refers to a Ῥούφου ("Rufus"), one of the sons of Σίμωνα Κυρηναῖον ("Simon of Cyrene"), who carried the cross of Jesus. This Rufus is also referred to by Paul in Rom 16:13 as living with his mother in Rome. A Roman audience would appreciate such recognition. In addition, Mark includes a number of Latin terms in his gospel and also explains Greek expressions with Latin equivalents (e.g., κοδράντης / "cent," Mark 12:42; πραιτώριον/ "Praetorium," 15:16 NASB).[84] Second, the fact that Mark is identified as Peter's interpreter may account for the Semitic flavor of the gospel as Mark faithfully recounted what Peter spoke in certain private settings where Aramaic most likely was spoken. Also, Mark's gospel is the only Synoptic that pays special attention to the word of Jesus' resurrection reaching Peter (Mark 16:7). Finally, if the

---

82. France, *Mark*, 9.

83. Harrison, *Introduction*, 183–84.

84. Gundry, *Survey*, 153. The mere use of a Roman loanword like κοδράντης does not conclusively imply a Roman origin of the gospel for Roman designation of coins was common in Palestine during the first century CE. See Schürer, *The History of Jewish People*, 64.

connection between Peter and Mark is accurate, then the Gospel of Mark represents a faithful account of an eyewitness of Jesus.

John Mark's ties to the apostolic mission and perhaps even his presence at the betrayal of Jesus as noted above affirm the close-knit circle of primary disciples who were actively involved in the dissemination of the gospel message. Despite John Mark's Judean background, he appears to be adequately equipped in Greek not only to participate in missionary activity throughout Palestine and in Rome but also to compose a gospel that targets Gentile readers.[85]

Luke the Physician

Λουκᾶς ("Luke") is the hellenized rendering for Lucius.[86] His name occurs three times in the epistles of Paul. He is listed among Paul's fellow workers along with Epaphras, Mark, Aristarchus, and Demas (Phlm 24). Shortly before Paul's martyrdom in Rome, Luke stands by him as a faithful companion (2 Tim 4:11). Paul also refers to Luke as ὁ ἰατρὸς ὁ ἀγαπητὸς ("the beloved physician," Col 4:14). The term ὁ ἰατρὸς is a professional designation for one who engages in the practice of helping people with their ailments (cf. Luke 4:23, 8:43).[87] The Muratorian fragment (ca. 170–180 CE) is the earliest tradition outside of the NT that identifies Luke as a physician and as the author of the Gospel of Luke and the book of Acts (Luke-Acts):[88]

> (2) Tertium evangelii librum secundum Lucam (3) Lucas Iste medicus, post ascensum Christi (4) cum Paulus quasi litteris studiosum (5) secum adsumpsisset, nomine suo (6) ex opinlone

---

85. This may explain why the Greek text of Mark is "unimpressive" and somewhat "prolix and clumsy" (Johnson, *Writings of the New Testament*, 150). Martin argues that the internal evidence in the Gospel of Mark "almost conclusively proves that Mark wrote for gentile readers" ("Mark," 254). See also Gundry, *Survey*, 129; Dodd, "Gospel Narrative," 396–400; Kümmel, *Introduction*, 97; Carson and Moo, *Introduction*, 177–79.

86. Danker, "Λουκᾶς," 603.

87. Danker, "ἰατρός," 465. Although as early as the third century BCE the practice of medicine was in full bloom among the Egyptians, medicine as a science owes its origins to the Greeks. See Graber and Müller, "ἰάομαι," 166.

88. The fragment containing a list of NT books written in Latin was discovered by Muratori and published in 1740 CE. See Hurtado, "Muratorian Fragment," 433. An older reference of a Western recension of Acts 20:13 that dates about 120 CE possibly includes Luke's name. Metzger notes that a variant reading for ἡμεῖς ("we") is found in the Armenian catena which is based upon the Old Syriac text and expands the "we" into "I, Luke, and those who with me went on board" (*Textual Commentary*, 423). See also Bruce, *Acts*, 7, 385; Garland, *Luke*, 21.

conscripsit, dominum tamen nec lpse (7) vidit in carne, et ideo prout assequl potuit 8ita et a nativitate lohannis incipit dicere.[89]

(2) The third book of the Gospel is that according to Luke. (3) Luke, the well-known physician, after the ascension of Christ, (4–5) when Paul had taken with him as one zealous for the law, (6) composed it in his own name, according to [the general] belief. Yet he himself had not (7) seen the Lord in the flesh; and therefore, as he was able to ascertain events, (8) so indeed he begins to tell the story from the birth of John.[90]

Additionally, Eusebius preserves the tradition of Luke's identity and authorship of Luke-Acts in the following passage:

Luke, who was by race an Antiochian and a physician [ἰατρός] by profession, was long a companion of Paul, and had careful conversation with the other Apostles, and in two books left us examples of the medicine for souls which he had gained from them—the Gospel, which he testifies that he had planned according to the tradition received by him by those who were from the beginning eyewitnesses and ministers of the word, all of whom he says, moreover, he had followed from the beginning, and the Acts of the Apostles which he composed no longer on the evidence of hearing but of his own eyes. And they say that Paul was actually accustomed to quote from Luke's Gospel since when writing of some Gospel as his own he used to say, "According to my gospel" (*Hist. eccl.* 3.4.6–8 [Lake, LCL]).

H. J. Cadbury notes that there is nothing in these early traditions that could not be inferred from the NT. Lucan authorship was probably derived from Luke's travels with Paul as found in the "we"-sections of Acts.[91] However, Donald Guthrie argues that what makes the tradition strong is the "undisputed sway among the Church Fathers" that the authorship of Luke-Acts was attributed to someone other than an apostle.[92] Why would Luke-Acts be attached to Luke's name if the tradition were spurious?[93]

89. Aland, *Synopsis*, 538.

90. Metzger, *Canon*, 191–201.

91. Cadbury, "The Tradition," 209–64. Cadbury provides the full text of primary references from the patristics and later traditions that relate to Luke (e.g., Irenaeus, Clement of Alexandria, Tertullian, Origen, Eusebius, Jerome, etc.).

92. Guthrie, *Introduction*, 115.

93. Fitzmyer, *Luke*, 41.

Based upon the information found in the NT and in the writings of the patristic fathers, Luke's biographical background can be summarized as follows:

(1) Luke's home might have been Antioch of Syria. Interestingly, the first integrated Christian congregation consisting of members representing both Jewish and Hellenistic backgrounds was established in Antioch. Luke attributes the impetus behind the establishment of the church in Antioch to the persecution that broke out against the church in Jerusalem:

> Οἱ μὲν οὖν διασπαρέντες ἀπὸ τῆς θλίψεως τῆς γενομένης ἐπὶ Στεφάνῳ διῆλθον ἕως Φοινίκης καὶ Κύπρου καὶ Ἀντιοχείας μηδενὶ λαλοῦντες τὸν λόγον εἰ μὴ μόνον Ἰουδαίοις. Ἦσαν δέ τινες ἐξ αὐτῶν ἄνδρες Κύπριοι καὶ Κυρηναῖοι, οἵτινες ἐλθόντες εἰς Ἀντιόχειαν ἐλάλουν καὶ πρὸς τοὺς Ἑλληνιστὰς εὐαγγελιζόμενοι τὸν κύριον Ἰησοῦν (Acts 11:19–20).

> Now those who were scattered because of the persecution that happened against Stephen made their way as far as Phoenicia and Cyprus and Antioch, speaking the word to no one except to Jews alone. But there were some of them, men of Cyprus and Cyrene, who came to Antioch and began speaking to the Greeks also, preaching the Lord Jesus.

If the tradition about Luke's place of origin is authentic, then one could reasonably speculate that Luke became a disciple of Jesus through the efforts of those who preached in Antioch where Paul, Barnabas, and John Mark were also engaged in ministry (Acts 12:25—13:1–2). This would also explain the relationship that developed between Luke and Paul.

(2) Luke was a medical doctor by trade and a companion of Paul. Medical science accelerated during the Hellenistic age. Driven by the seriousness and pathos of Hippocrates (ca. 460–370 BCE) and the famous Hippocratic oath, medical practitioners conserved the "research of the past by editing, copying and commenting on the works of previous doctors" in order to advance the science of medicine.[94] According to the list below, medical science forged new frontiers:[95]

> Herophilus (ca. fourth-third centuries BCE) was the first doctor to dissect human bodies.

> Erasistratus (third century BCE) was the first doctor to maintain that the human body was composed of atoms.

---

94. Caragounis, "Scholarship," 1078.

95. Ibid.

Heraclides (first century BCE) was the first doctor to explore the science of pharmacology.

Soranus (first-second centuries CE) was the first doctor to specialize in gynecology and obstetrics.

Although there is no record about where Luke received his education, the medical profession had advanced remarkably by the time Luke became a physician.

Interestingly, the Gospel of Luke contains evidence of a heightened sensibility to medical concerns. Tables 3.3, 3.4, and 3.5 indicate instances in which Luke supplies greater detail concerning medical issues than do his gospel counterparts:

Table 3.3. The healing of Peter's mother-in-law

Matthew 8:14–15	Mark 1:29–31	Luke 4:38–39
Καὶ ἐλθὼν ὁ Ἰησοῦς εἰς τὴν οἰκίαν Πέτρου εἶδεν *τὴν πενθερὰν αὐτοῦ βεβλημένην καὶ πυρέσσουσαν* καὶ ἥψατο τῆς χειρὸς αὐτῆς, καὶ ἀφῆκεν αὐτὴν ὁ πυρετός, καὶ ἠγέρθη καὶ διηκόνει αὐτῷ.	Καὶ εὐθὺς ἐκ τῆς συναγωγῆς ἐξελθόντες ἦλθον εἰς τὴν οἰκίαν Σίμωνος καὶ Ἀνδρέου μετὰ Ἰακώβου καὶ Ἰωάννου. *ἡ δὲ πενθερὰ Σίμωνος κατέκειτο πυρέσσουσα,* καὶ εὐθὺς λέγουσιν αὐτῷ περὶ αὐτῆς. καὶ προσελθὼν ἤγειρεν αὐτὴν κρατήσας τῆς χειρός καὶ ἀφῆκεν αὐτὴν ὁ πυρετός, καὶ διηκόνει αὐτοῖς.	Ἀναστὰς δὲ ἀπὸ τῆς συναγωγῆς εἰσῆλθεν εἰς τὴν οἰκίαν Σίμωνος. *πενθερὰ δὲ τοῦ Σίμωνος ἦν συνεχομένη πυρετῷ μεγάλῳ* καὶ ἠρώτησαν αὐτὸν περὶ αὐτῆς. καὶ ἐπιστὰς ἐπάνω αὐτῆς ἐπετίμησεν τῷ πυρετῷ καὶ ἀφῆκεν αὐτήν·παραχρῆμα δὲ ἀναστᾶσα διηκόνει αὐτοῖς.

Source: chart is based upon Aland, *Synopsis* (emphasis mine).

In contrast to Matthew and Mark who mention that Peter's mother-in-law had become sick with a fever, Luke describes in greater detail that συνεχομένη πυρετῷ μεγάλῳ ("she was ill with a high fever"). Luke provides two important observations: (1) The present passive participle συνεχομένη denotes that her sickness had caused an internal state of distress and torment.[96] (2) The addition of the adjective μεγάλῳ ("great") indicates that her condition was critical.

96. Danker, "συνέχω," 970–71.

Table 3.4. The cleansing of the leper

Matthew 8:1–2	Mark 1:40	Luke 5:12
Καταβάντος δὲ αὐτοῦ ἀπὸ τοῦ ὄρους ἠκολούθησαν αὐτῷ ὄχλοι πολλοί. *καὶ ἰδοὺ λεπρὸς προσελθὼν* προσεκύνει αὐτῷ λέγων κύριε, ἐὰν θέλῃς δύνασαί με καθαρίσαι.	*Καὶ ἔρχεται πρὸς αὐτὸν λεπρὸς παρακαλῶν αὐτὸν* [καὶ γονυπετῶν] καὶ λέγων αὐτῷ ὅτι ἐὰν θέλῃς δύνασαί με καθαρίσαι.	Καὶ ἐγένετο ἐν τῷ εἶναι αὐτὸν ἐν μιᾷ τῶν πόλεων *καὶ ἰδοὺ ἀνὴρ πλήρης λέπρας* ἰδὼν δὲ τὸν Ἰησοῦν, πεςὼν ἐπὶ πρόσωπον ἐδεήθη αὐτοῦ λέγων κύριε, ἐὰν θέλῃς δύνασαί με καθαρίσαι.

Source: Chart is based upon Aland, *Synopsis* (emphasis mine).

The use of the adjective πλήρης ("complete") provides a more precise description of the degree to which the disease of leprosy had affected the man's body.[97]

Table 3.5. The healing of the paralytic

Matthew 9:2	Mark 2:3	Luke 5:18
καὶ ἰδοὺ προσέφερον αὐτῷ *παραλυτικὸν* ἐπὶ κλίνης βεβλημένον. καὶ ἰδὼν ὁ Ἰησοῦς τὴν πίστιν αὐτῶν εἶπεν τῷ παραλυτικῷ·θάρσει, τέκνον, ἀφίενταί σου αἱ ἁμαρτίαι.	καὶ ἔρχονται φέροντες πρὸς αὐτὸν *παραλυτικὸν* αἰρόμενον ὑπὸ τεσσάρων.	καὶ ἰδοὺ ἄνδρες φέροντες ἐπὶ κλίνης ἄνθρωπον ὃς ἦν *παραλελυμένος* καὶ ἐζήτουν αὐτὸν εἰσενεγκεῖν καὶ θεῖναι [αὐτὸν] ἐνώπιον αὐτοῦ.

Source: Chart is based upon Aland, *Synopsis* (emphasis mine).

A subtle distinction is made by Luke when he refers to the lame man who was brought before Jesus. The NT employs four different terms to describe this condition: χωλός ("lame"), κυλλός ("maimed"), παραλθτικός ("paralytic"), and παραλελθμένος ("paralyzed").[98] The first three words represent the more common designations for this condition. However, Luke prefers the perfect passive participle which "better expresses the condition of the man."[99]

97. Danker, "πλήρης," 826–27.

98. Bock, *Luke,* 480.

99. Fitzmyer, *Luke,* 582. See also Luke 5:18, 24; Acts 8:7, 9:33.

The point of the above analysis is not to argue that Luke was a physician because he used technical medical terminology but to demonstrate that the evidence corroborates with what we know about Luke from ancient writers and the NT. Luke was a literate and educated person who certainly had a command of the Greek language.[100]

However, Luke might have revealed his medical bias in the following passage concerning an ill woman that Jesus healed:

> Καὶ γυνὴ οὖσα ἐν ῥύσει αἵματος ἀπὸ ἐτῶν δώδεκα, ἥτις [ἰατροῖς προσαναλώσασα ὅλον τὸν βίον] οὐκ ἴσχυσεν ἀπ᾽ οὐδενὸς θεραπευθῆναι, προσελθοῦσα ὄπισθεν ἥψατο τοῦ κρασπέδου τοῦ ἱματίου αὐτοῦ καὶ παραχρῆμα ἔστη ἡ ῥύσις τοῦ αἵματος αὐτῆς (Luke 8:43–44).

> And a woman, who had a hemorrhage for twelve years and could not be healed by anyone, came up behind to touch the fringe of his garment and immediately her hemorrhage stopped.

In the Greek passage above, the bracketed phrase ἰατροῖς προσαναλώσασα ὅλον τὸν βίον ("spent all her livelihood on physicians") denotes a textual variant not considered a part of the original text. The stronger manuscript witnesses exclude the phrase.[101] Consequently, the phrase was retained

---

100. Hobart argued that the medical language in Luke-Acts provided evidence for Luke's vocation. He compared Luke's vocabulary to extant Greek medical writings of Hippocrates, Aretaeus, Galen, and Dioscorides. His purpose was to "show, from an examination of the language employed in the third Gospel and the Acts of the Apostles, that both are the works of a person well acquainted with the language of the Greek Medical Schools" (*Luke*, xxix). However, Cadbury argued that much of Luke's alleged medical language can be found in the LXX and in the nonmedical writings of educated Hellenistic authors like Josephus, Lucian, and Plutarch. "The so-called medical language of these books," wrote Cadbury, "cannot be used as a proof that Luke was their author, nor even as an argument confirming the tradition of his authorship" (*Luke*, 50–51). See also Cadbury, "Lexical Notes," 190–209; Marx, "Luke," 168–72. Surprisingly, the studies by Hobart and Cadbury have actually shown that the author of Luke-Acts was highly educated and therefore more precise in his descriptions of medical issues. The evidence may not prove that Luke was a medical doctor but it certainly does not dispute the patristic tradition about Luke or the biblical references to him about his vocation. Although Hobart may have overstated his case, he nevertheless demonstrated that incidental medical interest appears in the writings of Luke-Acts. After a thorough study of the positions of Hobart and Cadbury, Robertson asserted that "most impressive of all is it to read Mark's reports of the miracles and then Luke's modifications. And then the reading of the Gospel and the Acts straight through leaves the same conviction that we are following the lead of a cultivated physician whose professional habits of thought have colored the whole in many subtle ways. This positive impression refuses to be dissipated" (*Luke*, 12).

101. The phrase is omitted in P[75] (early third century CE), B (fourth century CE),

within brackets and given a "C" rating, which indicates doubt as to whether the variant should remain in the text.[102] Mark's account is more critical of the medical professions:

> καὶ πολλὰ παθοῦσα ὑπὸ πολλῶν ἰατρῶν καὶ δαπανήσασα τὰ παρ' αὐτῆς πάντα καὶ μηδὲν ὠφεληθεῖσα ἀλλὰ μᾶλλον εἰς τὸ χεῖρον ἐλθοῦσα (Mark 5:26).

> And had endured much from many physicians and spent all that she had and was not helped at all but had become much worse.

Regardless of whether Luke summarized Mark 5:26, he has certainly softened Mark's harsh remarks about physicians.[103] "If Luke, the Beloved Physician, is the author of Luke-Acts," wrote Fitzmyer, "then one could understand his reluctance to incorporate the Marcan criticism."[104]

According to the book of Acts, Luke joins Paul on several occasions as a travel partner. When Luke accompanies Paul he switches from the third person to the first person plural.[105] These passages are referred to as the "we"-sections in Acts and provide the following details about Luke's travels with Paul:[106]

> Luke first joins Paul at Troas and sails with him to Philippi (Acts 16:10–17).

> When Paul returns to Philippi, Luke rejoins him and they sail back to Troas (Acts 20:5–15).

> Luke accompanies Paul on the way to Jerusalem and remains with Philip at Caesarea (Acts 21:1–18).

> Luke joins Paul again on the journey to Rome (Acts 27:1–28:16).

Additionally, Luke remains with Paul during his second imprisonment while he awaits his imminent execution (2 Tim 4:11).

---

and D (fifth century CE). See Metzger, *Text of the New Testament*, 41, 47, 49; Fitzmyer, *Luke*, 746.

102. Metzger, *Textual Commentary*, 121.

103. Bock, *Luke*, 806.

104. Fitzmyer, *Luke*, 746.

105. The "we"-sections have been variously explained that Luke provided an account of a genuine eyewitness, that Luke used sources written by someone else, or that Luke employed a literary technique to foster vividness and interest. See Garland, *Luke*, 22; Hemer, *Acts*, 312–34.

106. See Guthrie, *Introduction*, 116.

Hobart proposed that Luke joined Paul on these occasions because the apostle faced a number of delicate medical issues.[107] Joseph Lightfoot argued that the first "we"-section occurred during the time of Paul's physical malady mentioned in Gal 4:13–14 and that Luke may have joined Paul "partly in a professional capacity."[108] This would explain the arbitrary presence of Luke at key junctures during Paul's journeys and his sudden disappearance from the narrative. Since ancient physicians were known to travel as itinerants, Luke may have been Paul's personal physician.[109]

(3) Luke was a Hellenistic Jew. The debate about the ethnic identity of Luke is a controversial one.[110] However, there are a number of reasons that favor Luke's Hellenistic Jewish background.[111] First, in a discussion about Jewish patriotism and citizenship among foreign countries, Josephus made the following observation:

> All persons invited to join a colony, however different their nationality, take the name of the founders. It is needless to go outside our race for instances. Our Jewish residents in Antioch are called Antiochenes, having been granted rights of citizenship by its founder, Seleucus (*Ag. Ap.* 2.4 §39 [Thackeray, LCL]).

The reference above confirms that Jews were present in Antioch and were naturally called Antiochenes. Consequently, Luke's Jewish ethnicity cannot be ruled out because of the patristic tradition that connects him to a dominant Gentile city like Antioch.

Second, the method of shortening names was a common practice among the Jews. Similar to Luke's name being a shortened form of the Latin *Lucius*, the name of Paul's companion Σιλᾶς ("Silas") was also a hellenized contraction from the Latin name *Silvanus*. Despite these Latin derivatives, the names do not necessarily indicate the ethnicity of the individuals who bore them. Fitzmyer makes the following observation:

---

107. Hobart, *Luke*, 292–97.

108. Lightfoot, *Colossians and Philemon*, 241–42.

109. Witherington III, *Corinth*, 459–64; Hengel and Schwemer, *Paulus*, 18–22.

110. For a complete examination of the various positions, see Allen, *Lukan Authorship*, 261–323.

111. Burney states that "St. Luke was a Hellenistic Jew and not a Gentile would be—apart from other evidence to the contrary—the natural deduction from the fact that the LXX has coloured his Greek style in so marked a degree; since this surely implies that he was brought up upon the Greek Bible. Had he been a Gentile, and not converted to Christianity until he was a grown man, his Greek style would presumably have been already formed and would not have taken on a LXX colouring, at any rate to the extent that it has" (*Aramaic Origin*, 10–11).

Greek and Roman names were borne by many Jews in Palestine and Syria of this period. They were often indicative of their status with as *liberti*, "freedmen," descendants of Jews once sold into slavery during the Roman conquest of an area, or as *incolae*, "inhabitants," of the area, who in time had been granted the right of Roman citizenship.[112]

In light of this practice, there might be a connection between the name Luke and the name Λούκιος ("Lucius" NASB) to whom Paul referred as συγγενεῖς μου ("my kinsmen," Rom 16:21).[113] The term συγγενεῖς can refer specifically to an actual relative or more broadly to a fellow countryman. Contextually, the term appears to refer to the latter group since Paul uses it three times in his closing remarks to the Romans (16:7, 11, 21).[114] If this Lucius was a reference to Luke, albeit a reference to his Roman name, then he was a Jew and not a Gentile.[115]

Third, if the first "we"-section in Acts 16:10–17 extends to verse 20, then the author is more likely a Jew. Luke records below the accusations against Paul and Silas when they stood before the authorities for upsetting the local economy:

> καὶ προσαγαγόντες αὐτοὺς τοῖς στρατηγοῖς εἶπαν· οὗτοι οἱ ἄνθρωποι ἐκταράσσουσιν ἡμῶν τὴν πόλιν, Ἰουδαῖοι ὑπάρχοντες, καὶ καταγγέλλουσιν ἔθη ἃ οὐκ ἔξεστιν ἡμῖν παραδέχεσθαι οὐδὲ ποιεῖν Ῥωμαίοις οὖσιν (Act 16:20–21).

> Now having brought them to the chief magistrate, they said, "These men are throwing our city into confusion, being Jews; and they proclaim habits which are not proper for us to receive or to practice, being Romans."

Since Luke continues to use the first person plural ἡμῖν through v. 17 and reverts to a third person plural participle ἐξελθόντες ("they departed") in v. 40, he appears to have been present when the above incident occurred and to have remained in Philippi when the others departed. The significance of this event is that Luke, Paul, and Silas were called Ἰουδαῖοι ("Jews") while the accusers referred to themselves as Ῥωμαίοις ("Romans"). Although this may not be one of the strongest arguments for Luke's Jewish ethnicity, the fact that only Jews served as missionaries in the book of Acts argues in favor of

---

112. Fitzmyer, *Luke*, 43.

113. Luke is an "affectionate or pet name for Lucius" (Danker, "Λούκιος," 603).

114. Danker, "συγγενής," 950.

115. Wenham, "Luke," 3–44.

Luke's Jewish connections since he was also an evangelist.[116] Garland states that "Luke may have escaped arrest, since only Paul and Silas are mentioned, but all the missionaries in Acts are Jews [. . .] the missionaries in Acts, like Paul, represent what is truly Jewish."[117]

Finally, since Luke was a Hellenist, he was not associated with the rigidity of a certain sect of Jewish Christians known as "the circumcision party" that protested against letting Gentiles enter the church without first embracing certain aspects of Judaism. Luke indicates that this conservative group originated from believing Pharisees in Jerusalem who insisted that Gentile converts be circumcised (Acts 15:1, 5; Gal 2:12).[118] Although the influence of the circumcision party diminishes, Paul continues to face challenges of a lesser degree regarding the practice of circumcision. Paul's closing comments in his correspondence to the Colossians contain the following reference to his fellow workers:

Ἀσπάζεται ὑμᾶς Ἀρίσταρχος ὁ συναιχμάλωτός μου καὶ Μᾶρκος ὁ ἀνεψιὸς Βαρναβᾶ (περὶ οὗ ἐλάβετε ἐντολάς, ἐὰν ἔλθῃ πρὸς ὑμᾶς, δέξασθε αὐτόν) καὶ Ἰησοῦς ὁ λεγόμενος Ἰοῦστος, οἱ ὄντες ἐκ περιτομῆς, οὗτοι μόνοι συνεργοὶ εἰς τὴν βασιλείαν τοῦ θεοῦ, οἵτινες ἐγενήθησάν μοι παρηγορία. ἀσπάζεται ὑμᾶς Ἐπαφρᾶς ὁ ἐξ ὑμῶν, δοῦλος Χριστοῦ [Ἰησοῦ], πάντοτε ἀγωνιζόμενος ὑπὲρ ὑμῶν ἐν ταῖς προσευχαῖς, ἵνα σταθῆτε τέλειοι καὶ πεπληροφορημένοι ἐν παντὶ θελήματι τοῦ θεοῦ. μαρτυρῶ γὰρ αὐτῷ ὅτι ἔχει πολὺν πόνον ὑπὲρ ὑμῶν καὶ τῶν ἐν Λαοδικείᾳ καὶ τῶν ἐν Ἱεραπόλει. ἀσπάζεται ὑμᾶς Λουκᾶς ὁ ἰατρὸς ὁ ἀγαπητὸς καὶ Δημᾶς (Col 4:10–14).

Aristarchus, my fellow prisoner greets you and Mark, the cousin of Barnabas (concerning whom you received instruction; if he comes to you, welcome him) and Jesus who is called Justus; these are the only ones from the circumcision who are coworkers in the kingdom of God; who have been a comfort to me. Epaphras who is one of your number, a servant of Christ Jesus greets you; always laboring on your behalf in prayer, so that you may always stand complete fully assured in all the will of God. For I testify to you that he has deep concern for you and for those in Laodicea and Hierapolis. Luke, the beloved physician, greets you and also Demas.

116. Gundry, *Survey*, 208.

117. Garland, *Luke*, 23.

118. Bruce, *Acts*, 288–89; Jervis, *Galatians*, 4–7; DeLacey, "Circumcision," 226–28.

The phrase οἱ ὄντες ἐκ περιτομῆς (lit., "being of the circumcision") on the surface appears to imply that only Aristarchus, Mark, and Justus were Jewish and that Epaphras, Luke, and Demas were not.[119] However, the Greek phrase seems to refer to those who were associated with the "circumcision party," for Paul also applies the phrase τοὺς ἐκ περιτομῆς (lit., "the ones of the circumcision") to Jewish Christians associated with the circumcision party who came from Jerusalem to Galatia. W. F. Albright argued that Paul does not infer that Luke had not been circumcised but "designates the party which considered circumcision as a necessary prerequisite for salvation."[120] Even Fitzmyer does not consider the textual evidence compelling enough to demand the conclusion that Luke was a Gentile although he argues that Luke may have been a Semitic Gentile.[121]

There is some question about the degree to which a Semitic Gentile or Godfearer would have embraced Jewish lifestyle and thought. The Roman moralist Decimus Iunius Iuvenalis (ca. 50–130 CE) describes below an interesting problem about Gentiles who attached themselves to Jewish Synagogues without wholly adopting Jewish lifestyles:[122]

> Some who have had a father who reveres the Sabbath, worship nothing but the clouds, and the divinity of the heavens, and see no difference between eating swine's flesh, from which their father abstained, and that of man; and in time they take to circumcision. Having been wont to flout the laws of Rome, they learn and practice and revere the Jewish law, and all that Moses handed down in his secret tome, forbidding to point out the way to any not worshipping the same rites, and conducting none but the circumcised to the desired fountain. For all which the father was to blame, who gave up every seventh day to idleness, keeping it apart from all the concerns of life (*Sat.* 14:96–106 [Ramsay, LCL]).

Would a Semitic Gentile or a Godfearer be as well versed as Luke in Semitic thought, practice, knowledge, and lifestyle? David E. Garland provides the following summary:

> If it means that they are the only Jewish converts among his coworkers, it would appear to exclude Timothy, the coauthor of the letter. Possibly the phrase "of the circumcision" [lit. trans.]

119. Carson and Moo, *Introduction*, 206; Lightfoot, *Colossians and Philemon*, 238–40.

120. Munck, *Acts*, 266.

121. Fitzmyer, *Luke*, 44–47.

122. Ferguson, *Backgrounds*, 116.

refers to the circumcision party (see Acts 10:45; 11:2; Gal 2:12) and means: These are the only ones from that group who bring him comfort. If it refers to these three as Jews, it may be a lament (see Rom 9:1–3)—these are the only ones. In the context of Jewish opposition in Colosse, however, it is more likely that Paul wants to remind them that some Jews, whom they know or know about, have been willing to throw aside their religious entitlements for the sake of the gospel in which there is no Jew nor Greek, circumcised or uncircumcised. They also serve with him in the mission among the Gentiles.[123]

Luke's Hellenistic background had prepared him for a monumental opportunity—to write a two-part historical synopsis of Christian origins (Luke-Acts) skillfully integrating both Hellenistic[124] and Jewish components.[125] Luke was an "educated person, whose Greek was the most literary in the NT." As a Hellenistic Jew, he was also "thoroughly at home in Jewish culture and theology."[126] Luke's Hellenistic background also fits the pattern of the primary disciples of Jesus with similar backgrounds.

The Apostle Paul

Σαῦλος ("Saul") was probably named in honor of King Saul, the first monarch of Israel, since his family also descended from Benjamin, the same Jewish tribe as the king (1 Sam 9:1–2; Phil 3:5; Rom 11:1). Saul is also called Παῦλος ("Paul," Acts 13:9), a grecized version of the Roman surname

123. Garland, *Colossians and Philemon*, 278.

124. Luke has been called a "pragmatic Hellenistic historian" who incorporated elements of Hellenistic historiography in Luke-Acts (Plümacher, "Luke as Historian," 398–402). See also Gasque, "Luke," 179; Bock, *Luke*, 13; Hemer, *Book of Acts*, 312–34.

125. Despite the universal flair and the emphasis upon Gentile missions, Luke-Acts has a noticeable Jewish perspective. Joseph Tyson stated that "story after story in both the gospel and Acts tells of Jewish acceptance or rejection of the message of Jesus, the apostles, and Paul. In addition, verbal images of Jewish people, institutions, piety, and religious practices add color to the narratives. The interest in Jewish religious life is remarkable, especially in Acts, and, despite the author's sympathy with the mission to the Gentiles, there is no corresponding interest in Gentile religious life. What little there is pales into insignificance when compared with the rich detail about Jewish traditions" (*Luke-Acts*, 3); see also Strelan, *Luke the Priest*, 112; Richard, "Luke," 15–32; Garland notes that Luke also "adopts a Septuagintal style of Greek in opening chapters and makes allusions to the Scriptures without announcing that he is doing so" (*Luke*, 23–24); Gundry, *Survey*, 236; On the historicity of Acts, see Gasque, "Luke the Historian," 415–29.

126. Gasque, "Luke," 179. Gasque also notes that the epistle to the Hebrews ranks with Luke-Acts in literary quality.

Paulus.[127] Since Paul was a Roman citizen, he had three names—first name (*praenomen*), family name (*nomen gentile*), and an additional name (*cognomen*).[128] His additional name—Παῦλος—might have been chosen because of its assonance with Σαῦλος.[129] Only in the book of Acts is Paul known by the name Σαῦλος (Acts 7:58, 8:1, 3, 9:1, 8, 11, 22, 24, 11:25, 30, 12:25, etc.) and by the name of Σαούλ ("Saul"), which is a Greek transliteration of the Hebrew name שָׁאוּל ("Saul," Acts 9:4, 17, 22:7, 13, 26:14).[130] The transliterated form of Saul only appears in connection with Paul's conversion experience. On the other hand, Paul never refers to his Jewish name in any of his epistles, choosing rather to identifiy himself by his surname (e.g., Rom 1:1; 1 Cor 1:1; 2 Cor 1:1; Eph 1:1, etc.).[131] Helmut Koester makes the following observation about the custom of selecting surnames among Jews in the Diaspora:

> That Paul's name was originally "Saul" as reported in Acts 7:58; 81 and elsewhere is not improbable since diaspora Jews often chose a Greek or Roman name that sounded similar to their Hebrew name. But in his letters Paul always uses his Roman name "Paulus." If his Hebrew name was indeed Saul, the change of his name should not be connected with his call as an apostle but with the custom of Israelites in the diaspora to use a Greek or Roman name that had some similarity with their given Hebrew name.[132]

During Paul's defense before his fellow countrymen, the Jews began to call for his execution. The Roman commander ordered that Paul be scourged in order to find out the truth behind the protest against him. Luke records an interesting twist of events as the Romans prepared Paul for scourging:

> ὡς δὲ προέτειναν αὐτὸν τοῖς ἱμᾶσιν, εἶπεν πρὸς τὸν ἑστῶτα ἑκατόνταρχον ὁ Παῦλος· εἰ ἄνθρωπον Ῥωμαῖον καὶ ἀκατάκριτον ἔξεστιν ὑμῖν μαστίζειν; ἀκούσας δὲ ὁ ἑκατοντάρχης προσελθὼν τῷ χιλιάρχῳ ἀπήγγειλεν λέγων· τί μέλλεις ποιεῖν; ὁ γὰρ

---

127. Blass and Debrunner, *Greek Grammar*, 29 §53–54.

128. Bruce, *Heart Set Free*, 38.

129. Bruce, "Paul the Apostle," 709; Danker, "Σαῦλος," 917.

130. Danker, "Σαούλ," 913.

131. Betz, "Paul," 187.

132. Koester, *History and Literature*, 106. McRay postulates that "since the possibilities of Paul's family having been granted Roman citizenship probably lie in the generosity of Pompey, Julius Caesar, or Mark Antony. . . . Paul's Roman name could possibly have been Gnaeus Pompeius Paulus, Gaius Julius Paulus, or Marcus Antonius Paulus" (*Paul*, 28).

ἄνθρωπος οὗτος Ῥωμαῖός ἐστιν. προσελθὼν δὲ ὁ χιλίαρχος
εἶπεν αὐτῷ· λέγε μοι, σὺ Ῥωμαῖος εἶ; ὁ δὲ ἔφη· ναί. ἀπεκρίθη
δὲ ὁ χιλίαρχος· ἐγὼ πολλοῦ κεφαλαίου τὴν πολιτείαν ταύτην
ἐκτησάμην. ὁ δὲ Παῦλος ἔφη· ἐγὼ δὲ καὶ γεγέννημαι. εὐθέως
οὖν ἀπέστησαν ἀπ᾽ αὐτοῦ οἱ μέλλοντες αὐτὸν ἀνετάζειν, καὶ ὁ
χιλίαρχος δὲ ἐφοβήθη ἐπιγνοὺς ὅτι Ῥωμαῖός ἐστιν καὶ ὅτι αὐτὸν
ἦν δεδεκώς (Act 22:25–29).

But when they stretched him out with straps, Paul said to the
centurion standing by, "Is it permitted to whip a man who is a
Roman and uncondemned?" When the centurion heard this, he
went and reported it to the commander, saying, "What are you
about to do? For this man is a Roman." The commander came to
him and said, "Tell me, are you a Roman?" He answered, "Yes."
The commander answered, "I acquired this citizenship with a
large sum of money." And Paul answered, "But I was born a citizen." Therefore, those who were about to examine him withdrew
immediately; and the commander was afraid knowing that he
was a Roman and because he had been bound.

Paul's Roman citizenship came with certain privileges and advantages that
he invoked on several occasions.[133] Roman citizens were exempted from
degrading and inhumane forms of punishment as in the citation above.[134]
The chief magistrates in Philippi were likewise afraid when they learned
after they had beaten and imprisoned Paul and Silas that they were Roman
citizens (Acts 16:35–40). Roman citizens also had the right to appeal to
Rome (or Caesar) thereby exempting themselves from local jurisdictions
and governors.[135] Paul made such an appeal before the governor Porcius
Festus in Caesarea (Acts 25:11–12). And likely, because Paul was a Roman
citizen, he was afforded a swifter execution by beheading (cf. 2 Tim 4:6–8).
Eusebius wrote that "Paul was beheaded in Rome itself . . ." (*Hist. eccl.* 2.25.5
[Lake, LCL]).

The introduction of Paul's surname during his first missionary commission (Acts 13:9) appears to anticipate the shift in Paul's efforts from

133. Ferguson, *Backgrounds*, 63.

134. However, Roman citizens were still subject to the whims of Roman leaders
especially if one was suspected of being a spy as in the case of a certain man named
Publius Gavius who "there in the open market-place of Messana a Roman citizen,
gentlemen, was beaten with rods" and executed by order of Gaius Verres. Cicero
(106–43 BCE) bemoaned the incident and asked, "Does freedom, that precious thing,
mean nothing? Nor the proud privileges of a citizen of Rome?" (*Verr.* 5.62–63 §161–63
[Greenwood, LCL]).

135. Jones, "I Appeal to Casesar," 53–65. See also Sherwin-White, *Citizenship*,
245–50.

preaching the gospel to his countrymen to that of focusing his attention on reaching the Gentiles.[136] The pivotal event that prompted Paul's shift in direction occurred in Pisidian Antioch located in the southern province of Galatia.[137]

> παρρησιασάμενοί τε ὁ Παῦλος καὶ ὁ Βαρναβᾶς εἶπαν· ὑμῖν ἦν ἀναγκαῖον πρῶτον λαληθῆναι τὸν λόγον τοῦ θεοῦ· ἐπειδὴ ἀπωθεῖσθε αὐτὸν καὶ οὐκ ἀξίους κρίνετε ἑαυτοὺς τῆς αἰωνίου ζωῆς, ἰδοὺ στρεφόμεθα εἰς τὰ ἔθνη. οὕτως γὰρ ἐντέταλται ἡμῖν ὁ κύριος· τέθεικά σε εἰς φῶς ἐθνῶν τοῦ εἶναί σε εἰς σωτηρίαν ἕως ἐσχάτου τῆς γῆς. Ἀκούοντα δὲ τὰ ἔθνη ἔχαιρον καὶ ἐδόξαζον τὸν λόγον τοῦ κυρίου καὶ ἐπίστευσαν ὅσοι ἦσαν τεταγμένοι εἰς ζωὴν αἰώνιον·διεφέρετο δὲ ὁ λόγος τοῦ κυρίου δι᾽ ὅλης τῆς χώρας (Acts 13:46–49).

> Paul and Barnabas spoke boldly and said, "It was necessary that the word of God be spoken first to you; since you reject it and judge yourselves unworthy of eternal life; behold, we now turn to the Gentiles. For this reason the Lord has commanded us, 'I have placed you as a light among the Gentiles to bring salvation to the end of the earth.'" Hearing this, the Gentiles rejoiced and praised the word of the Lord and many who had been appointed unto eternal life believed. And the word of the Lord was spreading throughout the whole region.

The emphatic placement of ὑμῖν along with the words ἀναγκαῖον and πρῶτον in verse 46 underscore that Paul felt obligated to reach his countrymen. However, it was painfully clear that they were not receptive. The term ἀπωθεῖσθε ("you reject") signifies pushing something away forcefully.[138] Consequently, reaching the Jews would cease to be his main objective.

The primary biographical information about Paul's background is found in the book of Acts and in a few of his epistles (Acts 22:3–5, 23:6, 26:4–5, Phil 3:4–6, 2 Cor 11:22).[139] This information provides insight

---

136. Luke clearly presupposes that Saul had already had the surname "Paul" before its introduction and therefore "may well have used his Roman name when dealing with the Gentile world" (Riesner, *Paul's Early Period*, 144).

137. Pisidian Antioch was located in Galatia until the provincial lines were redrawn by the Romans in 74 CE and the city was under the provincial jurisdiction of Pamphylia. See Frend, "Pisidia," 874.

138. Danker, "ἀπωθέω," 126. See also Bock, *Acts*, 463.

139. For an evaluation of the historical reliability of the book of Acts see Hemer, *Acts*.

concerning Paul's place of birth, his education, his religious associations, and his work as a Christian apostle and missionary.

Paul was from Tarsus, a city in the region of Cilicia (Acts 9:11, 21:39, 22:3). Tarsus was located on an important route between Rome and Syria. The city was a significant one during Paul's time (Acts 21:39). According to Jerome, Paul's family moved to a village in Galilee near Hazor called Gischala (Γισχάλων) but returned to Tarsus when the Romans took it over (*Vir. ill.* 5).[140] Tarsus was also a thriving Hellenistic city.[141] Alexandria, Athens, and Tarsus were the three most important educational centers of the Mediterranean world in the first century CE.[142] Strabo (64 BCE–21 CE)[143] praised the people of Tarsus for their interest in education and philosophy.

> The people of Tarsus have devoted themselves so eagerly, not only to philosophy, but also to the whole round of education in general, that they have surpassed Athens, Alexandria, or any other place that can be named where there have been schools and lectures of philosophers. . . . Further, the city of Tarsus has all kinds of schools of rhetoric; and in general it not only has a flourishing population but also is most powerful, thus keeping up the reputation of the mother-city (*Geogr.*14.5.13 [Jones, LCL]).

While growing up in this environment, Paul certainly "imbibed many of the Hellenistic elements in the cultural atmosphere of his day"[144] to such an extent that he was able not only to write in Greek but also to think in Greek.[145]

Paul had the benefit of bridging two worlds—the world of the Hellenist and the world of the Jew. He was born in the Hellenistic city of Tarsus but appears to have received his formal training as a pupil in Jerusalem from Rabbi Gamaliel. Paul emphatically declared before the Jewish council ἐγὼ Φαρισαῖός εἰμι, υἱὸς Φαρισαίων ("I am a Pharisee, a son of a Pharisee," Acts 23:6). In his letter to the Philippians, he described himself as a genuine Ἑβραῖος ἐξ Ἑβραίων ("Hebrew of Hebrews," Phil 3:5). Bruce notes that "Paul might be called a Hellenist in that Greek was manifestly no foreign

---

140. See http://khazarzar.skeptik.net/books/hieronym/viris_g.htm and http://www.newadvent.org/fathers/2708.htm.

141. McRay, *Archaeology*, 234.

142. Hoerth and McRay, *Bible Archaeology*, 236. See also McRay, *Archaeology*, 234. Located at the entrance of the city of Tarsus is the Cleopatra Gate where Mark Antony and Cleopatra met in 51 CE.

143. Ferguson, *Backgrounds*, 118.

144. Bruce, "Paul the Apostle," 710. Murray referred to him as "one of the great figures in Greek literature." See Murray, *Greek Religion*, 199.

145. Bruce, *Heart Set Free*, 15.

language to him, but the designation on which he insists is not Hellenist but Hebrew."[146] Paul indicated in his letter to the Galatians that he had excelled in his Jewish education and orthodox commitments:

καὶ προέκοπτον ἐν τῷ Ἰουδαϊσμῷ ὑπὲρ πολλοὺς συνηλικιώτας ἐν τῷ γένει μου, περισσοτέρως ζηλωτὴς ὑπάρχων τῶν πατρικῶν μου παραδόσεων (Gal 1:14).

For I was advancing in Judaism beyond many of my contemporaries among my countrymen, being more zealous for my ancestral traditions.

Jerome H. Neyrey argues that Paul's strict Pharisaic Jewish conditioning was never lost in his conversion to Christianity. In fact, Paul's concerns for order, hierarchy, and boundaries in matters pertaining to purity show that his Jewish education continued to influence his theology and world view. "As a reformer [Paul] sees new and different patterns," writes Jerome Neyrey, "and so he sets out to rearrange maps, not to discard them entirely."[147]

Efforts were made by rabbis during the Hellenistic period to instruct in the law the Jewish population of the Diaspora and Palestine in order to preserve Judaism from its total assimilation into Greek culture and language. During the first century CE, a network of Jewish elementary schools taught the Hebrew Bible to boys who began school around age six or seven.[148] Advanced studies in hermeneutical and exegetical methods were drawn up by Rabbi Hillel and taught to older students. Rabbi Gamaliel under whom Paul studied was the son or grandson of Hillel.[149] He was considered to be more rigid and conservative than Rabbi Hillel.[150] A passage in the Mishnah lists many significant rabbis who had died and attributes to each a special epitaph. The entry about Gamaliel's death contains the following tribute: "When Rabban Gamaliel the elder died, the glory of the Torah came to an end, and cleanness and separateness perished" (m. Sot. 9.15).[151] Interestingly, the word "separateness" translates the Hebrew term פרש, which contains the idea of separating oneself.[152] Paul described himself and Gamaliel as a

146. Ibid., 42–43.

147. Neyrey, Cultural Readings, 71.

148. Stegner, "Paul," 505. See b. B. Bat. 21a (Neusner, Talmud, 82–84).

149. Youngblood, "Gamaliel," 393–94. Chilton questions the historical accuracy of Paul's contact with Gamaliel and Pharisaism, suggesting that Paul was "rather a provincial hanger-on of the movement, who turned a zeal for the Temple and purity into a zeal for the oral law" ("Gamaliel," 906).

150. Bruce, Heart Set Free, 51.

151. Neusner, Mishnah, 465.

152. See "פרש" in Brown, Hebrew and Englsih Lexicon, 831. See also Wyatt,

Φαρισαῖος ("Pharisee"), a term derived from the same Hebrew word that refers to one who has separated himself for religious purposes.[153]

Paul's letters reveal many *midrashic* techniques that he would have learned under Gamaliel's tutelage: the use of parallel secondary texts, key terms, citation formulas, and typology, to name a few.[154] Yet his Jewish training did not preclude a good Hellenistic education. In fact, Paul likely received formal instruction in Greek culture and language from Gamaliel "who probably gave his disciples prophylactic courses in this subject."[155] Paul's writings often mimic Greek rhetoric and style. His letters have become literary masterpieces.[156] Hans Dieter Betz remarks that Paul's letters reveal highly developed literary skills.

> These letters—with their skillful rhetoric, careful composition, and elaborate theological argumentation—reflect an author who was in every way uniquely equipped to become the "apostle of the gentiles" (Rom 11:13; cf. Gal 2:8, 9; Rom 1:5).[157]

Such a merger between Hellenism and Judaism was not unusual. In Jerusalem, the governing council of Jews had already embraced the Greek designation of συνέδριον ("Sanhedrin") since the days of Hyrcanus II (*Ant.* 14.9.3–5 §165–179).[158]

Paul's linguistic skills are apparent in two instances in the book of Acts. First, after Paul had given a report about his work among the Gentiles to James and the elders of the church in Jerusalem, some men from Asia saw him in the temple and began to stir up trouble accusing him of allowing Greeks to defile the temple by entering into it. Paul was seized and put in barracks because of the violence unleashed against him (Acts 21:15–36). Luke records the following conversation that took place between Paul and the Roman commander:

"Pharisees," 822–29.

153. Danker, "Φαρισαῖος," 1049.

154. Ellis, *Old Testament*, 79–101.

155. Bruce, "Paul the Apostle," 710. See also Knox, *Hellenistic Elements*, 33. Conzelmann states that "Paul's exegetical method utilized elements of the school of Hillel, which had appropriated the principles of Hellenistic hermeneutics" (*Acts*, 186).

156. Yamauchi ("Hellenism," 386) asserts that though Paul received at best a secondary Hellenistic education, his Hellenistic rhetorical and literary abilities are evident in his use of chiasmus (1 Cor 3:17), litotes (Rom 1:28), alliteration (2 Cor 6:3), climax (Rom 8:29–30), oxymorons (2 Cor 6:9), paronomasia (2 Cor 3:2), and sophistic replies to opponents (2 Cor 10–13).

157. "Paul," 187.

158. Danker, "συνέδριον," 967.

Μέλλων τε εἰσάγεσθαι εἰς τὴν παρεμβολὴν ὁ Παῦλος λέγει τῷ χιλιάρχῳ· εἰ ἔξεστίν μοι εἰπεῖν τι πρὸς σέ; ὁ δὲ ἔφη· Ἑλληνιστὶ γινώσκεις; οὐκ ἄρα σὺ εἶ ὁ Αἰγύπτιος ὁ πρὸ τούτων τῶν ἡμερῶν ἀναστατώσας καὶ ἐξαγαγὼν εἰς τὴν ἔρημον τοὺς τετρακισχιλίους ἄνδρας τῶν σικαρίων; εἶπεν δὲ ὁ Παῦλος· ἐγὼ ἄνθρωπος μέν εἰμι Ἰουδαῖος, Ταρσεὺς τῆς Κιλικίας, οὐκ ἀσήμου πόλεως πολίτης· δέομαι δέ σου, ἐπίτρεψόν μοι λαλῆσαι πρὸς τὸν λαόν (Acts 21:37–39).

As he was about to be brought into the barracks, Paul said to the commander, "May I say something to you?" And he said, "Do you know Greek? Then you are not the Egyptian who some time ago stirred up trouble and led 4,000 men from among the assassins into the desert, are you?" But Paul said, "I am a Jewish man of Tarsus in Cilicia, a citizen of no insignificant city. I beseech you; allow me to speak to the people."

Paul's ability to speak Greek takes the commander by surprise. The text indicates that the commander had assumed that Paul was associated with a Jewish revolt that occurred a few years earlier when Marcus Antonius Felix was the procurator of Judea.[159] However, because of his knowledge of Greek, it was evident to the commander that Paul was not ὁ Αἰγύπτιος ("the Egyptian"). After the commander granted him permission, Paul spoke to his countrymen:

ἐπιτρέψαντος δὲ αὐτοῦ ὁ Παῦλος ἑστὼς ἐπὶ τῶν ἀναβαθμῶν κατέσεισεν τῇ χειρὶ τῷ λαῷ. πολλῆς δὲ σιγῆς γενομένης προσεφώνησεν τῇ Ἑβραΐδι διαλέκτῳ λέγων· Ἄνδρες ἀδελφοὶ καὶ πατέρες, ἀκούσατέ μου τῆς πρὸς ὑμᾶς νυνὶ ἀπολογίας (Acts 21:40—22:1).

When he had given him permission, Paul, standing on the stairs, motioned to the people with his hand. And when it became quiet, he addressed *them* in the Hebrew language saying, "Brethren and fathers listen to my defense which I now *offer* to you."

After conversing with the Roman commander in Greek, Paul shifts easily into the Hebrew (Aramaic) language in order to arrest the attention of his countrymen.[160] The situation is calm for a moment until Paul refers to his

159. Bruce, *Acts*, 412.

160. McRay observes that "[Paul] told the crowd publicly in Aramaic that he was a zealous Jew, but only in Greek did he privately inform the tribune that he was a citizen of Tarsus, and only in the exclusively Roman context of the Antonia Fortress did Paul mention his Roman citizenship" (*Paul*, 220).

apostolic mission to the ἔθνη ("Gentiles," Acts 22:21) after which the mob erupts again.

Paul's educational background was not typical but extraordinary. Albrecht Oepke states the matter concisely: "Ein Diasporajude, der zwar durchweg LXX zitiert, aber den Urtext zweifellow auch kennt, ist keine allagliche Erscheinung."[161] Paul was able to transverse the diversity of cultures of his day. His background, training, and commitment were perfectly suited for the task that lay ahead of him.

Paul's conversion from Judaism to Christianity occurred on the road to Damascus as he sought to arrest Christians. His miraculous encounter with Jesus transformed him from a persecutor of Christians to a proclaimer of the gospel of Christ. The Lord sent a disciple named Ananias to Damascus to find Paul and deliver to him a special message. When Ananias showed signs of reservation, the Lord reassured him about Paul with the following words:

> εἶπεν δὲ πρὸς αὐτὸν ὁ κύριος· πορεύου, ὅτι σκεῦος ἐκλογῆς ἐστίν μοι οὗτος τοῦ βαστάσαι τὸ ὄνομά μου ἐνώπιον ἐθνῶν τε καὶ βασιλέων υἱῶν τε Ἰσραήλ . . . (Acts 9:15).

> But the Lord said to him, "Go, for he is a chosen instrument of mine to bear my name before the Gentiles and kings and the sons of Israel . . .

Despite Paul's record as a persecutor, he was chosen by the Lord's hand to preach the good news of Jesus to Gentiles, to those in positions of authority, and to his own countrymen. And that he did more extensively than anyone else.[162]

SUMMARY

Jesus formed a small band of twelve intimate disciples from a larger following to be his apostles. The question was raised as to why these particular individuals were selected. My analysis has revealed that the apostles had national, regional, and familial connections to Jesus. Judas Iscariot, a Judean, may have been the only exception. Since the apostles were from Galilee, the Hellenistic culture in which they lived prepared them socially to be messengers to both Gentiles and Jews. The apostles were bilingual. The ability to speak Greek was not just a necessity but a natural form of communication.

161. Oepke, "Paulus," 443.
162. Bruce, *Acts*, 187.

They appear to have been comfortable in both Hellenistic and Jewish settings as they ministered throughout Palestine, the Decapolis, and Syria.

Although they were not apostles, James and Jude played a significant role in the early church. As his brothers, they too were closely associated with Jesus. They became more involved in Christian ministry after Jesus' death. Despite scholarly division over the authenticity of the books attributed to them, James and Jude were indisputably capable of composing letters in Greek. The similarity of background links them tightly to the apostles.

John Mark was not a Galilean, but he had significant connections to the apostles Peter and Paul. He may also have been an eyewitness of Jesus' betrayal in the garden. Mark's background and experience certainly equipped him for Christian ministry. Luke, the beloved physican, was another companion of Paul. He was capable of composing the two-volume history of the early church. My assertion is that Luke was a Hellenistic Jew. His Jewish heritage is consistent with the schema employed by Jesus to select *Jewish* emissaries. His Hellenistic background associates him closely with the apostles—a more reasonable explanation than supposing that Luke was a Gentile or perhaps even a Semitic Gentile.

The most renowned disciple of Jesus was, of course, the Apostle Paul. He was for all practical purposes an orthodox Jew, having received his formal education from Gamaliel. Paul also had connections to the Hellenistic city of Tarsus. His education and experience were broad enough for him to engage the intellectual world as well as to minister to the less fortunate of society. Additionally, unlike most Jews of his day, Paul was a citizen of Rome and therefore had special privileges, access, and opportunities not afforded to others. Consequently, Paul was able to weave effortlessly through Roman, Greek, and Jewish cultures and to compose letters in Greek that addressed a wide range of issues confronting Christians in the first century CE.

Paul's appointment as an apostle was not unique, however, in respect to the general pattern of characteristics of their backgrounds that all the apostles and writers of the NT shared: (1) they were all Jews; (2) they were all connected in some way to the ministry of Jesus; (3) they were all members of a tight circle of early Christian emissaries; and (4) they were all at the very least bilingual and able communicators in both oral and written form.

In the final analysis, the backgrounds of the apostles, the brothers, and the primary disciples of Jesus reveal a particular intentionality of Jesus to select individuals who were not only Jewish but also fluent in Greek and who had connections with Hellenism in order to fulfill the divine mandate best explained by the apostle Paul:

Οὐ γὰρ ἐπαισχύνομαι τὸ εὐαγγέλιον, δύναμις γὰρ θεοῦ ἐστιν εἰς σωτηρίαν παντὶ τῷ πιστεύοντι, Ἰουδαίῳ τε πρῶτον καὶ Ἕλληνι (Rom 1:16).

For I am not ashamed of the gospel; for it is the power of God unto salvation to everyone who believes, to the Jew first and also to the Greek.

CHAPTER 4

Aramaic and Portions of
the Greek New Testament

THE QUESTION CONCERNING THE language that Jesus and his disciples spoke
is important because it relates to the historical authenticity of the NT and its
relevance to modern society. G. R. Selby states the matter plainly:

> It does not require . . . a great deal of reflection to realize how
> important the material found within the Gospels has been for
> the past. Of course, our present society is built upon the past,
> and so these documents have a contemporary importance for
> the part they have played in the historical development of all
> that might be described as Western culture. In addition, though,
> and equally important, is the major function the New Testament,
> and especially the Gospels, have in the lives of millions of people
> throughout the world who still call themselves Christians.[1]

The predominant assumption among scholars has been to connect authenticity to the Aramaic language since it was likely the native tongue of Jesus
and the early disciples.[2] However, evidence shows that Jesus and his disciples were capable of conversing and writing in Greek. Further still, Greek
rapidly became the medium of communication throughout the Roman Empire. Cicero (106–43 BCE) once wrote, "For if anyone thinks that the glory
won by the writing of Greek verse is naturally less than that accorded to the
poet who writes in Latin, he is entirely in the wrong. Greek literature is read

1. Selby, *Jesus,* 2.

2. For an overview of the historical development of debate over the quest for the
historical authenticity of Jesus' teachings, see Porter, *Criteria for Authenticity,* 17–125.

in nearly every nation under heaven, while the vogue of Latin is confined to its own boundaries, and they are, we must grant, narrow" (*Arch.* 10.23 [Watts, LCL]).[3]

Interestingly, every book of the NT was originally written in Greek. Despite the obvious Semitic influences upon the Greek documents, Helmut Koester asserts that "not a single early Christian Greek writing can be shown to have been translated from Hebrew or Aramaic."[4] Though Matthew Black insists that Jesus' teaching was in Aramaic, he does acknowledge the multilingual setting of first-century Palestine:

> Greek was the speech of the educated "Hellenized" classes and the medium of cultural and commercial intercourse between Jew and foreigner; Latin was the language of the army of occupation and, to judge from Latin borrowings in Aramaic, appears also to some extent to have served the purposes of commerce; Hebrew, the sacred tongue of the Jewish Scriptures, continued to provide the lettered Jew with an important means of literary expression and was cultivated as a spoken tongue in the learned coteries of the Rabbis; Aramaic was the language of the people of the land and, together with Hebrew, provided the chief literary medium of the Palestinian Jew of the first century; Josephus wrote his *Jewish War* in Aramaic and later translated it into Greek.[5]

Black admits that his position must expand to include the possibility that Jesus also communicated in Hebrew:

> We must nevertheless allow possibly more than has been done before for the use of Hebrew in addition to (or instead of) Aramaic by Jesus Himself, especially on solemn festive occasions; there is a high degree of probability that Jesus began his career as a Galilean rabbi who would be well versed in the Scriptures, and able to compose (or converse) as freely in Hebrew as in Aramaic.[6]

Since Jesus was able to compose and converse freely in Hebrew and in Aramaic, why would he not have been able to do the same in Greek? Perhaps Black's premise should expand even more in order to allow that possibility as well.

3. Although Cicero's comment does not relate directly to the *koinē* Greek of first-century CE Palestine, it does, however, indicate the overall elevated popularity of the Greek language.

4. Koester, *History, Culture, and Religion,* 111–12.

5. Black, *Aramaic Approach,* 15.

6. Ibid., 49.

My purpose has been to demonstrate that Jesus and his primary disciples did in fact converse in Greek. First, I surveyed the linguistic landscape of Palestine during the first century CE in order to demonstrate that the most common way to communicate was through the medium of the Greek language. Second, I explored the archaeological evidence and showed how it revealed the Hellenistic character of Galilee, the Decapolis, and Judea. Third, I investigated the backgrounds of the primary disciples of Jesus in order to stress that Jesus' selection was in fact intentional, for they shared a similar cultural background. Finally, in this chapter, I will analyze the premise behind the Aramaic Hypothesis by evaluating the linguistic character of the NT documents, the peculiarities of the Greek language, and the elusive Aramaic Gospel of Matthew. I will also address the various proposals concerning the presence of Aramaic words and expressions in the GNT before I offer my solution. The observation of Thomas K. Abbott serves as a fitting reminder as this study moves forward:

> The positive evidence of facts seems to be entirely in favour of the view that Greek was very generally spoken. The apostles were as to education average specimens of the Galileans who formed our Lord's audiences. It is certain that they were able to speak Greek fluently, and some of them at least were able to write Greek. *This is more than we can affirm of their knowledge of any other tongue.* . . .[7]

THE LINGUISTIC CHARACTER OF THE GREEK NEW TESTAMENT DOCUMENTS

Aramaic, Hebrew, Latin, and Greek were important languages in the first century CE and directly impacted the people living in Palestine. However, the evidence has revealed that during the ministry of Jesus and his disciples, Greek had emerged as the dominant language in Palestine and both Jews and Gentiles used it widely. The results that derived from the conquests of Alexander the Great and the sweeping impact of Hellenistic influence

---

7. Emphasis mine. Abbott, *Original Texts*, 181. Although this statement by Abbott was made prior to the discovery of the Aramaic Targums among the DSS and other Aramaic documents in Palestine, it remains true in the context in which he said it. No current discovery has enlightened scholars about the apostles' knowledge of any other language. For a full catalogue of Aramaic texts, see Fitzmyer and Harrington, *Palestinian Aramaic*.

produced the perfect linguistic environment that enabled Christianity to flourish.[8]

The Greek New Testament Manuscripts

The GNT is the best-attested set of ancient documents known today. Despite the fact that the original compositions of the NT are not extant, there are, however, approximately fifty-five hundred Greek manuscripts of the NT.[9] Some of these ancient manuscripts are dated fewer than a hundred years from the original date of composition. For instance, the Chester Beatty collection contains portions of Rom 15:29–16:3 (P[46]) and dates to about 200 CE.[10] Additionally, the John Rylands Library in Manchester, England, holds one of the earliest fragments of the Gospel of John, which dates near the beginning of the second century CE.[11] After comparing the manuscript witness of the NT to that of the classics, Koester makes the following observation:

> [T]he problems of New Testament textual criticism differ from those of its classical sister discipline. Classical authors are usually preserved in only a few manuscripts, and often in just one, but there are thousands of manuscripts of the New Testament in Greek, numerous translations that derive from an early stage of the textual development, a large number of lectionaries, and finally, beginning in the 2d century CE, an uncounted number of quotations in the writings of the church fathers. Moreover, while the only surviving manuscripts of classical authors often come from the Middle Ages, the manuscript tradition of the New Testament begins as early as the end of the 2d century CE; it is therefore divided only by as much as a century from the time at which the autographs were written. Thus it would seem that New Testament textual criticism possesses a base that is far more advantageous than that for the textual tradition of classical authors.[12]

The most interesting observation about the abundance of ancient manuscripts is that *none* are written in Aramaic. The absence of any Aramaic manuscripts is significant for two reasons. First, this absence of manuscript

8. Ferguson, *Backgrounds*, 13–15.

9. Porter, "Manuscripts," 670.

10. Portions of P[46] are held by the Chester Beatty Museum in Dublin, Ireland, and by the library of the University of Michigan. See Wegner, *Journey*, 236–37.

11. Ibid., 237; see also Guthrie, *Introduction*, 297.

12. Koester, *History and Literature*, 18.

evidence makes suspect the assumption that the NT, especially the Gospels, is a translation from Aramaic originals. Second, the premise that only that which can be traced back to Aramaic is historically reliable is questionable.[13] Nigel Turner states the matter succinctly:

> If Jesus spoke Aramaic, rather than the Greek of the New Testament writings, then the earliest records of his teaching and his apostles' teaching were transmitted in Aramaic, and the realization of this must influence our interpretation of them in their Greek dress. The presumption is that when these very early records were put into Greek, mistakes would be made, and at the very least there is the possibility that misunderstandings crept in because reverence would demand that his own language be translated as literally as possible.[14]

The opposite, however, may be closer to the truth. Jesus and his disciples were more likely to have spoken and written in a dialect of Greek that contained a high degree of Semitic characteristics. This Semitic influence upon the NT is precisely the reason that some scholars presume that there must have been Aramaic sources behind the GNT. For example, Black asserts that since Jesus was a Galilean Rabbi, he would have conversed and taught in Hebrew and Aramaic:

> The gospels were written in a predominantly Hellenistic environment, and they were written in Greek. But Greek was not the native language of their central Figure, nor of the earliest apostles, if it was not unfamiliar to them. Jesus must have conversed in the Galilean dialect of Aramaic, and His teaching was probably almost entirely in Aramaic. At the basis of the Greek Gospels, therefore, there must lie a Palestinian Aramaic tradition, at any rate of the sayings and teaching of Jesus, and this tradition must at one time have been translated from Aramaic into Greek.[15]

---

13. Turner notes that the issue of historicity centers upon the role of the historian in relation to the writers of the NT: "Did the Evangelists set out consciously to write history or something else which can be regarded as the raw material of history but not as prefabricated history in its own right. . . . The alternative is to regard the Gospels not as biographies of Jesus, but as something else, such as propaganda tracts of a particular kind, or as Gospel proclamations with supporting material given as a prelude to a more detailed preaching of the Cross" (*Historicity and the Gospels*, 50–51).

14. Turner, *Style*, 174.

15. Black, *Aramaic Approach*, 16.

Additionally, late in the nineteenth century, Emil Schürer argued that the presence of Aramaic words and expressions in the NT indicated the popularity of Aramaic within Palestine:

> That Aramaic was in the time of Christ the sole popular language of Palestine, is evident from the words mentioned in the New Testament: ἀββᾶ (Mark xiv. 36), ἀκελδαμάχ (Acts i.19), γαββαθᾶ (John xix. 13), γολγοθᾶ (Matt. xxvii. 33), ἐφφαθά (Mark vii. 34), κορβανᾶς (Matt. xvii. 6), μαμωνᾶς (Matt. Vi. 24), μαρὰν ἀθά (1 Cor. xvi. 22), Μεσσίας = שׁיחא (John i. 41), πάσχα (Matt. xxvi. 17), ῥακά (Matt. v. 22), σατανᾶς (Matt. xvi. 23), ταλιθὰ κούμι (Mark v. 41); to which may be added names of persons, such as Κηφᾶς, Μάρθα, Ταβιθά, and the numerous names compounded with bar (Barabbas, Bartholomew, Barjesus, Barjonas, Barnabas, Barsabas, Bartimæus). The words, too, of Christ upon the cross: Ἐλωῒ ἐλωῒ λαμὰ σαβαχθανεί (Mark xv. 34), are Aramaic.[16]

The problem with this line of reasoning is that it overlooks the one obvious fact: All the ancient documents of the NT are in Greek.[17] Occasional Aramaic words or expressions and Semitic influence upon the GNT do not warrant a conclusion that the sole popular language of Palestine was Aramaic. Stanley Porter offers the following corrective to an extreme bias in linguistic studies:

> The linguistic picture of the early Church ... is certainly far more complex than has often been appreciated ... In Roman Palestine of the first century CE, Jesus, as well as many of his closest followers, who also came from Galilee, was probably multilingual. He spoke Aramaic to be sure, and Greek to be almost as sure, and possibly even Hebrew.[18]

A greater case can be made that Greek was the most popular language of Palestine for it was the *lingua franca* of the Roman Empire during the first century CE.[19] However, Maurice Casey argues that among the Jews, Aramaic was the *lingua franca* in Palestine. He bases his argument upon the following evidence: (1) Aramaic was the *lingua franca* of the Jews from

16. Schürer, *History of Jewish People*, 8–10.

17. Dalman recognizes the problem and states that "the difficulty is increased by the fact that we do not possess any Jewish-Aramaic literary documents going back to the time of Christ, from which we would have been able to conclude with the highest degree of certainty what the language of Jesus was" (*Jesus—Jeshua*, 23).

18. Porter, *Criteria for Authenticity*, 131.

19. Ibid., 136–37; see also Hughes, "Languages Spoken by Jesus," 127–43.

the fifth century BCE onward and thus continued to be their vernacular in the first century CE; (2) there are numerous Aramaic documents extant from Israel from the third century BCE until the time of Jesus; (3) the Targums from the Dead Sea indicate that complete translations of the Hebrew Scriptures were made and were available during the first century BCE; (4) temple inscriptions, inscriptions on the shekel trumpets, letters dictated by Gamaliel, and some inscriptions found in the tomb of Caiaphas indicate the everyday use of Aramaic; and (5) Josephus originally wrote the first draft of his *Jewish Wars* in Aramaic.[20]

However, the evidence that Casey presents is selective and misleading for several reasons. First, although the Temple inscriptions that were written in Greek were written primarily to keep Gentiles out, the "Romans regularly had edicts and similar pronouncements written in Greek for the indigenous population."[21] The fact that some inscriptions have survived in Aramaic does not argue for an expansive use of Aramaic among the general population, for many more inscriptions have survived in Greek. In fact, evidence from among the funerary inscriptions found in Palestine indicates that a majority of Jewish communities in the region of Galilee and in Jerusalem probably spoke Greek and testifies to the "continuous use of Greek in the centre of the Jewish land" during the first two centuries CE.[22] Pieter van der Horst summarizes the significance of funerary inscriptions to linguistic studies in the first century CE:

> [F]or a great part of the Jewish population the daily language was Greek, even in Palestine. This is impressive testimony to the impact of Hellenistic culture on Jews in their mother country, to say nothing of the Diaspora. . . . In Jerusalem itself about 40 percent of the Jewish inscriptions from the first–century period (before 70 C.E.) are in Greek. We may assume that most Jewish Jerusalemites who saw the inscription *in situ* were able to read them. In a first–century C.E. tomb near Jericho, a Jewish family nicknamed the Goliaths (because of their extraordinary stature) inscribed more than half their epitaphs in Greek . . . this is not to say that Hebrew and Aramaic ever died out completely as languages for the Jews. . . . But in the first five centuries of the Common Era, exactly the period when rabbinic literature was being written in Hebrew and Aramaic, a majority of the Jews in Palestine and the western Diaspora spoke Greek. That is

20. Casey, *Aramaic Sources*, 76–78.

21. Porter, *Criteria for Authenticity*, 168.

22. Sevenster, *Do You Know Greek?*, 138–43, and Gundry, "Language Milieu," 405–6.

probably one reason why there is so little evidence of influence of the Mishnah outside rabbinic circles.[23]

Second, the more compelling observation in regard to Josephus is not that he wrote his original draft of the *Jewish Wars* in Aramaic but that he wrote the final composition in Greek. His acquisition of the Greek language is a testament to how important it was as a venue of communication in a multilingual society.[24]

The GNT is a microcosm of the linguistic world of the first century CE. Galilean Jews were more hellenized than their Judean counterparts since they lived closer to Gentile cities and regions. However, the evidence reveals that Greek was also prevalent in southern Palestine. In view of these facts, Gundry provides a compelling statement: "How much more likely it is, then, that Jesus the Galilean and the apostles, who were predominantly if not exclusively Galilean, commonly used Greek in addition to the Semitic tongues."[25]

Semitic Influences in the Greek New Testament

One of the major areas of difficulty relating to the languages Jesus and his disciples spoke is the observation that the GNT reveals a high degree of Semitic influence. Gustav Dalman sees such influence as conclusive evidence that Aramaic was *the* language of the Jews, especially since certain Aramaic words found in the GNT (Βηθζαθά, Γαββαθα, Γολγοθα, and Ῥαββουνί) were designated as Hebrew (or Aramaic).[26] The Semitic impact upon the GNT can be classified under two broad headings—Hebraisms and Aramaisms.[27]

In the first category, Hebraisms refer to the language, form, and content that are reflected in the Hebrew Bible and the LXX that may be found in the Greek of the NT.[28] Often, a Semitic style reveals itself in the manner in which the writers of the NT translated OT passages. Such translations might be a literal representation, a paraphrase, or even an allusion. The translations need not be lengthy. Some of these translations may be only small phrases or just a few words. The Gospel of Matthew contains a number of

---

23. Horst, "Jewish Funerary Inscriptions," 48. Horst's article contains a review of most of the important discoveries.

24. Sevenster, *Do You Know Greek?*, 61–76.

25. Gundry, "Language Milieu," 407.

26. Dalman, *Jesus—Jeshua*, 14–15.

27. Koester, *History and Literature*, 112–14.

28. Wilcox, "Semitic Influence," 1093–98.

quotations from the Hebrew Bible. One of the lengthier quotations of the OT is found in Matt 13:14–15 (Isa 6:9–10; cf. Mark 4:12; Acts 28:26–27; Luke 8:10; John 12:40):[29]

> καὶ ἀναπληροῦται αὐτοῖς ἡ προφητεία Ἡσαΐου ἡ λέγουσα· ἀκοῇ ἀκούσετε καὶ οὐ μὴ συνῆτε, καὶ βλέποντες βλέψετε καὶ οὐ μὴ ἴδητε. ἐπαχύνθη γὰρ ἡ καρδία τοῦ λαοῦ τούτου, καὶ τοῖς ὠσὶν βαρέως ἤκουσαν καὶ τοὺς ὀφθαλμοὺς αὐτῶν ἐκάμμυσαν, μήποτε ἴδωσιν τοῖς ὀφθαλμοῖς καὶ τοῖς ὠσὶν ἀκούσωσιν καὶ τῇ καρδίᾳ συνῶσιν καὶ ἐπιστρέψωσιν καὶ ἰάσομαι αὐτούς.

> And in them the prophecy of Isaiah is being fulfilled, which says: "Hearing, you will hear but not comprehend and seeing, you will see and not perceive. For the heart of this people has become dull, and with their ears they hardly hear and they have closed their eyes, lest they should see with their eyes and hear with their ears and understand with their hearts and repent and I should heal them."

Since the writers of the NT were Jews, quotations from and allusions to the Hebrew Bible and the LXX are not surprising and appear naturally.

An area of particular interest is the GNT's use of the LXX. The very existence of the LXX indicates that at least the Jews in Alexandria, Egypt, needed their sacred writings translated into Greek because Greek had become their first language. Additionally, the presence of the LXX translation in the GNT shows that such immersion in the Greek vernacular had continued and expanded to Palestine.[30] Edward W. Grinfield argued in the nineteenth century CE that the authenticity of the NT was related to the authenticity of the LXX since the former contained a goodly amount of the latter. He was so moved by his analysis that he was compelled to write an apology for the inspiration of the LXX:

> I gradually ascertained, that, almost every quotation in the New Testament, was either literally, or substantially, taken from the LXX. That it was perpetually present to the minds of the Evangelists and Apostles, nay, that, where I had least expected to find it, the Apocalypse, even there, it constituted the entire staple of thought and expression.

---

29. All quotations from the LXX are from *Septuaginta*. For an evaluation of the similarities/differences in the quotation relating to the MT, the LXX, and the GNT see Archer and Chirichigno, *Old Testament Quotations*, 93–94.

30. Silva, "Bilingualism," 220.

The inevitable inference I could not avoid it,—that the authenticity of the New Testament is bound up with the authenticity of this Greek version of the Old—that it stands pledged, not only for its general truth and historic authenticity, but, for its Scriptural and canonical authority.[31]

Grinfield's recognition of the pervasiveness of the LXX in the NT is well documented.

The importance of the LXX can be demonstrated in reference to Jesus' public ministry. The Gospel of Luke records an important event in the life of Jesus that served as his official commencement of public ministry. After the testing in the wilderness, Jesus returned to Galilee and began to teach in the synagogues of the region to the delight of those who heard him (Luke 4:14–15). However, in his hometown of Nazareth, Jesus met a less than cordial crowd when he attended the synagogue. Jesus stood up and read from the book of Isaiah (Luke 4:16–17). Afterwards, he closed the book, handed it back to the attendant, sat down, and declared to all who were present that the prophecy had been fulfilled in their hearing (Luke 4:20–21). The passage in Isaiah from which Jesus read parallels closely two Isaianic passages in the LXX.

Luke 4:18–19[32]

πνεῦμα κυρίου ἐπ᾽ ἐμὲ οὗ εἵνεκεν ἔχρισέν με εὐαγγελίσασθαι πτωχοῖς, ἀπέσταλκέν με, κηρύξαι αἰχμαλώτοις ἄφεσιν καὶ τυφλοῖς ἀνάβλεψιν, [ἀποστεῖλαι τεθραυσμένους ἐν ἀφέσει,] κηρύξαι ἐνιαυτὸν κυρίου δεκτόν.

The Spirit of the Lord is upon me because he has anointed me to preach the gospel to the poor. He has sent me to proclaim release to the captives and sight to the blind, [to set free those who are oppressed], *and to proclaim the favorable year of the Lord.*

Isa 61:1–2

---

31. Grinfield, *Apology*, viii.

32. The words in italics represent the verbal agreements between the GNT and the LXX regarding Isa 61:1–2. The words within brackets represent verbal agreements regarding Isa 58:6. Luke (1) omits ἰάσασθαι τοὺς συντετριμμένους τῇ καρδίᾳ from Isa 61:1 ("to heal the brokenhearted" [2007]), (2) omits καὶ ἡμέραν ἀνταποδόσεως παρακαλέσαι πάντας τοὺς πενθοῦντας ("and a day of redemption to comfort all those who mourn") from the last phrase of Isa 6:2, (3) changes καλέσαι ("to declare") in Isa 62:2 to κηρύξαι ("to proclaim"), and (4) changes the present active imperative ἀπόστελλε ("let") in Isa 58:6 to the aorist active infinitive ἀποστεῖλαι ("to set free"). See Archer and Chirichigno, *Old Testament Quotations*, 128–29.

πνεῦμα κυρίου ἐπ᾽ ἐμέ οὗ εἵνεκεν ἔχρισέν με εὐαγγελίσασθαι πτωχοῖς ἀπέσταλκέν με ἰάσασθαι τοὺς συντετριμμένους τῇ καρδίᾳ κηρύξαι αἰχμαλώτοις ἄφεσιν καὶ τυφλοῖς ἀνάβλεψιν καλέσαι ἐνιαυτὸν κυρίου δεκτὸν καὶ ἡμέραν ἀνταποδόσεως παρακαλέσαι πάντας τοὺς πενθοῦντας.

The Spirit of the Lord is upon me because he has anointed me to preach the gospel to the poor, to heal the brokenhearted, *to pro-claim release to the captives and sight to the blind, to declare the favorable year of the Lord* and a day of redemption to comfort all those who mourn.

Isa 58:6

οὐχὶ τοιαύτην νηστείαν ἐγὼ ἐξελεξάμην λέγει κύριος ἀλλὰ λῦε πάντα σύνδεσμον ἀδικίας διάλυε στραγγαλιὰς βιαίων συναλλαγμάτων [ἀπόστελλε τεθραυσμένους ἐν ἀφέσει] καὶ πᾶσαν συγγραφὴν ἄδικον διάσπα

"Is this not the fast that I have chosen," says the Lord, "in order to loosen all bonds of unrighteousness, to undo the bands of the yoke, [to set free those who are oppressed], and to break every yoke?"

The LXX was probably the customary version used in the synagogues throughout Galilee and no doubt would have been the translation that the Gentile Godfearers would have understood. One would have to wonder why the LXX is so pervasive in the NT if there were Aramaic originals lying behind the Gospels.[33] Consider the following observation by Grinfield:

> The number of direct quotations from the Old Testament in the Gospels, Acts, and Epistles may be estimated, I think, at about 350, of which, not more than 50 materially differ from the LXX. But the indirect verbal allusions would swell the number to a far greater amount. Though there be not a single professed quotation in the Apocalypse, it teems with verbal references in every chapter.

Further still, if the Gospels were translations from Aramaic originals, should not the references to the LXX in them be considered translations from hypothetical Aramaic originals? Table 4.1 delineates the linguistic character of OT quotations made by Jesus:

---

33. Selby, *Jesus*, 89.

Table 4.1. Quotations by Jesus in the Gospel of Matthew from the OT

NT Citation	OT Reference	LXX	Both	MT	None
Matt 4:4; Luke 4:4	Deut 8:3	●V[A]			
Matt 4:6 (Satan)	Ps 91:11–12 (MT); Ps 90:11–12 (LXX)	●			
Matt 4:7	Deut 6:16	●V			
Matt 4:10	Deut 6:13	●			
Matt 9:13; 12:7	Hos 6:6	●V			
Matt 11:10; Mark 1:2	Mal 3:1				●[B]
Matt 13:14–15; Mark 4:12; Luke 8:10	Isa 6:9–10	●			
Matt 15:8–9[C]	Isa 29:13	●			
Matt 19:5; Mark 10:7–8[D]	Gen 2:24	●			
Matt 19:18–19	Deut 24:4	●V			
Matt 19:19; 22:39	Lev 19:18	●V			
Matt 21:13; Mark 11:17; Luke 19:46	Isa 56:7; Jer 7:11			●	
Matt 21:16	Ps 8:3 (8:2)[E]	●V			
Matt 21:42; Mark 12:10; Luke 20:17	Ps 118:22–23	●V			
Matt 22:32; Mark 12:26; Luke 20:37	Exod 3:6, 15	●V			
Matt 22:37; Mark 12:30; Luke 10:27	Deut 6:5			●	
Matt 22:44; Mark 12:36; Luke 20:42	Ps 110:1 (MT) Ps 109:1 (LXX)	●V			
Matt 26:31	Zech 13:7	●V			
Matt 27:46	Ps 22:2 (22:1)		●		

A. V=Verbatim; differences in this citation are in word order only.

B. All three references in the NT are in agreement and differences with the LXX are relatively minor—word order and word substitutions.

C. Interestingly, the point that Jesus makes is dependent upon a reading of the LXX rendering of the OT reference. See Porter, "Septuagint/Greek Old Testament," 1105.

D. All four citations in the NT are identical (cf. 1 Cor 6:16; Eph 5:31).

E. The reference in parentheses indicates the reference in the English text which on occasions differs from the MT and LXX numbering.

Source: The chart is an adaptation of Grinfield's chart in *Apology for the Septuagint,* 185. Grammatical comments are based upon Archer and Chirichigno, *Old Testament Quotations,* and Beale and Carson, *Commentary on the New Testament.*

Table 4.1 reveals that the majority of quotations by Jesus as recorded in the heavily Semitic Gospel of Matthew are from the LXX. Most of these quotations are exact reproductions of the LXX. In several references, the quotations are based upon the LXX although they appear to be simple paraphrases. Only in one instance does a quotation come from the Hebrew (Aramaic) and not the LXX. The inclusion of a quotation from the Hebrew text seems to affirm the bilingual culture in which Jesus lived. Based upon Jesus' OT quotations, Grinfield offers the following observation:

> Out of the thirty–seven quotations made by Jesus himself from the Old Testament, thirty–three agree almost verbatim with the LXX, two agree with the Hebrew, and differ from the LXX, one differs from both, and one agrees partially with both. Only six agree exactly with the Hebrew. From this enumeration, it is plain that our Lord constantly used and quoted the version.[34]

The overwhelming preference for the LXX in the Gospels poses a significant problem for the Aramaic Hypothesis. Selby explains the difficulty as follows:

> Either, in the hypothetical documents, the quotations from the Old Testament were in Hebrew, which the Evangelists, for some inexplicable reason of their own, extracted, substituting for them the Septuagint quotations, or else, in these same hypothetical original documents, the original quotations were Jesus' own Aramaic translations of the Hebrew text, with which the Evangelists dispensed, in order to replace them with the Septuagint text. When the care . . . with which Mark and Luke appear to record the few Aramaic sayings of Jesus is appreciated, it seems highly unlikely that these same Evangelists would jettison Jesus' Aramaic translations in favor of the Septuagint version of the Scriptures. Once more it becomes apparent how devious the explanations have to be for the Aramaic Hypothesis to retain any credibility whatsoever.[35]

Another significant area where the LXX plays an important role in the GNT is in the OT references within the speeches recorded in the book of Acts. For example, while on his first missionary tour, Paul arrived in Pisidian Antioch and attended the synagogue service on the Sabbath day (Acts 13:14). After portions of the Law and Prophets were read, Paul was given an opportunity to speak (Acts 13:16). He gave a long speech in which he rehearsed God's work through Israel to bring forth a Savior for them (Acts

34. Grinfield, *Apology*, 30–31.
35. Selby, *Jesus*, 89.

13:15–41). In order to buttress his arguments, Paul cited a number of OT passages and concluded with a warning from a citation of Hab 1:5:

ἴδετε, οἱ καταφρονηταί, καὶ θαυμάσατε καὶ ἀφανίσθητε, ὅτι ἔργον ἐργάζομαι ἐγὼ ἐν ταῖς ἡμέραις ὑμῶν, ἔργον ὃ οὐ μὴ πιστεύσητε ἐάν τις ἐκδιηγῆται ὑμῖν (Acts 13:41).

Behold! You scoffers, and marvel and be destroyed; for I am accomplishing a work in your days, a work which you will never believe even if someone should describe it to you.

Table 4:2 provides a comparison between the LXX and the GNT citation:

Table 4.2. Paul's citation of Hab 1:5

LXX	GNT	Analysis
ἴδετε οἱ καταφρονηταί	ἴδετε, οἱ καταφρονηταί,	
καὶ		omission
ἐπιβλέψατε		omission
καὶ θαυμάσατε	καὶ θαυμάσατε	
θαυμάσια		omission
καὶ ἀφανίσθητε	καὶ ἀφανίσθητε,	
διότι ἔργον	ὅτι ἔργον	changed διότι to ὅτι
ἐγὼ ἐργάζομαι	ἐργάζομαι ἐγὼ	word order changed
ἐν ταῖς ἡμέραις ὑμῶν	ἐν ταῖς ἡμέραις ὑμῶν,	see above
	ἔργον	addition
ὃ οὐ μὴ πιστεύσητε	ὃ οὐ μὴ πιστεύσητε	
ἐάν τις ἐκδιηγῆται	ἐάν τις ἐκδιηγῆται	
	ὑμῖν.	addition

Source: Beale and Carson, *Commentary on the New Testament*, 587.

Paul's citation is nearly verbatim with the LXX.[36] His citation certainly aided the comprehension of those present whom Paul identified as those who feared God (Acts 13:16).

Another citation of the LXX occurs during the dispute over the influx of Gentiles into the church at the council in Jerusalem. James provided a resolution to the conflict:

Μετὰ δὲ τὸ σιγῆσαι αὐτοὺς ἀπεκρίθη Ἰάκωβος λέγων· ἄνδρες ἀδελφοί, ἀκούσατέ μου. Συμεὼν ἐξηγήσατο καθὼς πρῶτον ὁ θεὸς ἐπεσκέψατο λαβεῖν ἐξ ἐθνῶν λαὸν τῷ ὀνόματι αὐτοῦ. καὶ τούτῳ συμφωνοῦσιν οἱ λόγοι τῶν προφητῶν καθὼς γέγραπται (Acts 15:13–15).

---

36. Beale and Carson, *Commentary on the New Testament*, 587; Archer and Chirichigno, *Old Testament Quotations*, 159; Munck, "Acts," 123.

> Now after they became silent, James answered, saying, "Brothers, listen to me. Symeon has explained how God first concerned himself about taking from among the Gentiles a people for his name. And about this the words of the prophets agree just as it is written."

James encouraged the acceptance of the Gentiles and affirmed the work by Paul and Peter among them. As support for the eventual inclusion of the Gentiles, James refers to the prophetic literature to underscore his judgment. The particular quotation is from Amos 9:11–12:

> μετὰ ταῦτα ἀναστρέψω καὶ ἀνοικοδομήσω τὴν σκηνὴν Δαυὶδ
> τὴν πεπτωκυῖαν καὶ τὰ κατεσκαμμένα αὐτῆς ἀνοικοδομήσω
> καὶ ἀνορθώσω αὐτήν, ὅπως ἂν ἐκζητήσωσιν οἱ κατάλοιποι τῶν
> ἀνθρώπων τὸν κύριον καὶ πάντα τὰ ἔθνη ἐφ᾽ οὓς ἐπικέκληται
> τὸ ὄνομά μου ἐπ᾽ αὐτούς, λέγει κύριος ποιῶν ταῦτα γνωστὰ
> ἀπ᾽ αἰῶνος (Acts 15:16–18).

> "After these things I will return, and I will rebuild the tabernacle of David which has fallen, and I will rebuild what has been demolished, and I will restore it. So that the rest of humankind may seek the Lord and all the Gentiles among them who are called by my name," says the Lord who does these things known from long ago.

Table 4.3 shows a comparison between the LXX and the GNT citation:

Table 4.3. James's citation of Amos 9:11-12

LXX	GNT	Analysis
ἐν τῇ ἡμέρᾳ ἐκείνῃ ἀναστήσω	μετὰ ταῦτα ἀναστρέψω καὶ ἀνοικοδομήσω	cf. Jer 12:15 uses verb from omission below
τὴν σκηνὴν Δαυὶδ τὴν πεπτωκυῖαν καὶ ἀνοικοδομήσω τὰ πεπτωκότα αὐτῆς	τὴν σκηνὴν Δαυὶδ τὴν πεπτωκυῖαν	omission
καὶ τὰ κατεσκαμμένα αὐτῆς ἀναστήσω καὶ ἀνοικοδομήσω αὐτὴν, καθὼς αἱ ἡμέραι τοῦ αἰῶνος	καὶ τὰ κατεσκαμμένα αὐτῆς ἀνοικοδομήσω καὶ ἀνορθώσω αὐτήν,	shift of verb: "destroy/ overturn" repeats verb used above change of verb omission
ὅπως ἐκζητήσωσιν οἱ κατάλοιποι τῶν ἀνθρώπων	ὅπως ἂν ἐκζητήσωσιν οἱ κατάλοιποι τῶν ἀνθρώπων τὸν κύριον	adds ἂν addition
καὶ πάντα τὰ ἔθνη ἐφ᾽ οὓς ἐπικέκληται τὸ ὄνομά μου ἐπ᾽ αὐτούς λέγει κύριος ὁ θεὸς	καὶ πάντα τὰ ἔθνη ἐφ᾽ οὓς ἐπικέκληται τὸ ὄνομά μου ἐπ᾽ αὐτούς, λέγει κύριος	omission
ὁ ποιῶν ταῦτα	ποιῶν ταῦτα γνωστὰ ἀπ᾽ αἰῶνος.	omits ὁ Isa 45:21?

Source: Chart is adapted from Beale and Carson, *Commentary on the New Testament*, 590–93.

Despite the minor variances, the citation appears to show familiarity with the LXX for it "is closer to the LXX than the MT."[37] Additionally, the use of Peter's Jewish name Συμεών ("Symeon") reveals that he and the Jews in Jerusalem were comfortable with the LXX and accepted it as an authoritative reference. Johannes Munck argued that the incongruence of using the name Symeon and then citing the LXX "shows that the words of James have been thoroughly reworked."[38] One would wonder, however, why the citation of the LXX would be incongruent since it was used so widely among both Jews and Christians.[39]

37. Ibid., 589.
38. Munck, "Acts," 140 §39. See also Bock, *Acts*, 503–4, and Bruce, *Acts*, 294.
39. Selby, *Jesus*, 90–91.

The second category of Semitic influence upon the NT relates to Arama-isms. Aramaic expressions or words are mostly transliterated into Greek from Aramaic. The difficulty with identifying Aramaisms in the NT is the absence of any Aramaic originals with which to make comparisons. The vernacular language of many of the non-hellenized population of Palestine was probably Aramaic, especially within their familial circles where contact with Greek-speakers was minimal. Therefore, except within these close-knit circles, espe-cially among the Jews, Greek was likely the language of Palestine. The Greek spoken was a type of Greek that contained a Semitic flavor. Porter argues that some scholars have failed to appreciate the significance of the fact that Greek was extensively spoken throughout the Greco-Roman world:

> That Greek was the *lingua franca* of the Graeco–Roman world and the predominant language of the Roman Empire is ac-knowledged by virtually everyone who has considered this is-sue, although the full significance of this factor has not been fully appreciated by all New Testament scholars.[40]

Koester asserts that "Aramaisms are most frequent in the gospels, because Jesus, his disciples, and the members of earliest Palestinian churches spoke Aramaic."[41] Although the Gospels reveal various levels of Semitic influence, the actual number of Aramaic transliterations in the Gospels is not signifi-cant. In fact, does it not seem rather extreme to argue for Aramaic originals when the Gospel of Mark adopted the curious practice of reproducing only some, not all, of Jesus' sayings in Aramaic? According to Turner, this obser-vation seems to favor Greek as the dominical language:

> St. Mark gives no more than *talitha coum* 541, *qorban* 711, *ephphatha* 734, *abba* 1436, *eloi eloi lema sabachthani* 1534. One would think that the evangelist's reason for reproducing this particular selection of transliterations is that, *contrary to his usual way* [emphasis mine], Jesus spoke in Aramaic on these occasions. The reason why is not so clear, but on some of them he may have been addressing individuals whose sole language was Aramaic.[42]

Table 4.4 lists the non-translated Aramaic words and the context in which they were used in the Gospel of Mark.

40. Porter, "Did Jesus Ever Teach in Greek?," 205.

41. Koester, *History, Culture, and Religion*, 112.

42. Turner, *Style*, 181. Koester's assertion concerning Aramaic originals behind Mark seems extreme based upon the internal evidence: "Only the gospel of Mark seems to have used Greek that were straightforward translations of Aramaic originals" (*His-tory, Culture, and Religion*, 112).

Table 4.4. Non-translated Aramaic words in the Gospel of Mark

Verse	Aramaic Words	Literal Translation	Context
Mark 5:41 καὶ κρατήσας τῆς χειρὸς τοῦ παιδίου λέγει αὐτῇ·*ταλιθα κουμ*, ὅ ἐστιν μεθερμηνευόμενον τὸ κοράσιον, σοὶ λέγω, ἔγειρε.	Ταλιθα κουμ[A]	Little girl arise.	A room in a private home of a syna-gogue official
Mark 7:11 ὑμεῖς δὲ λέγετε·ἐὰν εἴπῃ ἄνθρωπος τῷ πατρὶ ἢ τῇ μητρί *κορβᾶν*, ὅ ἐστιν δῶρον, ὃ ἐὰν ἐξ ἐμοῦ ὠφεληθῇς	Κορβᾶν[B]	Gift to God	A semiprivate gathering of an unspecified number of Pharisees and scribes in the market place in Jerusalem
Mark 7:34 καὶ ἀναβλέψας εἰς τὸν οὐρανὸν ἐστέναξεν καὶ λέγει αὐτῷ *Εφφαθα*, ὅ ἐστιν διανοίχθητι.	Εφφαθα[C]	Be opened	A private meeting away from the multitude
Mark 14:36 καὶ ἔλεγεν·*αββα* ὁ πατήρ, πάντα δυνατά σοι παρένεγκε τὸ ποτήριον τοῦτο ἀπ᾽ ἐμοῦ ἀλλ᾽ οὐ τί ἐγὼ θέλω ἀλλὰ τί σύ.	Αββα[D]	Father	A private setting in the garden of Gethsemane
Mark 15:34 καὶ τῇ ἐνάτῃ ὥρᾳ ἐβόησεν ὁ Ἰησοῦς φωνῇ μεγάλῃ· ελωι ελωι λεμα σαβαχθανι; ὅ ἐστιν μεθερμηνευόμενον ὁ θεός μου ὁ θεός μου, εἰς τί ἐγκατέλιπές με;	ελωι ελωι λεμα σαβαχθανι[E]	My God, my God, why have you forsaken me?	A public setting involving an un-specified number of bystanders

A. Aramaic, טליתא קום or קום טלתא. See Danker, "κουμ," 563; ibid., "ταλιθα," 988.
B. Aramaic or Hebrew, קרבן. Ibid., "κορβάν," 559.
C. Aramaic, אתפתח . Ibid., "εφφαθα," 419. For a discussion relating to the hypothesis that Jesus used magical formulas when healing others, see Peisker and Brown, "Open," 560, 729. There is also some disagreement as to the proper linguistic classification of אתפתח.
D. Aramaic, אבא. Danker, "ἀββα," 1.
E. Aramaic, אלהי למא שבקתני אלהי. Ibid., "σαβαχθάνι," 909.

Source: NA[28]

A careful analysis of Table 4.4 may provide the reason that the Aramaic is transliterated and not translated into Greek. In each situation where the

Aramaic appears, Jesus is interacting with others in a private/semiprivate situation where he converses in the native language of others. Aramaic may have been routinely spoken in the household of Jairus. For Jesus to speak Aramaic in this private and intimate setting was appropriate and expected. However, to assert that Jairus or Jesus would not or could not converse in Greek is to go beyond the evidence. The preservation of the Aramaic may indicate a detour from the norm, not the norm itself. Alan Cole strongly denies that Jesus would not have taught or spoken in Greek but expresses the possibility that if he did, special circumstances would have led him to adapt to the situation as in the case of the crisis at the home of Jairus.

> Whether or no [sic] the Lord ever taught in Greek . . . is very doubtful: but even if He did at times, there would be a special appropriateness in using her own mother tongue to the little girl, as the risen Lord conversed with Mary in her own tongue (Jn. Xx. 16). Perhaps the emphasis laid on the fact that Aramaic was used on these occasions suggests that it was not so common on other occasions.[43]

The situation in Mark 7 is not necessarily an intimate moment as in the case of the healing of the daughter of Jairus. Jesus seems to have come out of Jerusalem (Mark 7:1; cf. Matt 15:1) along with a multitude of followers. However, Jesus appears to be engaged within a semiprivate conversation with an unspecified number of Pharisees and "some" scribes; afterward, he addresses the multitude (Matt 15:10). Jesus challenges the hypocritical accusation made against his disciples for eating with impure hands and thereby violating the tradition of the elders (Mark 7:2–5). He accuses the Pharisees and scribes of violating the commandment of God by circumventing familial obligations because of their religious commitments. One made a vow of dedication to God when declaring something κορβᾶν ("gift to God").[44] Jewish tradition was clear that family needs superseded voluntary acts of piety in order to provide the care necessary for one's family. This action was inherent in the basic law to honor one's father and mother. Josephus also refers to the Jewish practice of κορβᾶν in *Jewish Antiquities*:

> [T]hose who describe themselves as "Corban" to God—meaning what Greeks would call "a gift"—when desirous to be relieved of this obligation must pay down to the priests a fixed sum . . . for those whose means are insufficient to pay the appointed sum,

43. Cole, *Mark*, 106.

44. Brown, "κορβᾶν," 43–44. The emphasis seems to be placed on the consecration of a gift to God (Lev 1:2; 22:27; 23:14; Num 7:25; Ezek 20:28; 40:43) and later incorporated the idea of dedicating oneself to God.

the priests are at liberty to decide as they choose (*Ant.* 4.4 §73 [Thackeray and Marcus, LCL]).

In his treatise *Against Apion*, Josephus also refers to the oath of κορβᾶν:

Now this oath [κορβᾶν] will be found in no other nation except the Jews, and, translated from the Hebrew, one may interpret it as meaning "God's gift" (*Ag. Ap.* 1.22 §167 [Thackeray, LCL]).

The Mishnah contains several entries that discuss the practice of κορβᾶν. One entry in particular relates somewhat to the situation in Mark 7:

[If] he saw people eating figs [belonging to him] and said, "Lo, they are *qorban* to you!" and they turned out to be his father and brothers, and there were others with them—The House of Shammai say, "They are permitted, and those with them are prohibited." And the House of Hillel say, "These and those [men] are permitted [to eat the figs]" (*m. Ned.* 3:2).[45]

Since the κορβᾶν declaration was usually associated with those engaged in religious service or leadership, it was therefore pertinent to the discussion and directed specifically at the scribes and Pharisees who because of supposedly mitigating technicalities violated the commandments of God. Those who were not in the inner circle of the scribes and Pharisees were probably not touched religiously with such internal maneuvering. This was "insider" language and behavior; many may not have understood what Jesus meant by the term. Consequently, the Gospel of Mark provides the meaning for the technical use of κορβᾶν, which was an important concept that served as the pivotal issue in this semiprivate conversation between Jesus and his accusers.[46]

When Jesus was in the region of Decapolis, some people brought an individual who was deaf and entreated Jesus to help (Mark 7:31–32). Jesus took him aside privately and healed him (Mark 7:33–34). Again, Jesus employed an Aramaic word that is left untranslated in the text. However, the meaning of the word is supplied. The word Εφφαθα is an Aramaic command uttered in a private setting and perhaps was the very first word that the deaf man ever heard. The implication may be that some in the region spoke Aramaic or that Jesus used his native language in a private prayer on behalf of the deaf man.[47] This is another unique situation in which Jesus spoke Aramaic.

---

45. Neusner, *Mishnah*, 410.

46. Black, *Aramaic Approach*, 139; France, *Mark*, 286–87.

47. Ibid., 304.

One of the most difficult moments in Jesus' life was the agony he went through while praying in the garden of Gethsemane. Jesus wanted Peter, James, and John to accompany him in the garden and to lend him support as he prayed. In his prayer, Jesus used the Aramaic word Ἀββά when addressing the Father. Dalman states that the use of Ἀββά "shows that this was the language in which our Lord converses with His Father" and then attempts to reconstruct the entire prayer in Aramaic.[48] The only problem is that Dalman assumes that the entire prayer was spoken in Aramaic. This might have been the case, but the assumption goes beyond the evidence. Would it not have been appropriate for Jesus to use Ἀββά, a term of endearment since his childhood, and to combine it with ὁ πατήρ ("father") because such expressed the "perfect relation" between him and the Father?[49] France sees the combination symbolic of a conflict between two wills:

> It is summed up in the filial address Ἀββὰ ὁ πατήρ, the more striking because given to us in both Aramaic and Greek, and it is revealed as a blending of two wills, which pull in different directions but are brought together by the Son's willing submission to the Father's purpose.[50]

The Hebrew term אב ("Father") and the Aramaic term אבה (or אבא) are closely related. The former represents a more dignified address while the latter emphasizes a familial and revered relationship that children have with their fathers.[51] James Dunn associates Ἀββά as expressing a relationship of endearment:

> The reason why 'abbā' would be so little used presumably because it was typically a family word, or expressive of a degree of intimacy with reverence which would be characteristic of children (but not just little children) within the family circle, or of disciples of a loved and revered teacher.[52]

48. Dalman, *Jesus—Jeshua*, 20.

49. Ibid. By the time of the first century CE, there was a tendency for the nominative to substitute for the place of the vocative, especially when the vocative was understood. See Blass and Debrunner, *Greek Grammar*, 81 §147.

50. France, *Mark*, 580.

51. See "אב" in Brown, *Hebrew and English Lexicon*, 3. France states that "the term conveys the respectful intimacy of a son in a patriarchal family" (*Mark*, 584).

52. Dunn, "Prayer," 619. Dunn's position is actually an adaption of the position of J. Jeremias which initially equated αββα with "Daddy." See Jeremias, *Prayers*, 11–65; Barr, "Abba," 28–47; Green, "Gethsemane," 265; Baur, "Son of God," 772. Hurtado states that "it is remarkable that Mark (like Paul) in addressing Greek—speaking (and largely Gentile) readers used this Aramaic expression alongside the Greek term for 'father.' . . . Mark probably intended his readers to see in Jesus' Gethsemane prayer both

Additionally, Jesus may be using a Semitic expression by combining both Ἀββά and the Greek ὁ πατήρ similar to the way God addressed Moses on Mount Sinai:

> ויעבר יהוה| על־פניו ויקרא יהוה| יהוה אל רחום וחנון ארך אפים
> ורב־חסד ואמת|:

(Exod 34:6)

> Then the Lord passed by before him and proclaimed, "*Lord! Lord God!* Compassionate and gracious, slow to anger, and abounds in loving kindness and truth."

This proclamation confirms the unique relationship that Moses had with God. The use of the covenant name יהוה (*Yahweh*, "Lord") in conjunction with the more general address אל (*el*, "God") is similar to Jesus' address to God in the garden. The Aramaic that is found in the text during this troubling and private time in Gethsemane conforms to the pattern as illustrated in the previous contexts where Aramaic is spoken by Jesus.

Finally, the Gospel of Mark records a cry to the Father on the lips of Jesus as he hung on the cross, overwhelmed by a feeling of desperation—ελωι ελωι λεμα σαβαχθανι ("My God, my God, why have you forsaken me?," Mark 15:34). The Aramaic that is spoken is not a direct quotation of the Hebrew in Ps 22:1 but a "colloquial paraphrase of His own familiar mother-tongue."[53] Though Jesus probably conversed freely in Greek on many occasions, would not his anguish during the crucifixion have been expressed naturally in Aramaic?[54] Actually, Jesus appears to be quoting Ps 22:2 from the Aramaic Targum, which was written partly in Hebrew and in Aramaic.[55] Dalman notes that the words spoken by Jesus provide insight into the degree to which Scripture shaped his life.

---

a precedent for their own submission to God and a reminder that the basis of their filial relationship to God lay in Jesus' own." See Hurtado, "God," 273.

53. Cole, *Mark*, 242.

54. Porter considers the estimate that 10–15 percent of the Jews who lived in Jerusalem spoke Greek as their first language to be a conservative estimate. He says that "it is less likely that in a given instance Jesus would have spoken Greek to Jews from Jerusalem, and more likely that he would have spoken Aramaic. With Jews from outside of Palestine and from areas of high probability regarding the speaking of Greek, even if now in Jerusalem, it is very likely that Jesus would have spoken with them in Greek" (*Criteria for Authenticity*, 145).

55. CAL Targumic Studies Module online: http://cal1.cn.huc.edu/get_a_chapter?file=81002&sub=022&cset=H (accessed May 5, 2013). See also Wilcox, "Semitic Influence," 1095–96.

> Jesus was now not speaking for others, but bursting out of the trance of silence, He gave vent to His gathered emotions, and this, not in a word of prayer formed by Himself, but in a Psalm–verse which forced itself to His lips. This proves His familiarity with Scripture, and reveals, above all, what was going on in His mind; but it is also in keeping with the need of the Dying who cannot any longer find words of His own.[56]

Maurice Casey indicates that for Jesus to quote the Aramaic version of Scripture during a "moment of extreme stress" would be "entirely natural" and infers that Aramaic was his first language.[57]

The fact that Jesus' words are in the form of a quotation rather than in the form of his own speech emphasizes the trust that he placed in the Father during this moment of crisis.[58] The last cry (Mark 15:37) just before his death may offer an alternate way to interpret Jesus' words during this crisis. The φωνὴν μεγάλην ("loud shout," Mark 15:37) may have been a shout of exultation, knowing that the Father would not forsake him as the Psalmist ultimately proclaimed:[59]

כי לא־בזה ולא שקץ ענות עני ולא־הסתיר פניו ממנו ובשועו אליו שמע:

(Ps 22:25)

> For he has not despised or detested the affliction of the afflicted;
> Nor hidden his face from him; But when he cried to him for help, he heard (Ps 22:24).

Regardless of the characterization of Jesus' words—despair or exultation—the context illustrates the consistency of Mark's record of the Aramaic words of Jesus.

The above analysis of the Aramaic words left untranslated in the Gospel of Mark demonstrates that Jesus did indeed speak Aramaic on occasions, especially in contexts characterized by private or semiprivate situations. The significance of the inclusion of these Aramaic words and expressions is not to bolster the opinion that Jesus spoke and taught in Aramaic and that the Gospel of Mark is a composition based entirely upon Aramaic sources. The opposite is true: the significance of Mark's inclusion of the few Aramaic terms is to bring to the forefront the adaptability of Jesus to the need of the moment. In fact "Mark's language switch implies that Jesus switched

56. Dalman, *Jesus—Jeshua*, 205.

57. Casey, *Aramaic Sources*, 88.

58. See France, *Mark*, 652.

59. Ibid., 655; see also France, "Teaching of Jesus," 101–36; Beale and Carson, *Commentary on the New Testament*, 236–37.

languages," which would indicate that he did not normally teach or speak Aramaic.[60] The Aramaic that is found in the Gospel of Mark argues favorably for the bilingual character of Palestine.

Alexander Roberts argued in the late 1900s that the preservation of Aramaic in the GNT served as evidence against the proposition that Aramaic was habitually employed by Jesus. Roberts explains the situation as follows:

> The fact seems to be that the occasional occurrence of Aramaic expressions in the Gospels, instead of proving that Christ *habitually* made use of that dialect, rather tends to prove the contrary. If it be maintained that Syro–Chaldaic was the language which He generally employed, the question at once occurs, why we have a few such words, and a few only, preserved to us as having been used by Him on rare occasions. On the supposition that He spoke usually in Greek, these words, we may see, come in naturally enough as exceptions to the general rule, and are specially inserted as such, just as in the reported discussion of Cicero we often find a few Greek terms introduced; and, as in our language, a French or German expression may every now and then occur. But if, on the other hand, it be supposed that Christ really for the most part made use of the Aramaic, so that the Greek was the exception and not the rule in His discourses, it seems impossible to give any satisfactory, or even tolerable, explanation of the manner in which the few Aramaic words found in the Gospels are introduced. They certainly *appear* to be brought in as exceptional to our Saviour's practice; and when regarded in that light their occurrence can cause little difficulty, even although no evident reason may be found for His use of Aramaic on these particular occasions. But when the opposite opinion is maintained, and when these words are looked on as being really specimens of His ordinary language, there is no principle of reason which can be suggested as likely to have guided the evangelist in their preservation and insertion.[61]

Although Roberts admits that there is "no principle of reason" why the Gospels preserved selected Aramaic words and expressions, the most plausible reason for Aramaic in Palestine was that it was the language closely associated with private and intimate settings, such as the home where people spoke their vernacular.[62] Therefore, Jesus unsurprisingly spoke Aramaic when ad-

60. Buth, "Aramaic Language," 89.

61. Roberts, *Greek*, 98.

62. Selby argues that the attention to detail indicates "that the Gospel accounts are

dressing a child to arise, a blind man to open his eyes, some Pharisees and scribes in a religious discussion, and the Father in a prayer of anguish and in a cry of desperation at the onset of death. Roberts does not think that "the most plausible of such solutions is that which conceives of these particular Aramaic expressions having been preserved rather than others, on account of the peculiar *solemnity* which belongs to them" for the simple reason that there are many solemn moments preserved in the Gospels that contain no Aramaic.[63] What Roberts does not recognize is that the solemnity of the above Aramaic expressions appears to be connected to unique private and semiprivate settings. Roberts makes the following conclusion based upon his survey of the textual evidence found in the GNT:

> It appears, then, from a general survey of the whole New Testament, that there are manifold and decisive reasons to conclude that Greek was commonly known and used in Palestine in the days of Christ and His apostles: that that accordingly was the language which He and they *usually* employed; and that, while both the Master and His disciples sometimes made use in public of the Aramaic dialect, such an occurrence was quite *exceptional* to their ordinary practice, and is on that account specially noticed in the evangelic history.[64]

Based upon the evidence, there seems to be a vast difference between recognizing Semitic influences in the GNT and asserting that Semitic influence demands the presence of Aramaic original documents behind the GNT. The most obvious document lying behind the GNT is the LXX. Henry Swete acknowledges that the LXX is the principal source upon which the GNT demonstrates reliance:

> [I]t may at once be said that every part of the N.T. affords evidence of a knowledge of the LXX., and that a great majority of the passages cited from the O.T. are in general agreement with the Greek version ... the LXX. is the principal source from which the writers of the N.T. derived their O.T. quotations.[65]

Semitic influence does not demand the conclusion that Jesus and his disciples spoke and taught in Aramaic exclusively. The habitual use of the LXX

---

most probably a good deal more accurate and reliable than contemporary New Testament critics will allow" (*Jesus*, 75).

63. For example, an atmosphere of solemnity surrounds the raising of Lazarus (John 11) and the appointment of the apostle John as Mary's caregiver (John 19:26–27). See Roberts, *Greek*, 99–100.

64. Ibid., 110.

65. Swete, *Introduction to Old Testament*, 392.

by Jesus and his disciples argues for a wider recognition of their facility with the Greek language.

> The presence of Semitisms in the Greek of the gospels does not necessarily indicate an exclusively Semitic (Aramaic or Hebrew) linguistic situation in the first century. In polylingual areas, languages tend to interpenetrate one another in their vocabulary and manner of expression. The Septuagint is full of Semitic forms of expression. This would have influenced powerfully the type of Greek spoken in Palestine. The fact that Greek had been imported into an originally Semitic language milieu also gives one reason to expect that the Greek spoken there will reflect Semitic idiom and thought patterns.[66]

Is the Greek New Testament a Translation?

Essential to the Aramaic Hypothesis is the presumption that the Gospels of the GNT were primarily translations of Aramaic sources. In other words, the Gospels are not necessarily original compositions. Black explains the issue as follows:

> The Gospels were written in a predominantly Hellenistic environment, and they were written in Greek. But Greek was not the native language of their central Figure, nor of the earliest apostles, if it was not unfamiliar to them. Jesus must have conversed in the Galilean dialect of Aramaic, and His teaching was probably almost entirely in Aramaic. At the basis of the Greek Gospels, therefore, there must lie a Palestinian Aramaic tradition, at any rate of the sayings and teaching of Jesus, and this tradition must at one time have been translated from Aramaic into Greek.[67]

In regard to the Gospel of John, Charles Burney argues that it shows evidence "that the Greek text of the Fourth Gospel is a translation from Aramaic with the broad general characteristics of the Aramaic language."[68] Additionally,

66. Thomas and Gundry, *Harmony*, 310.

67. Black, *Aramaic Approach*, 16.

68. Burney, *Aramaic Origin*, 27. Burney attempts to separate himself from previous attempts to identify the Aramaic source behind the Gospel of John: "Thus it was that the writer turned seriously to tackle the question of the original language of the Fourth Gospel; and quickly convincing himself that the theory of an original Aramaic document was no chimera, but a fact which was capable of the fullest verification, set himself to collect and classify the evidence in a form which he trusts may justify the

Charles C. Torrey states that "the evidence of translation, in each and all of the Four Gospels, is perfectly clear and very complete."[69] In fact, Torrey attempted to retranslate the Greek of the Gospels back into Aramaic in order to provide a more reliable English translation of the original Aramaic. Similarly, Casey holds to the premise that Jesus' original sayings found in the GNT are likely to be authentic if they retained their original Aramaic form.[70] Dalman's position, however, is more reserved than the positions of both Black and Torrey:

> From the very beginning it [Christian Church] thus used two
> languages, and in gatherings of the community the deeds and
> words of Jesus must have been recounted in Greek and in Ara-
> maic. The "Hebraists" would mostly all have understood some
> Greek, but the Hellenists very often no Aramaic or Hebrew.
> A gospel–source in Greek need not, by reason of its language,
> have been any later than one written in a Semitic dialect. It is
> thus *possible* that the oldest Christian writing may have been
> composed in Greek; and its Semitisms, so far as they are not

---

reasonableness of his opinion not merely to other Aramaic scholars, but to all New Testament scholars who will take the pains to follow out his arguments" (p. 3). In order to prove his thesis, Burney compares Semitic stylistic peculiarities of the Gospel of John with (1) the Aramaic sections of the OT, (2) the Aramaic paraphrases (Targums) of the OT, (3) the Palestinian Talmud, and (4) the Palestinian Syriac lectionary (pp. 20–27). Burney's analysis reveals significant Semitic stylistic and grammatical features in the Greek text of the Gospel of John that mirror Aramaic linguistic features in regard to sentence structure, conjunctions, pronouns, verbs, etc., that indicate translation Greek. There is one important area where Burney finds the significant evidence for his Aramaic Hypothesis mistranslations: "The most weighty form of evidence in proof that a document is a translation from another language is the existence of difficulties or peculiarities of language which can be shown to find their solution in the theory of mistranslation from the *assumed* original language (emphasis mine)" (p. 101). Burney's hypothesis, of course, cannot be proven because comparisons cannot be made with an actual Aramaic text of the Gospel of John. Therefore Burney commits the same two errors as his predecessors and others such as Black and Casey who also sympathize with his position: (1) the lack of any Aramaic manuscripts of the NT that can serve as a reference in order to compare translation peculiarities in the GNT (Much of Burney's evidence is dependent upon Aramaic MSS that are not from the first century CE) and (2) the reluctance to attribute Semitic characteristics of the GNT to the Semitic backgrounds of the writers. Semitic similarities of the GNT when compared to other Aramaic sources do not necessitate reliance upon Aramaic sources. Burney finds in the Fourth Gospel a "remarkable" coincidence of relationship to psalms and odes of Aramaic documents and to the writings of Ignatius (See his Appendix, p. 169). For an analysis of Aramaisms in the Fourth Gospel that directly relate to Burney's assertions, see Turner, *Style*, 64–79. See also Hughes, "Languages Spoken by Jesus," 141.

69. Torrey, *Four Gospels*, ix–x.

70. Casey, *Aramaic Sources*, 1. See also Dalman, *Words of Jesus*, 71.

Biblicisms, are in that case due to the Aramaic oral archetype [*Urgestalt*] of the Christian tradition.[71]

Interestingly, even Black must admit his uncertainty of whether there was actually an Aramaic written or oral source for "it is not possible from the evidence to decide."[72] Additionally, Black acknowledges that the Semitic style of the Gospel of Mark may be ultimately attributed to Jewish bilingualism:

> It is difficult . . . to decide whether such typical features of Mark's Semitic style allow of any interference as to his use of sources outside the sayings of Jesus. They may conceivably be construed as evidence of the kind of Greek which an Aramaic-speaking Jew would write . . . apart from the sayings of Jesus, there are far fewer indications of Aramaic influence.[73]

One could reasonably argue that the kind of Greek Mark employs is equally consistent with that of an "Aramaic-speaking Jew" who was also capable of communicating Greek in oral and written form. In view of the influence of the LXX upon the GNT and the Semitic *sitz im leben* of Jesus and his disciples, must the Semitisms, therefore, contained in the Gospels infer an Aramaic source?[74]

One important consideration is whether the Gospels of the GNT show evidence of being translations demonstrating reliance upon Aramaic sources. In order to identify aspects of this phenomenon, the LXX serves as a notable example of the characteristics of translation Greek. Mussies notes a number of characteristics in the Greek of the LXX that demonstrate its reliance upon a Semitic source.

71. Ibid.

72. Black, *Aramaic Approach*, 271.

73. Ibid., 271–72.

74. See Hughes, "Languages Spoken by Jesus," 134.

Table 4.5. Semitic characteristics in the Greek of the LXX

Characteristic	MT	LXX	Translation
(1) Frequent use of καί ("and") to translate the Hebrew conjunctive ו ("and"), especially at the beginning of sentences	Gen 1:3–5 **ויאמר** אלהים יהי אור **ויהי**־אור: **וירא** אלהים את־האור כי־ טוב **ויבדל** אלהים בין האור **ובין** החשך: **ויקרא** אלהים לאור יום **ולחשך** קרא לילה **ויהי**־ ערב **ויהי**־בקר יום אחד:	Gen 1:3–5 καὶ εἶπεν ὁ θεός γενηθήτω φῶς καὶ ἐγένετο φῶς καὶ εἶδεν ὁ θεὸς τὸ φῶς ὅτι καλόν καὶ διεχώρισεν ὁ θεὸς ἀνὰ μέσον τοῦ φωτὸς καὶ ἀνὰ μέσον τοῦ σκότους καὶ ἐκάλεσεν ὁ θεὸς τὸ φῶς ἡμέραν καὶ τὸ σκότος ἐκάλεσεν νύκτα καὶ ἐγένετο ἑσπέρα καὶ ἐγένετο πρωί ἡμέρα μία	Gen 1:3–5 *And* God said, "Let there be light." *And* there was light. *And* God saw the light that it was good. *And* God separated from between the light *and* between the darkness *and* God called the light "Day" *and* the darkness he called "Night." *And* there was evening *and* there was morning, one day.
(2) Frequent use of (καὶ) ιδού ("behold" or "and behold") to translate the Hebrew interjection הנה	Amos 7:1 כה הראני אדני יהוה **והנה** יוצר גבי בתחלת עלות הלקש **והנה**־לקש אחר גזי המלך:	Amos 7:1 οὕτως ἔδειξέν μοι κύριος καὶ ἰδοὺ ἐπιγονὴ ἀκρίδων ἐρχομένη ἑωθινή καὶ ἰδοὺ βροῦχος εἷς Ιωγ ὁ βασιλεύς	Amos 7:1 Thus the Lord God showed to me. *And behold*, He was forming a swarm of locusts when the spring crop began to sprout. *And behold*, The spring crop was after the king's mowing.
(3) Frequent use of genitive pronouns immediately following substantives	Judg 1:3 ויאמר יהודה לשמעון **אחיו** עלה אתי בגורלי ונלחמה בכנעני והלכתי גם־אני אתך בגורלך וילך אתו שמעון:	Judg 1:3 καὶ εἶπεν Ιουδας τῷ Συμεων ἀδελφῷ αὐτοῦ ἀνάβηθι μετ᾽ ἐμοῦ ἐν τῷ κλήρῳ μου καὶ παραταξώμεθα πρὸς τοὺς ανανιους καὶ πορεύσομαι κἀγὼ μετὰ σοῦ ἐν τῷ κλήρῳ σου καὶ ἐπορεύθη μετ᾽ αὐτοῦ Συμεων	Judg 1:3 Then Judas said to Symeon *his brother*, "Come up with me into my allotment that we may fight against the Canaanites and I will go with you unto your allotment."So Symeon went with him.

(4) Omission of the article with a substantive which is then followed by a genitive	Nahum 1:1 משא נינוה **ספר חזון** נחום האלקשי:	Nahum 1:1 λῆμμα Νινευη [?] βιβλίον [?]ὁράσεως Ναουμ τοῦ Ελκεσαίου	Nahum 1:1 The oracle of Nineveh. *The book of the vision* of Nahum the Elkoshite.
(5) Tendency not to separate the article from the substantive followed by an adjective with the article	Jonah 1:2 קום לך אל־נינוה **העיר הגדולה** וקרא עליה כי־ עלתה רעתם לפני:	Jonah 1:2 ἀνάστηθι καὶ πορεύθητι εἰς Νινευη τὴν πόλιν τὴν μεγάλην καὶ κήρυξον ἐν αὐτῇ ὅτι ἀνέβη ἡ κραυγὴ τῆς κακίας αὐτῆς πρός με.	Jonah 1:2 "Arise and go to Nineveh *the great city* and cry against it, for their wicked-ness has come up before me."
(6) Use of the nomi-native preceded by the article mim-icking a vocative[A]	Psalm 41:2 כאיל תערג על־אפיקי־ מים כן נפשי תערג אליך **אלהים:**	Psalm 41:2 ὃν τρόπον ἐπιποθεῖ ἡ ἔλαφος ἐπὶ τὰς πηγὰς τῶν ὑδάτων οὕτως ἐπιποθεῖ ἡ ψυχή μου πρὸς σέ ὁ θεός.	Psalm 42:1 As the deer pants for the water brooks, So my soul pants for Thee, O God.
(7) Use of the dative instead of a pos-sessive genitive	2 Kings 13:1 בשנת עשרים ושלש **שנה ליואש בן־אחזיהו** מלך יהודה מלך יהואחז בן־יהוא על־ישראל בשמרון שבע עשרה שנה:	2 Kings 13:1 ἐν ἔτει εἰκοστῷ καὶ τρίτῳ ἔτει τῷ Ιωας υἱῷ Οχοζιου βασιλεῖ Ιουδα ἐβασίλευσεν ωαχας υἱὸς Ιου ἐν Σαμαρείᾳ ἑπτακαίδεκα ἔτη	2 Kings 13:1 In the twenty third *year of Joash son of Ahaziah*, king of Judah, Jehoahaz reigned, Son of Jehu, over all Israel at Samaria seventeen years.
(8) Use of parono-mastic datives or accusatives with verbs for the Hebrew infinitive absolute	Genesis 2:17 ומעץ הדעת טוב ורע לא תאכל ממנו כי ביום אכלך ממנו **מות** תמות:	Genesis 2:17 ἀπὸ δὲ τοῦ ξύλου τοῦ γινώσκειν καλὸν καὶ πονηρὸν οὐ φάγεσθε ἀπ' αὐτοῦ ᾗ δ' ἂν ἡμέρᾳ φάγητε ἀπ' αὐτοῦ θανάτῳ ἀποθανεῖσθε	Genesis 2:17 But from the tree of knowledge of good and evil you shall not eat of it, for in the day that you eat from it you shall *surely* die.

(9) Frequent occurrence of nominal sentences	2 Kings 14:2	2 Kings 14:2	2 Kings 14:2
	בן־עשרים וחמש שנה היה מלכו ועשרים ותשע שנה מלך בירושלם **אמו ושם (יהועדן)** [**יהועדין**] מן־ירושלם:	υἱὸς εἴκοσι καὶ πέντε ἐτῶν ἦν ἐν τῷ βασιλεύειν αὐτὸν καὶ εἴκοσι καὶ ἐννέα ἔτη ἐβασίλευσεν ἐν Ιερουσαλημ καὶ ὄνομα τῆς μητρὸς αὐτοῦ Ιωαδιν ἐξ Ιερουσαλημ	A son *who* was twenty–five years old when he became king, and he reigned twenty–nine years. *His mother's name was Jehoaddin of* Jerusalem.
A. See also Pss 42:1 (43:1), 43:2 (44:1), and 44:7 (45:6).			

Source: The chart is based upon Mussies, "Greek in Palestine," 1048–49. I have selected only key characteristics from the fifteen Mussies highlights that best illustrate the dependency of the LXX upon the Hebrew text.

Table 4.5 indicates that the translators of the LXX adapted the Greek language to reflect the Semitic characteristics of the Hebrew text. These adaptations reveal that the translators in many respects were careful to maintain a certain degree of literalness. Interestingly, a Semitic language commonly holds to a much more rigid syntax than does the Greek language. Rife notes that the most common distinguishing factors of a Semitic language are as follows: (1) The word order is typically verb, subject, and object;[75] (2) the article and its noun are inseparable; (3) the adjective always immediately follows its substantive; (4) the conjunction is never a postpositive; (5) the genitive always immediately follows its construct; and (6) the direct, personal, pronominal object always follows its governing verb.[76] In Rife's judgment, these characteristics are reasonable criteria for evaluating a Greek text to determine Semitic source dependency:

> It seems reasonable to suppose, *a priori* this time, that any piece of Greek which exhibits the above [characteristics], along with other less common features of Semitic word–order, must be a translation from a Semitic original.[77]

An important aspect that bears upon whether or not the GNT is translation Greek is the recognition that the Gospels are themselves literary

75. The sentence structure in biblical Aramaic is less rigid than in biblical Hebrew and may exhibit the following characteristics: (1) verb, subject, and object; (2) subject and verb with no direct object; and (3) object, verb, and subject with a direct object. Consequently, word order similarities between the GNT and Aramaic are insufficient proof of translation Greek. See Steinmann, *Biblical Aramaic*, 332 §4.

76. Rife, "Translation Greek," 247.

77. Ibid.

compositions in their own right and admittedly, as Black observes, do not as a whole represent literalistic translations:

> What is the character of the Greek "translation" in the Gospels where Aramaic sources can be shown to have been employed? In view of the results already obtained, we are bound to consider the Greek of the sayings of Jesus only; and in this connexion, it cannot, I think, be sufficiently emphasized that in the majority of the longer connected parables, for example in Q, the "translation" is not literal but literary; in other words, it is *doubtful* if it can be justly described as translation at all in some cases, even where the evidence points to the existence and use of an Aramaic source. The Evangelists, that is to say, are for the most part writing Greek Gospels, even where they are dependent upon sources.[78]

After an analysis of the above characteristics and with an emphasis on uncovering the word order typically found in the GNT, Rife acknowledges that there appears to be close affinity to the word order of biblical Aramaic. However, contrary to proving translation Greek, Rife offers the following conclusion:

> It still appears *unlikely* that the facts of word–order will offer much support to the theory that any NT books are translation Greek, but they clearly indicate, per se, that Judith, I Maccabees, and other LXX books, are from Semitic originals.[79]

Semitic characteristics in the GNT may indicate translation Greek; however, Semitisms may equally indicate original Greek compositions by authors who have Semitic backgrounds. In fact, Mussies suggests that the "Semitizing of Greek" of both the NT and later apocryphal literature was a "spontaneous product of bilingual Jews . . . growing into some kind of genre–language."[80] In many respects, the Semitisms in the LXX and in the GNT were related more to preserving an element of Semitic style than to indicating translation Greek. A. T. Robertson states that "there is a certain dignity and elevation of style so characteristic of the Heb OT that reappears in the NT. The frequent use of *kai* in parts of the NT reminds one of the LXX and the Heb *waw* (See characteristic #1 in chart above). There is, besides, an indefinable

---

78. Emphasis mine; see Black, *Aramaic Approach*, 274. See also Porter, "Did Jesus Ever Teach in Greek?," 209.

79. Emphasis mine; see Rife, "Translation Greek," 252.

80. Mussies, "Greek in Palestine," 1049.

tone in the NT that is found in the OT."[81] Would it not be natural for the NT writers, whose minds were probably saturated with the phraseology of the LXX, to compose and speak Greek with Semitic flair?[82] Additionally, if the LXX played such an important role in the life of Jesus and his disciples and in the composition of the GNT, "then there can remain no doubt that Greek was the language which a public instructor naturally employed, and the language in which the people habitually expected to be addressed."[83]

The GNT exhibits a number of peculiar linguistic characteristics. These characteristics are found in the form of special words, wordplays, and grammatical constructions. If the GNT is a translation, then the presence of these linguistic peculiarities is difficult to explain on the basis of the Aramaic Hypothesis.

First, one of the linguistic peculiarities of the GNT is the inclusion of special Greek words that are used on occasions that lack a Semitic referent. Many Aramaic words were actually loanwords carried over from the Greek language that related to certain aspects of Jewish culture.[84] The borrowing was the result of the close contact between Aramaic and Greek. Saul Lieberman shows that many of these borrowed words from the Greek language occur in later Rabbinic literature and appear to have their own *raison d'être* for their inclusion.[85] Interestingly, the Jewish adoption of the Greek word συνέδριον to refer to their high council in Jerusalem, the Sanhedrin, has no equivalent in Aramaic and illustrates the deep level of incursion upon Judaism. Originally, συνέδριον (Latin, *senatus*) generally referred to a place where a council met and then to the group itself. The term was often used by the Romans for various governmental bodies, special authoritative groups, and judicial assemblies. The word appears in the LXX twelve times, primarily in the book of Proverbs, and typically translates the Hebrew term

81. Robertson, "Language," 1831.

82. Roberts, *Greek*, 137. Robertson states that "Christ spoke the *koinē* . . . and that the NT is not an idiom that was unknown to the Master" ("Language," 1832).

83. Roberts, *Greek*, 144.

84. Some Greek words were borrowed for special circumstances (e.g., λῃστής ["robber"], λογιστής ["calculator/auditor"], κύριε ["master/owner"], and κατήγωρ ["accuser"]). Several Greek words that were assimilated related to the trade of working with wood (e.g., ἐξέδρα ["wooden bench"], ἄσιλλα ["wooden yoke for carrying"], γλύψω ["to carve"], ζυγόν ["wooden yoke for animals"], τράπεζα ["table"], and πύξινον ["wooden tablet"]) which is interesting since Jesus is identified as ὁ τοῦ τέκτονος υἱός ("the carpenter's son," Matt 13:55). See Argyle, "Greek Among the Jews," 87–88. Most interesting is that the headquarters of the Jewish nationalistic sect called Ζηλωτής ("Zealot") were located in the cities of Galilee and bear witness to the influence of Greek in a bilingual culture. See Selby, *Jesus*, 80.

85. Lieberman, *Greek in Jewish Palestine*, 6.

סוד ("council/counsel")[86] though in most cases the LXX supplies the word without a Hebrew referent.[87]

Josephus records the first literary reference of συνέδριον to a Jewish governing body. After the Roman governor of Syria, Gabinius (57–55 BCE), defeated an uprising by Alexander, the son of Aristobulus, he established regional governing authorities in Palestine:[88]

> And so Gabinius demolished them. For Alexander's mother, who was on the side of the Romans, since her husband and her other children were held at Rome, came to him with the request that he do this, and he granted it; and after settling matters with her, he brought Hyrcanus to Jerusalem, to have charge of the temple. He also set up five councils (συνέδρια) and divided the nation into as many districts; these centres of government were: first, Jerusalem, next, Gadara, third, Amathūs, fourth Jericho, and fifth, Sepphoris in Galilee. And so the people were removed from monarchic rule and lived under an aristocracy (*Ant.* 14.5.4 §90–91 [Marcus, LCL]).

Shortly afterwards, the council in Jerusalem assumed authority over all the land, and the Jews adopted the word συνέδριον as the name for its high council, which was composed of seventy-one members over which the high priest presided.[89] After the destruction of Jerusalem in 70 CE the Jews formed a somewhat different council in Jabne called in Hebrew בית דין ("house of justice").[90]

The GNT references the συνέδριον on many occasions, often casting it and its leaders in a dark light.[91] But the inclusion of συνέδριον in the GNT has a broader significance than merely identifying the group that sought the death of Jesus (cf. Matt 26:3–5, 57–67) and encouraging the Apostle Paul's efforts to persecute the early church (Acts 9:1–2). Linguistically, συνέδριον symbolizes the pervasiveness of the Greek language employed by Jewish leaders. Paul's instructor, Rabbi Gamaliel, is purported to have been given permission to instruct his children in Greek because of their interaction

86. See "סוד" in Brown, *Hebrew and English Lexicon*, 691.

87. See Ps 25:4; Prov 11:13, 15:22, 22:10 (twice); 24:8, 26:26, 27:22, 31:23; Song 4:1; and Jer 15:17. See Marshall, "συνέδριον," 363–64.

88. The establishment of the Sanhedrin was the natural progression first begun during the Hasmonean era when elders gathered and formed a council of elders (γερουσία) for legislative purposes (*Ant.* 12.3.3 §138); see Ferguson, *Backgrounds*, 567–70.

89. Marshall, "Sanhedrin," 363.

90. Schürer, *History of Jewish People*, 165–84.

91. The Greek term συνέδριον appears twenty-two times in the GNT.

with the Roman government.[92] Simeon, the son of Gamaliel, indicates that hundreds in the house of Gamaliel devoted themselves to the study of Greek literature.[93] According to the GNT, a Pharisee named Νικόδημος ("Nicodemus") was a member of the συνέδριον in Jerusalem (John 3:1, 4, 9; 7:50; 19:39) and perhaps an associate of Gamaliel.[94] Does it not seem somewhat peculiar that a member of the Jewish συνέδριον had a Greek name?[95] Interestingly, the ancient city Mareshah (Tel Maresha) was one of the cities in southern Judah near Lachish[96] where settlers from the time of Alexander the Great hellenized the culture.[97] In Hellenistic times, Mareshah was called Marisa and became a prosperous city located in a crossway along a highway that ran north and south where roads led west to the Mediterranean coast and east to Hebron and Jerusalem. John Hyracanus I, the Hasmonean ruler, conquered the city and allowed the Idumeans who lived there to stay if they converted to Judaism. Although the city had a sparse population, the Romans granted the city's independence in 63 BCE only for it to be destroyed again by the Parthians in 40 BCE.[98] Sixty underground tombs were discovered in 1902 CE that date from the third and second centuries BCE. The inscriptions and graffiti were all in Greek and suggest that although the fathers had Semitic names, they gave Greek names to their sons. Although the date of these inscriptions is outside of the NT period of the first century CE, it does show an entrenched Hellenistic culture. These Greek inscriptions along with Greek iconoclasts uncovered from the nearby village of Beit Jibrin point to the widespread Hellenistic influence in the region of Judea.[99] Arnaldo Momigliano notes the deep penetration of Greek language and thought into Palestine during the Hasmonean era:

> There is no end to the story of the penetration of Greek words, customs, and intellectual habits into Judaea during the rule of the Hasmoneans and the subsequent reign of Herod. The

92. Lieberman, *Greek in Jewish Palestine*, 20.

93. Ibid.

94. Josephus mentions that one of the five sons of the high priest Annas bore the Greek name Theophilus ("Lover of God") and also served as high priest from 37–41 CE (*Ant.* 18.5.3 §123; 19.6.2 §297); see Allen, *Lukan Authorship*, 326–30.

95. Fagal, "Nicodemus," 533.

96. Lachish was one of the principal cities in Judea that served as a royal fortress to protect against foreign invaders and was located between Jerusalem and Gaza. Lachish is identified with Tell ed-Duweir about five miles southwest from Beit Jibrin (ancient Eleutheropolis). See Gold and Schoville, "Lachish," 55–58.

97. DeVries, "Mareshah," 244–45.

98. See *Ant.* 13.9.1 §256–58.

99. Langfur, "Maresha"; see Ortiz, "Archaeology," 104–5.

contradictory statements in Talmudic literature about the value and legitimacy of Greek are based on the reality of the power and influence of Greek culture in Palestine. Hermeneutic rules derived from Greek tradition were adopted by rabbis; Greek legal terminology was borrowed; Greek was used in inscriptions on ritual objects of the Temple; a synagogue in Caesarea used Greek in the liturgy. A famous Talmudic passage (Bab. Sotah 49f.) speaks of 500 students of Greek wisdom and 500 of Hebrew wisdom in the school of Gamaliel (A.D. 100) which is a *symbolic indication of the penetration of Greek culture into rabbinic schools.*[100]

The above circumstances provide insight into Paul's rabbinical training that must have included studies in Greek literature and culture. Paul was able to quote lines from Greek poets (1 Cor 15:33), converse with Greek philosophers (Acts 17:16–21), and adopt the characteristics of Greek rhetoric in his speech and his writings (1 Cor 2:1–4).[101] Paul's letter to Philemon is an example of a letter containing Hellenistic features:

> Although it is Paul's briefest letter and concerns only a single, personal request on behalf of a runaway slave, the Letter to Philemon is one of the purest examples of the Hellenistic letter–writing format as adapted by Paul to fit his own rhetorical style.[102]

Additionally, Paul employs the *paraenetic* style characterized by certain Greek cynics (philosophers) in order to build trusting relationships among the people to whom he ministered (1 Thess 2:1–11).[103] The linguistic territory of Judea, despite its fragmented population, was nonetheless united by the Greek language.[104]

Second, another peculiarity relating to the linguistic character of the GNT is the use of special wordplays that have no equivalent in Aramaic. For example, Jesus posed an important question to his disciples as they travelled into the district of Caesarea Philippi (Matt 16:13).[105] Jesus asked them what

100. Emphasis mine; Momigliano, "Greek Culture," 357–58.

101. Yamauchi, "Hellenism," 386.

102. Huber, *Bible*, 149.

103. Cynics were travelling moral philosophers. Abraham Malherbe argues that the Apostle Paul followed the example of the gentle philosopher in order to differentiate himself from other Greek cynics who had less favorable reception among communities (*Popular Philosophers*). See also Malherbe, "Gentle as a Nurse," 203–17; Paige, "Philosophy," 716–18; Ferguson, *Backgrounds*, 323–26.

104. Mussies, "Greek in Palestine," 1040.

105. The authenticity of this pericope is a matter of dispute among some scholars. For an overview of the historical authenticity of the Gospel of Matthew, see Nolland,

others were saying about him. The disciples responded by offering several notable rumors about his identity—John the Baptist, Elijah, Jeremiah, or one of the other prophets (16:14). Ultimately, however, Jesus wanted to know who they understood him to be. The narrative in the Gospel of Matthew records a monumental confession:

> λέγει αὐτοῖς· ὑμεῖς δὲ τίνα με λέγετε εἶναι; ἀποκριθεὶς δὲ Σίμων Πέτρος εἶπεν· σὺ εἶ ὁ χριστὸς ὁ υἱὸς τοῦ θεοῦ τοῦ ζῶντος. ἀποκριθεὶς δὲ ὁ Ἰησοῦς εἶπεν αὐτῷ· μακάριος εἶ, Σίμων Βαριωνᾶ, ὅτι σὰρξ καὶ αἷμα οὐκ ἀπεκάλυψέν σοι ἀλλ᾽ ὁ πατήρ μου ὁ ἐν τοῖς οὐρανοῖς (Matt 16:15–17).

> He said to them, "But who do you say that I am?" And Simon Peter answered and said, "You are the Christ, the Son of the living God." And Jesus answered and said to him, "Blessed are you Simon Barjonah, for flesh and blood did not reveal *this* to you but My Father who is in heaven."

In response to Peter's confession, Jesus employs a wordplay in order to heighten the truth of Peter's words. The narrative continues as follows:

> κἀγὼ δέ σοι λέγω ὅτι σὺ εἶ Πέτρος, καὶ ἐπὶ ταύτῃ τῇ πέτρᾳ οἰκοδομήσω μου τὴν ἐκκλησίαν καὶ πύλαι ᾅδου οὐ κατισχύσουσιν αὐτῆς (Matt 16:18).

> "And I say to you that you are Peter, and upon this rock I will build my church and the gates of Hades shall not prevail against it."

The wordplay involves the masculine nominal Πέτρος and the feminine nominal πέτρα. At first glance, one notices that the genders of πέτρα and Πέτρος are different. Πέτρος means a "stone" and πέτρα means a "bedrock or massive rock formation" (cf. Luke 8:6 and 13).[106] The LXX translates the Hebrew terms צור ("rock," e.g., Exod 17:6) and סלע ("crag or cliff," e.g., Num 20:8) and כף ("rock," e.g., Job 30:6) with πέτρα.[107] The thought seems to be that although Peter shows himself to be what his surname means—a rock— the truth that he confesses, not he himself, will be the foundational bedrock for the church (cf. Acts 4:8–12).[108] Charles Abraham notes that the pun

---

Matthew, 12–23.

106. Danker, "Πέτρος" and "πέτρα," 809.

107. See צור in Brown, *Hebrew and English Lexicon*, 495. Also צור and כף on pages 700–701 and 849 respectfully.

108. This is contra to Mundle who argues that Jesus declared in this event the primacy of Peter. See Mundle, "Rock," 383–85. See also Wilcox, "Peter and the Rock," 73–88; Caragounis, *Peter*, 44–57, 88–113.

Πέτρος / πέτρα appears to be a spontaneous literary wordplay that shows a high degree of sophistication that affirms that Jesus must have spoken and taught in Greek.[109] The alternation of Greek words is consistent with the way both words were commonly used in Greek.[110] Joseph Fitzmyer argues that the pun also works with Κηφᾶς (*Kēphās*), which is Simon's grecized Semitic surname that corresponds to the Greek surname Πέτρος and with the Aramaic term כאפא (*Kēphā*), which also means "rock."[111] However, the proposed Aramaic version Κηφᾶς / כאפא lacks the sharp distinction of meaning and emphasis that is found in the Greek and overlooks the fact that Jesus did not use Peter's Aramaic name.[112] If the source underlying the pun is Aramaic, there is no reasonable explanation for the switch from direct address to indirect address as indicated by presence of the feminine form of οὗτος ("this").[113] Leon Morris observes that "it is sometimes said dogmatically that Jesus spoke in Aramaic in which there is no distinction of gender, but it must be borne in mind that Jesus may well have spoken in Greek . . . it is

---

109. Abraham's response to "Did Jesus Speak Greek?," 68.

110. Porter, "Did Jesus Ever Teach in Greek?," 231.

111. Fitzmeyer, "Did Jesus Speak Greek?," 68 and 70; Danker, "Κηφᾶς," 544.

112. Bruce makes an interesting observation concerning efforts to appeal to the Syriac Peshitta as evidence of the actual words that might have been spoken by Jesus in Aramaic: "Because the Syriac of the Bible is written in a variant dialect of the language that Jesus spoke, extreme views are sometimes expressed about the forms in which his sayings appear in the Syriac Gospels, as though his actual words in the language in which they were uttered might be found there. The ordinary reader, for example, may readily infer from the writings of Mr. George Lamsa that the Peshitta Gospels preserve the very words of our Lord better than the Greek Gospels do. This, of course, is quite wrong; the Peshitta New Testament is simply a translation of the Greek" (*Books and Parchments*, 200). Ferguson notes that some Syriac traditions distinguish between Peter and rock. The Syriac rendition of the pun in Matt 16:18 is ܟܐܦܐ . . . ܟܐܦܐ (*Kēphā . . . kēphā*, "Rock . . . rock") in the Curetonian version (third/fourth centuries CE) and the Peshitta (fifth century CE); however, the Harclean version (seventh century CE) transliterates the Greek name Πέτρος (*Petros*, "Rock") into the Syriac ܦܛܪܘܣ (*Petros*) and employs the term ܫܘܥܐ (*shoā*, "rocky hill") in order to make the distinction that is found in the Greek text. Since Syriac is a later development of Aramaic, the attempt to preserve the difference suggests that the translators were aware of it. See Ferguson, *Church of Christ*, 48–49; Vööbus, "Versions," 974–78; Jennings, *Syriac New Testament*, 98, 173, and 218; Smith, *Syriac Dictionary*, 567; Sokoloff, *Syriac Lexicon*, 1531; Kiraz, *Syriac Gospels*, 242–43.

113. Nolland states that "the wordplay, particularly when based on a name given by Jesus, lacks meaning unless the name points towards the identity of 'this rock.' The change of words encourages the linking of αὕτη ('this') not to the immediately preceding Πέτρος ('Peter'), but back via v. 17 to the confession of v. 16. This confession will, however, be 'this rock' precisely as Peter's confession since this is what gives substance to the wordplay" (*Matthew*, 669).

hazardous to rest its meaning on a hypothetical Aramaic original."[114] There is an obvious distinction made in the Greek text by the contrasting emphases found in the emphatic second-person pronoun σὺ ("you") and the demonstrative οὗτος.[115] Since the wordplay is a single occurrence of its kind in the Gospel of Matthew, it does not appear to be an intentional fabrication and therefore cannot simply be dismissed as an editorial redaction.[116] Additionally, one might recall that this event occurs north of Palestine in a heavily saturated Gentile population. The city of Ceasarea Philippi (modern Banias) had long been a Hellenistic city before King Agrippa enlarged it and renamed it "Neronias" in honor of the emperor Nero.[117] Though the geographical location does not necessarily demand that Jesus spoke Greek on this occasion, it certainly would have been the best place to do so.[118] As to the matter of whether this narrative is a translation in Greek of the underlying Aramaic, how likely would "translators" of the words of Jesus pointlessly "indulge in clever adornments, and interest in language for its own sake"?[119] The wordplay recorded in Matt 16:18 is too complex to be classified as translation Greek and therefore is more likely to represent the actual words spoken by Jesus.[120]

Third, the GNT shows evidence of grammatical peculiarities that are uncharacteristic of translation Greek. Turner notes that the Greek genitive absolute is a rare construction in translated books of the LXX.[121] The rarest occurrence of the genitive absolute is found in Ecclesiasticus where it is used one time in the book's 1,406 verses. The book of Job, however, has thirteen genitive absolutes out of 1,074 verses which is one in eighty-three verses. When these figures are compared to the original compositions of the Greek books below, the contrast is striking:

---

114. Morris, *Matthew*, 423 n. 29.

115. Ferguson, *Church of Christ*, 48.

116. Carson, *Matthew*, 366–67.

117. McRay, *Archaeology*, 172; Hoerth and McRay, *Bible Archaeology*, 170–71.

118. Porter, "Did Jesus Ever Teach in Greek?," 229.

119. Turner, *Grammatical Insights*, 181.

120. Selby provides a summary of additional words and complex wordplays in the GNT in *Jesus*, 57–81.

121. See chart in Turner, *Grammatical Insights*, 179. Turner also addresses many other grammatical peculiarities found in the GNT.

Table 4.6. The genitive absolute in original Greek compositions

Book	# of Genitive Absolutes / Total # of Verses	Ratio
Wisdom	13 / 439	1 in 34 verses
4 Maccabees	21 / 484	1 in 23 verses
3 Maccabees	27 / 228	1 in 8 verses
2 Maccabees	80 / 555	1 in 7 verses

Source: Turner, Grammatical Insights, 179.

There is wide difference in the frequency of genitive absolutes employed between the translation Greek of the LXX and the free Greek compositions listed above. Consequently, it seems reasonable to assume that the frequency of the genitive absolute is less likely to be used when translations are made from Semitic originals because translators sought to retain a high degree of literalness when translating sacred books.

The frequency of the genitive absolute in the GNT varies between books that are primarily narratives and books that are primarily doctrinal or philosophical in character. For example, the genitive absolute is used on average one in every twenty verses in the Gospel of Matthew, one in every twenty-two verses in the Gospel of Mark, and one in every twenty-six verses in the Gospel of Luke. The genitive absolute is less frequent in the philosophical Gospel of John (one in every seventy-three verses) and even less in the doctrinal books of the Apostle Paul (one in every ninety-seven verses). In the sections of the Synoptic Gospels characterized as sayings or Q sections, the genitive absolute is also used less frequently:[122]

Table 4.7. The occurrence of the genitive absolute in Q and non Q sections

Section	# of Genitive Absolutes / Total # of Verses	Ratio
Non Q (Matt)	48 / 855	1 in 18 verses
Non Q (Luke)	34 / 943	1 in 28 verses
Q in Matt	4 / 213	1 in 53 verses
Q in Luke	9 / 272	1 in 30 verses

Source: Turner, Grammatical Insights, 178.

122. For an overview of the contents of Q, see Stein, Synoptic Gospels, 97–123.

In regard to the statistical information above, Turner offers the following summary:[123]

> Inevitably [the genitive absolute] occurs less frequently in the Q–sections, as there is a predominance of teaching and sparsity of narrative, but in spite of this the incidence of the genitive absolute is very marked when compared with translated books of the Septuagint. For instance, in subject–matter Q is most comparable with Ecclesiasticus and yet even in St. Matthew's version of Q, where it occurs less often than in St. Luke's, the genitive absolute occurs *twenty-eight times as often* as in Ecclesiasticus. If the Q–material was ever in Hebrew or Aramaic—most improbable, in view of these figures—then both versions were very free translation indeed, even paraphrases. Yet that is impossible, for no Christian translator would render the holy sayings of Jesus so freely. Veneration demanded literal treatment, and in this the Septuagint affords the parallel. As reverence for the sacred books increased, so did the degree of literalness in the translation.

The linguistic peculiarities involving special Greek words, wordplays, and grammatical constructions found in the GNT favor an original Greek composition. One must bear in mind that any speculation in regard to the translation Greek of the Gospels is based upon *hypothetical* Aramaic sources. Gundry provides a fitting conclusion:

> We cannot naïvely work on the assumption that everything was originally in Aramaic, that we should seek Aramaic equivalents wherever possible, and that wherever Aramaic equivalents cannot be traced we must reject authenticity. Whether we like it or not, the matter is a great deal more complex. But with the added complications of a trilingual milieu in first-century Palestine, there is the compensation that parts of the gospel tradition which may have sounded too Hellenistic to be authentic may be authentic after all, and that many of the dominical sayings in the present Greek text of the gospels may be closer to the *ipsissima*

---

123. Turner, *Style*, 177. Casey misses the point of Turner's evidence when he states, "Turner's argument from statistics comparing Gospel with LXX usage presupposes that Gospel translator could not differ from LXX translators" (*Aramaic Sources*, 64). Turner's point is that the gospel translators were more likely to have been literal rather than loose when translating an Aramaic Gospel because of its perceived sacredness (Turner, *Style*, 177). If the Gospels of Matthew, Mark, and Luke were written in translation Greek, the genitive absolute would not be so abundant! Therefore, the point is not whether they *could* differ from the habits of the LXX translators, but *would* they intentionally differ from those habits?

verba of Jesus than has been supposed. Many may, in fact, be identical with dominical sayings originally spoken in Greek.[124]

THE IDENTITY OF MATTHEW'S *LOGIA*

The hypothesis that portions of the GNT were dependent upon Aramaic written sources cannot be sustained for the following reasons: (1) the NT was written completely in Greek, (2) there are no extant Aramaic original documents that can provide a reference for comparison as in the case of the Hebrew text and the LXX, and (3) the linguistic peculiarities of the GNT are uncharacteristic of translation Greek. However, there remains one more important area of evidence that directly relates to the origin of the Gospels and particularly to the Gospel of Matthew: the patristic fathers. Since the earlier church writers provide information about gospel origins, the evidence of their testimonies needs to be carefully considered. Before evaluating this tradition, an important question must be addressed: Are there any copies of original Semitic Gospels extant today?

Rabbi Shem–Tob ben Shaprut's Treatise Even Bohan

George Howard wrote a riveting article, "Was the Gospel of Matthew Originally Written in Hebrew?," in which he claimed that new evidence had come to light that might indicate a Semitic original of Matthew's gospel:

> New evidence indicates that the Gospel of Matthew was an original Hebrew composition. Indeed, it is now possible to recover much of this original Hebrew composition from an extant manuscript . . . were the canonical Gospels originally written in Greek? Over the centuries, scholars have argued various positions. Some indeed have suggested that one or more of the Gospels were originally written in Hebrew and then translated into Greek. Others have argued that one or more of the Gospels were written in Aramaic and then translated into Greek. Still others have contended that the Gospels were written in Greek, but that their authors used collections of Aramaic or Hebrew sayings or traditions then extant but now lost. But no original Hebrew or Aramaic manuscripts of the Gospels have ever been recovered.[125]

---

124. Gundry, "Language Milieu," 408.

125. Howard, "Gospel of Matthew," 15–16.

Unfortunately, the last statement indicates that the "new evidence" remains in the realm of hypothetical speculation since no original Semitic manuscripts "have ever been recovered." Howard claims that he has found evidence in a fourteenth-century CE treatise called *Even Bohan* ("the Touchstone") written by Rabbi Shem–Tob ben Shaprut, a native of Tudela in Castile.[126] *Even Bohan* was a polemical treatise arguing for the superiority of Judaism over Christianity. Shem–Tob's treatise contains a Hebrew text of the Gospel of Matthew that Howard believes to be "an original Hebrew composition, not a translation. . . . [T]he kind of Hebrew in which it was written is just what one would expect of a document composed in the first century A.D. and preserved by Jews during the Middle Ages."[127] However, after comparisons were made between *Even Bohan* and the Greek text of the Gospel of Matthew, Howard is forced to make the following conclusion:

> The final question we must ask is whether the Greek Matthew is a translation from the Hebrew. This does not appear to be the case. Although the Greek and the Hebrew are accounts of the same events, basically in the same order, careful analysis of their lexical and grammatical features—and their lack of correspondence—indicates the Greek is not a translation. All efforts to prove that the Greek Matthew is a translation (and that the other canonical Gospels are as well) have utterly failed to convince. Although the canonical Gospels reflect a Semitic background, they are nonetheless Greek compositions, not translations.[128]

Eusebius and the Testimony of Papias

The support for an Aramaic source for the Gospel of Matthew has traditionally been linked to early Christian writers. The earliest record that appears

126. Howard's major work is *The Gospel of Matthew According to a Primitive Hebrew Text* in which he includes a critical edition of "Shem-Tob's 'Hebrew Matthew'" presented along with an English translation (pp. 2–151). This work is also found in a second edition under the title *Hebrew Gospel of Matthew*. See also Howard, "Short Ending of Matthew," 117–20; "Primitive Hebrew Matthew," 60–70; "Codex Sinaiticus," 46–47; and "Shem-Tob's 'Hebrew Matthew,'" 117–26.

127. Howard, "Gospel of Matthew," 20.

128. Ibid., 24. Petersen has shown that "Shem-Tob's 'Hebrew Matthew'" contains readings that match those of the Dutch "Liege Harmony" (copied before Shem-Tob wrote his treatise ca. 1280 CE). Petersen concluded that the textual similarities show that "Shem-Tob's 'Hebrew Matthew'" is likely dependent upon a medieval text of Matthew's gospel that is closely related to the textual traditions of the Vetus Latina, the Vetus Syra, and Tatians's *Diatessaron*. See also Petersen, "Review of The Gospel of Matthew," 722–26; Petersen, "Shem-Tob's 'Hebrew Matthew,'" 490–512.

to indicate that the Gospel of Matthew was originally written in Aramaic or Hebrew comes from a statement made by Papias, a bishop of Hierapolis in Phrygia, in the early second century CE.[129] Unfortunately, the writings of Papias are known only through the writings of others. Eusebius records the testimony of Papias regarding Matthew's gospel:

> This is related by Papias about Mark, and about Matthew this was said, "Matthew collected (συνετάξατο) the oracles (τὰ λόγια) in the Hebrew language (Ἑβραΐδι διαλέκτῳ), and each interpreted (ἡρμήνευσεν) them as best he could" (*Hist. eccl.* 3:39.16 [Lake, LCL]).

The difficulty with this statement concerns the identity of τὰ λόγια ("the oracles"). Traditionally, τὰ λόγια has been identified with a Hebrew or Aramaic Gospel of Matthew from which other translations might have been made.[130] Eusebius records the words of Irenaeus who also refers to the origin of the Gospel of Matthew:

> At the beginning of this work we made a promise to quote from time to time the sayings of the presbyters and writers of the church of the first period, in which they have delivered the traditions which came down to them about the canonical Scriptures. Now Irenaeus was one of these, so let us quote his words, and in the first place those which refer to the sacred Gospels, as follows: "Now Matthew published among the Hebrews a written gospel also in their own tongue, while Peter and Paul were preaching in Rome and founding the church. But after their death Mark also, the disciple and interpreter of Peter, himself handed down to us in writing the things which were preached by Peter" (*Hist. eccl.* 5.8.2 [Lake, LCL]).

Eusebius appears to understand the reference of Irenaeus to τὰ λόγια as the activity that eventually produced the Gospel of Matthew as Peter's sermons provided the source material for Mark's gospel.[131] However, the reference of Papias to the collection of τὰ λόγια is found in his work entitled Λογιῶν κυριακῶν ἐξηγήσεως ("Interpretation of the Oracles of the Lord," *Hist. eccl.* 3.39.1), which appears not to refer to Matthew's gospel but to the sayings or oracles of Jesus that were collected by Matthew. The Greek word ἐξήγησις ("exposition") and the cognate verb ἐξηγέομαι ("to explain") primarily re-

---

129. Michaels, "Apostolic Fathers," 211–12; McKnight, "Matthew," 527; Hagner, "Matthew," 281; Meier, "Matthew," 622–23.

130. Orchard and Riley, *Order of Synoptics*, 111–226.

131. Nolland, *Matthew*, 3.

late to the idea of providing an exposition or an explanation rather than to composing a translation.[132] However, John Nolland argues that since Papias combines Ἑβραΐδι διαλέκτῳ ("Hebrew dialect") with the verb ἡρμήνευσεν ("they interpreted"), the context appears to describe the act of translating; that is, translations were made from the Hebrew into Greek.[133] The implication may be that there were multiple renderings into Greek of the oracles or sayings of Jesus that Matthew had collected.[134] Therefore, τὰ λόγια probably refers to a Sayings Source rather than to an Aramaic Gospel from which the canonical Gospel of Matthew derived. Nolland offers the following observation:

> It is easier to suggest that Matthew's activity (if Papias is working from historically reliable tradition) provided the initial stimulus for the creation of such documents than that Matthew's collection of "oracles" directly underlies them, but the latter is certainly quite possible.[135]

Nolland's argument appears sound. However, in another passage that immediately precedes the reference to Matthew's collection, Eusebius quotes Papias:

> And the Presbyter used to say this, "Mark became Peter's interpreter (ἑρμηνετής) and wrote accurately all that he remembered, not, indeed, in order, of the things said or done by the Lord. For he had not heard the Lord, nor had he followed him, but later on, as I said, followed Peter, who used to give teaching as necessity demanded but not making, as it were, an arrangement (σύνταξιν)[136] of the Lord's oracles (κυριακῶν λογίων), so

---

132. Danker, "ἐξήγησις," 349; ibid., "ἐξηγέομαι"; Thiselton, "ἐξηγέομαι," 573–79.

133. Nolland, *Matthew*, 3. The verb ἑρμηνεύω can mean (1) to explain or to provide an interpretation and (2) to render words into a different language; that is, to translate. See Danker, "ἑρμηνεύω," 393; Thiselton, "ἑρμηνεύω," 579–84.

134. See Nolland, *Matthew*, 3.

135. Ibid. Donald Guthrie notes that the problem with identifying τὰ λόγια as a Sayings Source is that "it is highly unlikely that a source which has left no trace should still have circulated in the time of Papias. The only form in which this theory might be held is to suppose that Papias knew of the report but not of the source itself," Guthrie, *Introduction*, 45. Schleiermacher was the first scholar to propose the existence of an original source of sayings. See Schleiermacher, "Zeugnisse des Papias," 735. There are at least three primary interpretations regarding τὰ λόγια: (1) Matthew originally composed an Aramaic Gospel, (2) Matthew compiled a collection of Aramaic sayings of Jesus that has become the source referred to as "Q," or (3) Matthew gathered a collection of OT oracles relating to Jesus. Guthrie provides a good summary of the various positions (Guthrie, *Introduction*, 44–53).

136. The Greek term means "an orderly account" (Danker, "σύνταξις," 974).

that Mark did nothing wrong in thus writing down single points as he remembered them. For to one thing he gave attention, to leave out nothing of what he had heard and to make no false statements in them" (*Hist. eccl.* 3.39.15 [Lake, LCL]).

That Mark was the interpreter of Peter in that he collected, arranged (though not as orderly as others), and wrote down what Peter taught seems clear from the statement of Papias. In other words, the "interpretation" that Mark provides is not a translation but a presentation of what Peter taught.[137] The phrase κυριακῶν λογίων must not be restricted to refer only to the Lord's sayings but to Mark's gospel as a whole.[138] Consequently, the juxtaposition of κυριακῶν λογίων and τὰ λόγια argues in favor of the view that Papias is not referring simply to the actual sayings of Jesus but to the gospels that both Mark and Matthew composed.

The Testimony of Irenaeus and Pantaenus

As indicated above, the patristic tradition regarding an original Aramaic Gospel of Matthew also finds support from Irenaeus (120–202 CE):

> Matthew also issued a written Gospel among the Hebrews in their own dialect, while Peter and Paul were preaching at Rome, and laying the foundations of the Church. After their departure, Mark, the disciple and interpreter of Peter, did also hand down to us in writing what had been preached by Peter. Luke also, the companion of Paul, recorded in a book the Gospel preached by him. Afterwards, John, the disciple of the Lord, who also had leaned upon His breast, did himself publish a Gospel during his residence at Ephesus in Asia (*Haer.* 3.1.1 [Roberts and Donaldson, *ANF*]).

Eusebius corroborates the above testimony by quoting the words of Irenaeus: "Now Matthew published among the Hebrews a written gospel also in their own tongue (διαλέκτῳ)" (*Hist. eccl.* 5.8.2 [Lake, LCL]). Additionally, Eusebius refers to a tradition concerning an evangelist and teacher named Pantaenus (late second century CE)[139] who discovered a Semitic copy of Matthew's gospel:

137. See McKnight, "Matthew," 527.

138. The statement of Papias concerning the oracles of the Lord cannot be restricted to including only the sayings of Jesus for he indicated that Mark wrote about the things that Jesus said *and* did.

139. Eusebius identifies Pantaenus as head of the school in Alexandria during the time of the Roman Emperor Commodus (180–192 CE, *Hist. eccl.* 5.9.1–4). See also

For indeed there were until then many evangelists of the word who had forethought to use inspired zeal on the apostolic model for the increase and the building up of the divine word. One of these was Pantaenus, and it is said that he went to the Indians, and the tradition is that he found there that among some of those there who had known Christ the Gospel according to Matthew had preceded his coming; for Bartholomew, one of the apostles, had preached to them and had left them the writing of Matthew in Hebrew letters, which was preserved until the time mentioned (*Hist. eccl.* 5.10.2–3 [Lake, LCL]).

The Testimony of Origen

Origen (ca. 185–254 CE) likewise continues to pass down the tradition of the Semitic origin of Matthew's gospel: "As having learnt by tradition concerning the four Gospels, which alone are unquestionable in the Church of God under heaven, that first was written that according to Matthew, who was once a tax-collector but afterwards an apostle of Jesus Christ, who published it for those who from Judaism came to believe, composed as it was in the Hebrew language" (*Hist. eccl.* 6.25.4 [Lake, LCL]).

The Testimony of Epiphanius

Epiphanius (310–403 CE), bishop of Salamis, makes the claim that "Matthew put the setting forth and the preaching of the Gospel into the NT in the Hebrew language and alphabet" (*Pan.* 30.3.7 [Williams, LCL]; see also *Pan.* 29.9.4). He quotes directly from a copy of it on at least seven separate occasions[140] and complains that the manuscript is "not entirely complete, but is corrupt and mutilated—and they call this thing 'Hebrew'!" (*Pan.* 30.13.2 [Williams, LCL]).

Ferguson, *Backgrounds*, 40, 290; Placher states that Pantaenus "apparently set up a special school for intellectually sophisticated converts" (*Christian Theology*, 61).

140. See (1) *Pan.* 30.13.2–3, (2) 4–5, (3) 6, (4) 7–8, (5) 15.4, (6) 16.5, and (7) 22.4. It is likely that Epiphanius is referring to an Ebionite Gospel. The Ebionites were a heretical sect of Christian Jews who found refuge in the Transjordan after the destruction of Jerusalem in 70 CE and remained hostile toward the writings of Paul and Gentiles because of their libertine attitudes toward the law of Moses. See Ferguson, *Backgrounds*, 615–17.

The Testimony of Jerome

The strongest witness to the Semitic origin of the Gospel of Matthew is found in the writings of Jerome (348–420 CE). In *De viris illustribus*, Jerome writes the following:

> Matthew, surnamed Levi, first a publican, then an apostle, composed a Gospel of Christ at first in Judea in Hebrew for the sake of those of the circumcision who believed, but this was afterwards translated into Greek, though by what author is uncertain. Moreover, the Hebrew itself has been preserved until the present day in the library at Caesarea which Pamphilus the martyr so diligently gathered. I have also had the opportunity of having the volume described to me by the Nazarenes of Beroea, a city of Syria, who use it. In this it is to be noted that wherever the Evangelist, whether on his own account or in the person of our Lord the Savior, quotes the testimonies of the Old Testament, he does not follow the authority of the translators of the Septuagint, but the Hebrew. Wherefore these two forms exist: "Out of Egypt have I called my son," and "for he shall be called a Nazarene." (*Vir. ill.* 3.1–4 [Richardson, *NPNF²*]).[141]

Additionally, in another treatise, Jerome provides further insight about the character of the Semitic Gospel of Matthew:

> In the Gospel according to the Hebrews, which is written in the Chaldee and Syriac language, but with Hebrew letters, and is used to this day by the Nazoraeans (I mean the Gospel according to the Apostles, or, as many maintain, the Gospel according to Matthew, a copy of which is in the library at Caesarea) . . . (*Pelag.* 3:2 [Richardson, *NPNF²*]).

The designation "Nazoraeans" seems to have been employed by Jerome to identify a sect of Jewish Christians. "Nazoraeans" probably alludes to the more orthodox strain of the Ebionites who "used the Gospel of Matthew but also produced their own Gospel of the Ebionites" (which would have been an Aramaic translation of the Greek text of Matthew).[142]

---

141. See also *Epist.* 20.5; 120.8; and *Comm. Os.*

142. Ibid.; see also Wessel, "Ebionites," 9–10; Wright, "Ebionites," 313–17; Hagner, "Jewish Christianity," 584–85.

Summary

In light of the patristic witness, Theodor Zahn argued that τὰ λόγια in the writings of Papias originally referred to the original Aramaic Gospel written by Matthew around 61–65 CE and later translated into Greek around 90 CE. Zahn offers the following explanation:

> When now, Papias sets in contrast to the fact that Matthew compiled the Logia in Hebrew, the other fact that for this reason a ἑρμηνεύειν was necessary, which everyone exercised according to his ability, it is self–evident (1) that ἑρμηνεύειν here can mean only translating; and (2) that this was a translation into the Greek language, which did not need to be mentioned expressly, because this was the language of Papias and his readers. Those who knew Hebrew required no translation of a Hebrew document, and the Phrygian bishop knew nothing of hearers or readers unfamiliar with both Hebrew and Greek. (3) The fact deserves more attention than has been paid to it heretofore, that Papias does not speak of the translation of Matthew's writing, but of the words of Jesus which it contained. . . . The language in which Matthew wrote could have been no other than the language of Jesus, "the original language of the gospel" [. . .] the Aramaic vernacular of Palestine.[143]

The problem with Zahn's position is that the Gospel of Matthew does not show evidence of being a translation. Additionally, the patristic writers appear to have alluded to a Semitic translation of the Gospel of Matthew and thereby have incorrectly assumed that Papias inferred that Matthew's original gospel was composed in Hebrew or Aramaic. Robert Gundry argues that the phrase Ἑβραΐδι διαλέκτῳ ("Hebrew language") should be understood as describing the *style* in which Matthew chose to present Jesus as the Messiah, not an Aramaic composition.[144] The obvious Jewishness of Matthew's gospel lends strong support to Gundry's view.[145] Leon Morris makes the following observation about the Jewish characteristic of the Gospel of Matthew:

> The writer seems concerned throughout to show that Christianity is the true continuation of the Old Testament—the true Judaism, if we may put it that way. He was clearly a knowledgeable

143. Zahn, *Introduction*, 511–12, 522.

144. Gundry, *Matthew*, 620.

145. For an overview of the Semitic style of Matthew's gospel see Carson and Moo, *Introduction*, 135–52.

Jew, well acquainted with the kind of teaching we find in the Mishnah and the Talmud, and some would say not averse to the use of Midrash.[146]

Therefore, it is likely that Papias was unconcerned about the language in which Matthew wrote his gospel but very much aware that "Matthew composed a more Jewish, orderly styled Gospel" originally in Greek—the canonical Gospel of Matthew.[147]

146. Morris, *Matthew*, 2–3.

147. McKnight, "Matthew," 527–28.

Conclusion

WHY DOES THE GNT contain an abundance of Semitic characteristics? The principal reason proposed by scholars is that the GNT shows evidence of being dependent upon Aramaic sources. These sources are variously identified as original Aramaic compositions, Aramaic oral traditions, or perhaps a collection of Aramaic sayings of Jesus from which translations were made, normally referred to as "Q" in Synoptic studies.

The Aramaic Hypothesis, however, faces many obstacles, the principal one being that original compositions of the NT in Aramaic have never been found. The absence of Aramaic compositions renders the hypothesis inadequate for the following reasons: (1) The manuscripts of the NT are in Greek, (2) the Greek of the NT is uncharacteristic of translation Greek, and (3) the patristic tradition regarding Aramaic original compositions (e.g., Gospel of Matthew) is less than convincing. Speculations about Aramaic sources underlying the GNT remain theoretical in nature despite the confidence of scholars like Torrey, Burney, Black, and Casey who attempt to provide retro translations of the assumed underlying original Aramaic. It is my contention that the Aramaic Hypothesis is untenable. The question as to whether Jesus spoke in Aramaic is, of course, not assailable. Jesus and his disciples were conversant in several languages. Consequently, the premise that the only authentic statements or words of Jesus are those that have been preserved or reproduced in Aramaic is egregious for several reasons.

First, the Aramaic Hypothesis implies that the writers of the GNT were religious propagandists and not historians and therefore are classified as representatives of later Greek tradition. Joseph Fitzmyer asserts that since the Greek tradition (stage III) was a later development, it therefore should not be confused with the early Aramaic stage (stage I), which includes the historical period of Jesus' teaching and ministry, or with the preaching of Jesus' words and deeds during the apostolic period (stage II).[1] These stages

---

1. Fitzmyer, "Did Jesus Speak Greek?," 63.

represent arbitrary gaps and infer that the information obtained by the writers of the GNT about Jesus was somehow distorted at best and deceptive at
worst.

Second, the Aramaic Hypothesis incorrectly assumes that Aramaic was
the dominant language of Palestine during the first century CE. Rather, the
evidence shows that Greek was the common medium of communication,
not only in Palestine but also throughout the Roman Empire. Additionally,
the impact of Hellenism was extensive in Galilee, in the Decapolis, in Judea,
and in the city of Jerusalem.

Third, the Aramaic Hypothesis is built upon a hypothetic premise that
Aramaic sources existed in the first century CE. There is no Aramaic NT
referent to which comparisons can be made to validate the premise that
the Greek of the NT is a translation. More evidence exists that Jesus and his
disciples knew Greek than that they knew any other language. Nigel Turner
makes a pertinent observation: "Biblical Greek is so powerful and fluent, it
is difficult to believe that those who used it did not have at hand a language
all ready for use."[2]

My premise that Jesus and his primary disciples spoke in Greek is
based upon a collection of key factors, none of which standing alone in-
controvertibly proves my premise. The evidence, however, can be compared
to tent pegs that have been driven into the ground in order to keep a tent
erect and taut. A tent held by an incomplete set of tent pegs is lacking a
secure footing. That Jesus and his disciples utilized the Greek language to
communicate orally in addition to Aramaic and Hebrew is held up by the
following well-driven tent pegs.

First, in chapter 1 I provided an overview of the evidence that supports my thesis. The purpose was to build a context for interpretation and
to provide a methodological road map of investigation. Three significant
overviews formed the introduction in order to lay the groundwork for my
investigation: (1) an overview of languages that existed in the first century
CE, (2) an overview of evidence of Greek in Palestine, and (3) the biblical
evidence that Jesus spoke Greek. The overviews acknowledged the linguistic
diversity of the times, but more importantly they recognized the emergence
of Greek as the medium of communication for gospel in both oral and written form.

Second, in chapter 2 I addressed the emerging linguistic dominance of
Greek by analyzing how Latin, Hebrew, Aramaic, and Greek functioned in
Palestine. Each language had its particular place in society. Latin primarily
served as the language of the Roman administration. Hebrew more or less

2. Turner, *Grammatical Insights*, 183.

functioned as the sacred language of the Jews because it was the medium of the ancient Scripture. Although the native language of many in Palestine was Aramaic, it was fading by the time of the first century CE because Greek had emerged as the *lingua franca* of the Roman Empire. Greek served as the common language that bridged the gap between the government, religion, and commerce. Additionally, the archaeological and literary data revealed that Greek flourished in the region of Galilee. The Hellenistic cities of Caesarea, Tiberias, and Sepphoris along with the cities of the Decapolis formed the cultural background of much of Jesus' ministry.

Third, I presented a detailed investigation of the background of the primary disciples of Jesus in chapter 3. The disciples whom Jesus selected shared a common national and regional connection with him. Their backgrounds were perfectly suited for a bilingual ministry. They were experienced enough with Greek to navigate among Hellenistic Jews, Hebrew (Aramaic) speaking Jews, and Gentiles in Galilee and in Judea.

Finally, in chapter 4 I challenged the hypothesis that the GNT was dependent upon Aramaic oral and written sources. My investigation demonstrated that the main written source utilized by the writers of the GNT was the LXX—an observation difficult to explain by the Aramaic Hypothesis. Additionally, the grammatical peculiarities found in the GNT are indications of original compositions and not Greek translations. The strongest argument for the existence of Aramaic compositions is found in the writings of the early church fathers. However, it is questionable whether the patristic tradition from Papias to Jerome provides clear evidence to support the Aramaic Hypothesis. The matter is unclear and speculative. The Papias reference to the τὰ λόγια of Jesus is difficult to understand, and any hypothesis that rests heavily upon it is suspect. In summary, the following evidence I have presented undergirds my thesis that Jesus and his disciples did in fact communicate in the Greek language:

1. Greek was the common language of the people in Palestine.

2. Galilee was predominantly a Hellenistic region.

3. Jesus and his disciples shared a common Hellenistic and Jewish background.

4. The books (esp. Synoptic Gospels) of the NT were original compositions.

Although the support for the thesis of this study is reasonable and based upon corroborating evidence, there is one most important question yet to address: How does one account for the Semitic characteristics of the

GNT? Since the Aramaic Hypothesis is inadequate to explain the Semitic character of the GNT, another alternative is necessary.

That the GNT is saturated with Semitisms is not disputed. The Semitic elements of structure, style, and grammar in the GNT are noteworthy. Such Semitic impregnation is characteristic of Greek-speaking Jews whose biblical knowledge and spiritual formation most likely grew out of the LXX. Additionally, in a bilingual culture, languages often intertwine, particularly during a period of transition as one might move from predominantly speaking in one's native language to communicating in a second language more often. Greek-speaking Jews during the transition from Aramaic to Greek in the first century CE would naturally have a pronounced Semitic quality and, of course, such a Semitic quality would reveal itself in the GNT.[3] Robinson notes regarding the Gospel of John that it was "written in correct but simple Greek, with what might be called an Aramaic accent."[4] Turner calls it a Semitic "coloring."[5] Roberts makes the following observation concerning the Semitic nature of the Greek characteristic of the writers of the NT:

> Palestine alone can be said to be the country in which the dialect exhibited in the New Testament flourished. In their native land did the apostles learn the style of Greek in which their writings are composed; though, of course, subsequent practice and travel in other Greek–speaking countries somewhat modified the diction which they employed. With far great reason, therefore, might the Greek of the New Testament be styled *Hebraic*, or *Palestinian*, than Hellenistic—a term which is in every respect inappropriate; and the vigorous existence of such a dialect in Palestine, in the days of Christ and His apostles, can only, I believe, be accounted for on the ground that it was the prevailing public language of the country.[6]

I indicated in chapter 1 that the Greek of the NT may have been a hybrid *Palestinian* Greek containing occasional Aramaic words or Semitic expressions. The nature of the evidence has caused me to make a few adjustments that better explain the Semitic qualities contained in the GNT. It is my view, after a thorough investigation, that the common language of Palestine was *koinē* Greek, of which the GNT is a perfect example of the dialect in written form. Additionally, in view of the Semitic background, the influence of the Greek of the LXX, and the Hellenistic influence upon the Jews in Palestine,

3. Turner, "Language of the New Testament," 660 §577e.
4. Robinson, *New Testament*, 82.
5. Turner, "Language of the New Testament," 660.
6. Roberts, *Greek*, 291–92.

a distinctive dialect emerged within *koinē* Greek that characterized the way Jews utilized the Greek language. Therefore, what we have in the GNT is a hybrid *Palestinian* Greek—*koinē* Greek with a Semitic flair—containing an admixture of Aramaic words used in private and semiprivate contexts along with Semitic linguistic peculiarities as spoken by Jesus, his disciples, and the Jews in Palestine during the first century CE.

Bibliography

Abbott, Thomas K. *Essays Chiefly on the Original Texts of the Old and New Testaments.* London: Longmans, Green, 1891.

Abegg, Martin G., Jr. "Hebrew Language." Pages 459–63 in *Dictionary of New Testament Background.* Edited by Craig A. Evans and Stanley E. Porter. Downers Grove: InterVarsity, 2000.

Abraham, Charles. Review of "Did Jesus Speak Greek?" by Joseph A. Fitzmyer. *BAR* 19 (1993) 68.

Achtemeier, Paul J., et al. *Introducing the New Testament: Its Literature and Theology.* Grand Rapids: Eerdmans, 2001.

Adams, J. N. *Bilingualism and the Latin Language.* Cambridge: Cambridge University Press, 2004.

Agnew, F. "On the Origin of the term *Apostolos.*" *CBQ* 38 (1996) 49–53.

Aland, Kurt, ed. *Synopsis of the Four Gospels.* 7th ed. Stuttgart: German Bible Society, 1984.

Albright, William F. *Recent Discoveries in Bible Lands.* Pittsburgh: Biblical Colloquium, 1956.

Albright, William F., and William Foxwell. "The Names 'Nazareth' and 'Nazaraean.'" *JBL* 65 (1946) 397–401.

Allen, David L. *Lukan Authorship of Hebrews.* Nashville: B & H, 2010.

Angus, S., and A. M. Renwich. "Roman Empire and Christianity." Pages 207–21 in vol. 4 of *The International Standard Bible Encyclopedia.* Edited by Geoffrey W. Bromiley. 4 vols. Grand Rapids: Eerdmans, 1988.

Archer, Gleason L. *A Survey of Old Testament Introduction.* 3rd ed. Chicago: Moody, 1994.

Archer, Gleason L., and Gregory C. Chirichigno. *Old Testament Quotations in the New Testament: A Complete Survey.* Chicago: Moody, 1983.

Argyle, A. W. "Did Jesus Speak Greek?" *ExpTim* (December 1955) 92–93.

———. "Greek Among the Jews of Palestine in New Testament Times." *NTS* 20 (1973) 87–89.

Ash, Anthony L. "Jeremiah and Lamentations." *The Living Word Commentary.* Vol. 13. Edited by John T. Willis. Abilene: Abilene Christian University Press, 1987.

Ashkenazi, Eli. "2000 Year Old Amphitheatre Discovered Near Tiberias." *Haaretz,* http://www.haaretz.com/print-edition/news/2-000-year-old-amphitheater-discovered-near-tiberias-1.7564 (accessed on January 22, 2013).

Bagatti, Bellarmino. *The Church from the Circumcisions.* Jerusalem: Franciscan, 1971.

Barr, James. "Abba Is Not Daddy." *JTS* 39 (1988) 28–47.

———. "Hebrew, Aramaic and Greek in the Hellenistic Age." Pages 79–114 in vol. 2 of *The Cambridge History of Judaism*. Edited by W. D. Davies and L. Finkelstein. 4 vols. Cambridge: Cambridge University Press, 1989.

———. "Which Language Did Jesus Speak? Some Remarks of a Semitist." *BJRL* 53 (no date) 9–29.

Batey, Richard A. "Did Antipas Build the Sepphoris Theater?" *Jesus and Archaeology* (2006) 111–19.

———. *Jesus and the Forgotten City: New Light on Sepphoris and the Urban World of Jesus*. Grand Rapids: Baker, 1991.

———. "Jesus and the Theatre." *NTS* 30 (1984) 563–74.

———. "Sepphoris—An Urban Portrait of Jesus." *BAR* 18:3 (1992) 50–64.

Bauckham, Richard J. "2 Peter and the Apocalypse of Peter." In *The Fate of the Dead: Studies on the Jewish and Christian Apocalypses. NovTSup* 93 (1998) 290–303.

———. *Jude, 2 Peter*. Word Biblical Commentary. Edited by Ralph P. Martin. Nashville: Thomas Nelson, 1983.

Baur, David R. "Son of God." Pages 769–75 in *Dictionary of Jesus and the Gospels*. Edited by Joel B. Green et al. Downers Grove: InterVarsity, 1992.

Beale, G. K., and D. A. Carson, eds. *Commentary on the New Testament Use of the Old Testament*. Grand Rapids: Baker Academic, 2007.

Benoit, Pierre, et al. *Les Grottes de Murabba'at*. Discoveries in the Judean Desert 2. Oxford: Clarendon, 1961.

Betz, Hans Dieter. "Paul." Pages 186–201 in vol. 5 of *Anchor Bible Dictionary*. Edited by David Noel Freedman. 6 vols. New York: Doubleday, 1992.

Biblia Hebraica Stuttgartensia. 4th ed. Stuttgart: Deutsche Bibelgesellschaft, 1977.

Black, Matthew. *An Aramaic Approach to the Gospels and Acts*. 3rd ed. Oxford: Clarendon, 1967.

———. "The Recovery of the Language of Jesus." *NTS* 3 (1957) 305–13.

Black, Matthew, and Georg Fohrer, eds. "In Memoriam Paul Kahle." *Beihefte zur Zeitschrift fur die alttestamentliche Wissenschaft* 103 (1968) 17–28. Reprinted in Stanley E. Porter. *The Language of the New Testament: Classic Essays*. Sheffield: Sheffield Academic, 1991.

Blass, Friedrich, and Albert Debrunner. *A Greek Grammar of the New Testament and Other Early Christian Literature*. Translated by Robert W. Funk. Chicago: The University of Chicago Press, 1961.

Blomberg, Craig L. "Thomas." Pages 841–42 in vol. 4 of *The International Standard Bible Encyclopedia*. Edited by Geoffrey W. Bromily. 4 vols. Grand Rapids: Eerdmans, 1988.

Bock, Darrell L. *Acts*. Baker Exegetical Commentary on the New Testament. Grand Rapids: Baker Academic, 2007.

———. *Luke 1:1–9:50*. Baker Exegetical Commentary on the New Testament. Vol. 1. Edited by Moises Silva. Grand Rapids: Baker Academic, 1994.

Bornkamm, Gunther. *Jesus of Nazareth*. Augsbury: Fortress, 1995. Translator of 3rd ed. of *Jesus von Nazareth*. Stuttgart: Verlag W. Kolhammer, GMBH, 1959.

Bowman, Raymond A. "Arameans, Aramaic, and the Bible." *JNES* 8 (1948) 65–90.

———. "Ezra." *Interpreter's Bible*. Edited by George A. Buttrick. Vol. 3. New York: Abingdon, 1954.

————. "Nehemiah." *Interpreter's Bible.* Edited by George A. Buttrick. Vol. 3. New York: Abingdon, 1954.

Brashler, James A. "Jesus, Brothers and Sisters of." Pages 819–20 in vol. 3 of *Anchor Bible Dictionary.* Edited by David Noel Freedman. 6 vols. New York: Doubleday, 1992.

Britto, Francis. *Diglossia: A Study of the Theory with Application to Tamil.* Washington, DC: Georgetown University Press, 1986.

Brown, Colin. "Gift, Pledge, Corban." Pages 34–44 in *New International Dictionary of New Testament Theology.* Edited by Colin Brown. 4 Vols. Grand Rapids: Regency Reference Library, 1986.

————. "Historical Jesus, Quest of." Pages 322–44 in *Dictionary of Jesus and the Gospels.* Edited by Joel B. Green et al. Downers Grove: InterVarsity, 1992.

Brown, Francis. *The Brown-Driver-Briggs Hebrew and English Lexicon (BDB).* Based on the lexicon of William Gesenius as translated by Edward Robinson and edited by E. Rodiger. 1927. Reprint, Peabody, MA: Hendrickson, 2007.

Brown, Raymond E., et al., eds. *The New Jerome Biblical Commentary.* Englewood Cliffs, NJ: Prentice-Hall, 1990.

Bruce, F. F. *The Book of the Acts.* The New International Commentary on the New Testament. Rev. ed. Grand Rapids: Eerdmans, 1988.

————. *The Books and the Parchments.* 5th ed. London: Marshall Pickering, 1991.

————. *Paul: Apostle of the Heart Set Free.* Grand Rapids: Eerdmans, 1996.

————. "Paul the Apostle." Pages 696–720 in vol. 3 of *The International Standard Bible Encyclopedia.* Edited by Geoffrey W. Bromiley. 4 vols. Grand Rapids: Eerdmans, 1986.

Buchanan, George. "Essenes." Pages 147–55 in vol. 2 of *The International Standard Bible Encyclopedia.* Edited by Geoffrey W. Bromiley. 4 vols. Grand Rapids: Eerdmans, 1982.

Burge, Gary M., et al. *The New Testament in Antiquity.* Grand Rapids: Zondervan, 2009.

Burney, C. F. *The Aramaic Origins of the Fourth Gospel.* Oxford: Clarendon, 1922.

Buth, Randall. "Aramaic Language." Pages 86–91 in *Dictionary of New Testament Background.* Edited by C. A. Evans and S. E. Porter. Downers Grove: InterVarsity, 2000.

————. "Aramaic Targumim: Qumran." Pages 91–93 in *Dictionary of New Testament Background.* Edited by C. A. Evans and S. E. Porter. Downers Grove: InterVarsity, 2000.

————. "Mark 3:17 BONEPΓEΣ and Popular Etymology." *JSNT* 10 (1981) 29–33.

Butler, Basil C. *The Originality of St. Matthew.* Cambridge: Cambridge University Press, 1951.

Buttrick, George Arthur, ed. *Interpreter's Bible.* 12 vols. Nashville: Abingdon, 1951–1956.

Cadbury, Henry J. "Lexical Notes on Luke-Acts: The Recent Arguments for Medical Language." *JBL* 45 (1926) 190–209.

————. *The Style and Literary Method of Luke.* Cambridge: Harvard University Press, 1920.

————. "The Tradition." Pages 207–264 in *The Beginnings of Christianity.* Vol. 2. Edited by F. J. F. Jackson and K. Lake. London: Macmillan, 1933.

Caird, G. B. "Ben Sira and the Dating of the Septuagint." *BIOSCS* 7 (1974) 21–22.

Caldecott, W. Shaw, and Samuel J. Schultz. "Ahaz." Pages 76–78 in vol. 1 of *The International Standard Bible Encyclopedia*. Edited by Geoffrey W. Bromiley. 4 vols. Grand Rapids: Eerdmans, 1979.

Caragounis, Chrys C. *Peter and the Rock*. Berlin: Walter de Gruyter, 1990.

———. "Scholarship, Greek and Roman." Pages 1065–86 in *Dictionary of New Testament Background*. Edited by Craig A. Evans and Stanley E. Porter. Downers Grove: InterVarsity, 2000.

Carson, D. A. *Matthew: Chapters 1–12*. The Expositor's Bible Commentary. Edited by Frank E. Gaebelein. Grand Rapids: Zondervan, 1995.

———. *Matthew: Chapters 13–28*. The Expositor's Bible Commentary. Edited by Frank E. Gaebelein. Grand Rapids: Zondervan, 1995.

Carson, D. A., and Douglas J. Moo. *An Introduction to the New Testament*. 2nd ed. Grand Rapids: Zondervan, 2005.

Casey, Maurice. *Aramaic Sources of Mark's Gospel*. Cambridge: Cambridge University Press, 1998.

Chancey, Mark, and Eric M. Meyers. "How Jewish Was Sepphoris in Jesus' Time?" *BAR* 26 (2000) 18–33, 61.

Chilton, Bruce. "Gamaliel." Pages 903–6 in vol. 2 of *Anchor Bible Dictionary*. Edited by David Noel Freedman. 6 vols. New York: Doubleday, 1992.

Cicero. *The Verrine Orations*. Translated by L. H. G. Greenwood. 2 vols. Loeb Classical Library. Cambridge: Harvard University Press, 1935.

Cole, R. Alan. *The Gospel According to Mark: An Introduction and Commentary*. Tyndale New Testament Commentaries. 2nd ed. Grand Rapids: Eerdmans, 1989.

Collins, Raymond F. "John (Disciple)." Pages 383–86 in vol. 3 of *Anchor Bible Dictionary*. Edited by David Noel Freedman. 6 vols. New York: Doubleday, 1992.

———. "Thomas." Pages 528–29 in vol. 6 of *Anchor Bible Dictionary*. Edited by David Noel Freedman. 6 vols. New York: Doubleday, 1992.

Comprehensive Aramaic Lexicon Targumic Studies Module: http://cal 1.cn.huc.edu/ get_a_chapter?file=81002&sub =022&cset=H (accessed May 5, 2013).

Conzelmann, Hans. *Acts of the Apostles*. Philadelphia: Fortress, 1987.

Cotton, Hannah M., and Ada Yardeni. *Aramaic, Hebrew, and Greek Texts from Nahal Hever and Other Sites with an Appendix Containing Alleged Qumran Texts*. Discoveries in the Judean Desert 27. Oxford: Clarendon, 1997.

Cullman, Oscar. *Peter: Disciple, Apostle, Martyr*. 2nd ed. Translated by Floyd V. Filson. Philadelphia: Westminster, 1962.

Dalman, Gustav. *Jesus—Jeshua: Studies in the Gospels*. Translated by P. P. Levertoff. London: KTAV, 1929.

———. Jewish Virtual Library. http://www.jewishvirtuallibrary.org/jsource/judaic/ ejud_0002_0005_0_04821. htm (accessed July 15, 2013).

———. *Sacred Sites and Ways: Studies in the Topography of the Gospels*. Translated by Paul P. Levertoff. New York: Macmillan, 1935.

———. *The Words of Jesus Considered in the Light of Jewish Writings and the Aramaic Language*. Translated by D. M. Kay. Edinburgh: T. & T. Clark, 1902.

Danker, Frederick William, ed. *A Greek English Lexicon of the New Testament and Other Early Christian Literature (BDAG)*. 3rd ed. Chicago: University of Chicago Press, 2000.

Davids, Peter H. *The Epistle of James*. Grand Rapids: Eerdmans, 1982.

————. "Rich and Poor." Pages 701–10 in *Dictionary of Jesus and the Gospels*. Edited by Joel B. Green et al. Downers Grove: InterVarsity, 1992.

De Lacey, Douglas R. "Circumcision." Pages 226–30 *in Dictionary of Later New Testament and Its Developments*. Edited by Ralph P. Martin and Peter Davids. Downers Grove: InterVarsity, 1997.

DeVries, Carl E. "Mareshah." Pages 244–45 in vol. 3 of *The International Standard Bible Encyclopedia*. Edited by Geoffrey W. Bromiley. 4 vols. Grand Rapids: Eerdmans, 1986.

Dio, Cassius. *Dio's Roman History*. Translated by Earnest Cary. 9 vols. Loeb Classical Library. Cambridge: Harvard University Press, 1914–1927.

Dodd, C. H. "The Framework of the Gospel Narrative." *ExpTim* 43 (1932) 396–400.

Draper, H. Mudie. "Did Jesus Speak Greek?" *ExpTim* 67 (1956) 317.

Dunn, James D. G. *Jesus Remembered*. Grand Rapids: Eerdmans, 2003.

————. "Prayer." Pages 617–25 in *Dictionary of Jesus and the Gospels*. Edited by Joel B. Green et al. Downers Grove: InterVarsity, 1992.

————. *Unity and Diversity in the New Testament*. 3rd ed. London: SCM, 2006.

Dvorjetski, Estee. "Healing Waters." *BAR* 30 (2004) 16–27, 60.

Ehrman, Albert. "Judas Iscariot and Abba Saqqara." *JBL* 97 (1978) 572–73.

Ellis, E. Earle. *The Gospel of Luke*. 2nd ed. Grand Rapids: Eerdmans, 1974.

————. *The Old Testament in Early Christianity*. Grand Rapids: Baker, 1991.

Emerton, John A. "The Problem of Vernacular Hebrew in the First Century A. D. and the Language of Jesus." *JTS* 24 (1973) 1–23.

Epiphanius of Salamis. *The Panarion*. Translated by Frank Williams. New York: Brill, 1997.

Eusebius. *Die Praeparatio Evangelica, Die Griecheschen Christlichen Schriftsteller der Ersten Jahrhunderte* 2. Berlin: Akademie-Verlag, 1982.

————. *The Ecclesiastical History*. Translated by Kirsopp Lake. 2 vols. Loeb Classical Library. Cambridge: Harvard University Press, 1926 and 1932.

Evans, Craig A. "Life of Jesus Research: An Annotated Bibliography." *New Testament Tools and Studies* 24. Leiden: Brill, 1996.

Fagal, Harold E. "Nicodemus." Page 533 in vol. 3 of *The International Standard Bible Encyclopedia*. Edited by Geoffrey W. Bromiley. 4 vols. Grand Rapids: Eerdmans, 1986.

Fant, Clyde E., and Mitchell G. Reddish. *Lost Treasures of the Bible*. Grand Rapids: Eerdmans, 2008.

Feldman, Louis H. *Jew and Gentile in the Ancient World*. Princeton, NJ: Princeton University Press, 1993.

Ferguson, Everett. *Backgrounds of Early Christianity*. 3rd ed. Grand Rapids: Eerdmans, 2003.

————. *The Church of Christ: A Biblical Ecclesiology for Today*. Grand Rapids: Eerdmans, 1996.

Fine, Steven. "Synagogue Inscriptions." Pages 114–18 in *Oxford Encyclopedia of Archaeology in the Near East*. Edited by E. M. Myers. Oxford: Oxford University Press, 1996.

Fitzmyer, Joseph A. "Did Jesus Speak Greek?" *BAR* 17–18 (1991–1992) 58–77.

————. *Essays on the Semitic Background of the New Testament*. London: Geoffrey Chapman, 1971.

————. *The Gospel According to Luke I–IX.* Anchor Bible. Garden City, NY: Doubleday, 1981.

————. "The Languages of Palestine in the First Century A.D." *CBQ* 32 (1970) 501–31.

————. *The Semitic Background of the New Testament.* Grand Rapids: Eerdmans, 1997.

————. *A Wandering Aramean: Collected Aramaic Essays.* Missoula, MT: Scholars, 1979.

Fitzmyer, Joseph A., and Daniel J. Harrington. *A Manual of Palestinian Aramaic Texts.* Rome: Editrice Pontificio Istituto Biblico, 1978.

Fraade, Steven D. "Rabinic Views on the Practice of Targum." Pages 258–88 in *The Galilee of Late Antiquity.* Edited by Lee I. Levine. Cambridge: Harvard University Press, 1992.

France, R. T. *The Gospel of Mark.* The New International Greek Testament Commentary. Grand Rapids: Eerdmans, 2002.

————. "Mark and the Teaching of Jesus." Pages 101–36 of *Studies of History and Tradition in the Four Gospels.* Vol. 1 of *Gospel Perspectives.* Edited by R. T France and D. Wenham. Sheffield: JSOT, 1980.

Frend, W. H. C. "Pisidia." Pages 873–74 in vol. 3 of *The International Standard Bible Encyclopedia.* Edited by Geoffrey W. Bromiley. 4 vols. Grand Rapids: Eerdmans, 1986.

Garland, David E. *Colossians and Philemon.* NIV Application Commentary. Grand Rapids: Zondervan, 1998.

————. *Luke.* Exegetical Commentary on the New Testament. Edited by Clinton E. Arnold. Grand Rapids: Zondervan, 2011.

————. "Moses' Seat." Page 425 in vol. 3 of *The International Standard Bible Encyclopedia.* Edited by Geoffrey W. Bromiley. 4 vols. Grand Rapids: Eerdmans, 1986.

————. "Philip the Apostle." Page 833 in vol. 3 of *The International Standard Bible Encyclopedia.* Edited by Geoffrey W. Bromiley. 4 vols. Grand Rapids: Eerdmans, 1986.

Gasque, W. Ward. "Luke." Pages 178–79 in vol. 3 of *The International Standard Bible Encyclopedia.* Edited by Geoffrey W. Bromiley. 4 vols. Grand Rapids: Eerdmans, 1986.

————. "Luke the Historian." Pages 415–29 of *Sir William M. Ramsay: Archaeologist and New Testament Scholar.* Bound in William M. Ramsay's *St. Paul the Traveller and Roman Citizen.* Grand Rapids: Baker, 1982.

Geraty, Lawrence T. "The Khirbet el-Kom Bilingual Ostracon." *BASOR* 220 (1975) 55–61.

————. "Kom, Khirbet el-." Pages 99–100 in vol. 4 of *The Anchor Bible Dictionary.* Edited by David Noel Freedman. 6 vols. New York: Doubleday, 1992.

Gill, David. "Erastus the Aedile." *TynBul* 40:2 (1989) 293–302.

Gillman, Florence Morgan. "James, Brother of Jesus." Pages 620–21 in vol. 3 of *Anchor Bible Dictionary.* Edited by David Noel Freedman. 6 vols. New York: Doubleday, 1992.

Gleason, Archer L. *Encyclopedia of Bible Difficulties.* Grand Rapids: Zondervan, 1992.

Gold, Victor P., and Keith N. Schoville. "Lachish." Pages 55–58 in vol. 3 of *The International Standard Bible Encyclopedia.* Edited by Geoffrey W. Bromiley. 4 vols. Grand Rapids: Eerdmans, 1986.

Gonzalez, Justo L. *The History of Christianity.* Vol. 1. San Francisco: Harper, 1984.

Gordon, Victor R. "Nathanael." Pages 491–92 in vol. 3 of *The International Standard Bible Encyclopedia*. Edited by Geoffrey W. Bromiley. 4 vols. Grand Rapids: Eerdmans, 1986.

Graber, Friedrich, and Dietrich Müller. *New International Dictionary of New Testament Theology*. Edited by Colin Brown. 4 vols. Grand Rapids: Regency Reference Library, 1986.

Green, Joel B. "Gethsemane." Pages 265–68 in *Dictionary of Jesus and the Gospels*. Edited by Joel B. Green et al. Downers Grove: InterVarsity, 1992.

Grinfield, Edward W. *An Apology for the Septuagint*. London: William Pickering, 1850.

Guelich, Robert A. "Mark, Gospel of." Pages 512–25 in *Dictionary of Jesus and the Gospels*. Edited by Joel B. Green et al. Downers Grove: InterVarsity, 1992.

Gundry, Robert. "The Language Milieu of First-Century Palestine." *JBL* 83:4 (1964) 404–8.

———. *Matthew: A Commentary on His Literary and Theological Art*. Grand Rapids: Eerdmans, 1982.

———. *A Survey of the New Testament*. 5th ed. Grand Rapids: Zondervan, 2012.

Guthrie, Donald. *New Testament Introduction*. 4th rev. ed. Downers Grove: InterVarsity, 1990.

Hagner, Donald A. "Gospel According to Matthew." Pages 280–88 in vol. 3 of *The International Standard Bible Encyclopedia*. Edited by Geoffrey W. Bromiley. 4 vols. Grand Rapids: Eerdmans, 1986.

———. "James." Pages 617–18 in vol. 3 of *Anchor Bible Dictionary*. Edited by David Noel Freedman. 6 vols. New York: Doubleday, 1992.

———. "Jewish Christianity." Pages 584–85 in *Dictionary of the Later New Testament and Its Development*. Edited by Ralph P. Martin and Peter H. Davids. Downers Grove: InterVarsity, 1997.

Hanan, Eshel. "The Pools of Sepphoris: Ritual Baths or Bathtubs?" *BAR* 26 (2000) 42–45.

Hanson, K. C., and Douglas E. Oakman, translators. "The Theodotus Inscription." http://www.kchanson.com/ancdocs/greek/theodotus.htm.

Harris, R. Laird. "James." Pages 958–59 in vol. 2 of *The International Standard Bible Encyclopedia*. Edited by Geoffrey W. Bromiley. 4 vols. Grand Rapids: Eerdmans, 1982.

Harrison, Everett F. *Introduction to the New Testament*. Rev. ed. Grand Rapids: Eerdmans, 1971.

Harrison, Robert. "Hellenization in Syria-Palestine: The Case of Judea in the Third Century B. C. E." *BA* 57 (1994) 54–65.

Hayes, John H., and Stuart A. Irvine. *Isaiah*. Nashville: Abingdon, 1987.

Heard, Warren J. "Revolutionary Movements." Pages 688–98 in *Dictionary of Jesus and the Gospels*. Edited by Joel B. Green et al. Downers Grove: InterVarsity, 1992.

Hemer, Colin J. *The Book of Acts in the Setting of Hellenistic History*. Edited by H. Gempf. Winona Lake, IN: Eisenbrauns, 1990.

Hendriksen, William. *Exposition of the Gospel According to Luke*. New Testament Commentary. Grand Rapids: Baker, 1978.

Hengel, Martin. *Judaism and Hellenism: Studies in Their Encounter in Palestine During the Early Hellenistic Period*. Translated by John Bowden. Vol. 2. Philadelphia: Fortress, 1974.

Hengel, Martin, and Anna Maria Schwemer. *Paulus zwischen Damaskus und Antiochian wissenschaftliche Untersuchungen zum Neuen Testament 108.* Tubingen: Mohr-Siebeck, 1998.

Herron, Robert. "The Origin of the New Testament Apostolate." *WTJ* 45 (1983) 101–31.

Hess, Richard. "פרש." Pages 700–701 in vol. 3 of *New International Dictionary of Old Testament Theology and Exegesis.* Edited by Willem A. Van Gemeren. 5 vols. Grand Rapids: Zondervan, 1997.

Hirschfeld, Yizhar. "Excavations at Tiberias Reveal Remains of Church and Possibly Theatre." *BA* 54:3 (1971) 70–71.

Hobart, William K. *The Medical Language of Luke.* Dublin: Hodges, Figgis, 1882. Repr., Ann Arbor, MI: Cushing-Mallory, 1954.

Hoehner, Harold W. "Hasmoneans." Pages 21–27 in vol. 2 of *The International Standard Bible Encyclopedia.* Edited by Geoffrey W. Bromiley. 4 vols. Grand Rapids: Eerdmans, 1982.

———. "Herod." Pages 694–96 in vol. 2 of *The International Standard Bible Encyclopedia.* Edited by Geoffrey W. Bromiley. 4 vols. Grand Rapids: Eerdmans, 1982.

Hoerth, Alfred, and John McRay. *Bible Archaeology: An Exploration of the History and Culture of Early Civilizations.* Grand Rapids: Baker, 2005.

Holladay, Carl R. "Eupolemus." Pages 671–72 in vol. 2 of *Anchor Bible Dictionary.* Edited by David Noel Freedman. 6 vols. New York: Doubleday, 1992.

———. *Fragments from Hellenistic Jewish Authors.* Vol. 1 of Historians, Society of Biblical Literature Texts and Translations 20; Pseudepigrapha Series 10. Chico, CA: Scholars, 1983.

Holladay, William L., ed. *A Concise Hebrew and Aramaic Lexicon of the Old Testament.* Grand Rapids: Eerdmans, 1988.

Horsley, Richard A. *Archaeology, History, and Society in Galilee: The Social Context of Jesus and the Rabbis.* Valley Forge: Trinity Press International, 1996.

Horst, Pieter W. van der. "Jewish Funerary Inscriptions—Most Are in Greek." *BAR* 18:4 (1992) 46–49, 54–57.

Howard, George. *The Gospel of Matthew According to a Primitive Hebrew Text.* Macon, GA: Mercer University Press, 1987.

———. *Hebrew Gospel of Matthew.* Macon, GA: Mercer University Press, 1995.

———. "A Note on Codex Sinaiticus and Shem-Tob's Hebrew Matthew." *NovT* 34 (1992) 46–47.

———. "A Note on Shem-Tob's Hebrew Matthew and the Gospel of John." *JSNT* 47 (1992) 117–26.

———. "A Note on the Short Ending of Matthew." *HTR* 81 (1988) 117–20.

———. "A Primitive Hebrew Gospel of Matthew and the Toldoth Yeshu." *NTS* 34 (1992) 60–70.

———. "Was the Gospel of Matthew Originally Written in Hebrew?" *BRev* (1986) 15–16.

Howard, Wilbert F. *John.* Interpretor's Bible. Edited by George A. Buttrick. 12 vols. New York: Abingdon, 1952.

Huber, Robert V., ed. *The Bible Through the Ages.* Pleasantville, NY: Reader's Digest, 1996.

Hughes, Philip. "The Languages Spoken By Jesus." Pages 127–43 in *New Dimensions in New Testament Study.* Edited by Richard N. Longenecker and Merrill C. Tenney. Grand Rapids: Zondervan, 1974.

Hurtado, Larry W. "God." Pages 270–76 in *Dictionary of Jesus and the Gospels*. Edited by Joel B. Green et al. Downers Grove: InterVarsity, 1992.

———. "Muratorian Fragment." Pages 33–34 in vol. 3 of *The International Standard Bible Encyclopedia*. Edited by Geoffrey W. Bromiley. 4 vols. Grand Rapids: Eerdmans, 1986.

Jefford, Clayton N. "Mark, John." Pages 557–58 in vol. 4 of *Anchor Bible Dictionary*. Edited by David Noel Freedman. 6 vols. New York: Doubleday, 1992.

Jennings, William. *Lexicon to the Syriac New Testament*. Oxford: Clarendon, 1926.

Jeremias, Joachim. *The Prayers of Jesus*. Naperville, IL: Allenson, 1967.

Jerome. *De viris illustribus*. http://khazarzar.skeptic.net/books/hieronym/viris_g.htm and http://www.newadvent.org/fathers/2708.htm (accessed April 10, 2013).

Jervis, L. Ann. *Galatians*. New International Bible Commentary. Vol. 9. Edited by W. Ward Gasque. Peabody, MA: Hendrickson, 1999.

Johnson, Luke T. *The Writings of the New Testament: An Interpretation*. Philadelphia: Fortress, 1986.

Jones, A. H. M. "I Appeal to Caesar." *Studies in Roman Government and Law*. New York: Praeger, 1960.

Josephus. Translated by H. St. J. Thackeray et al. 12 vols. Loeb Classical Library. Cambridge: Harvard University Press, 1926–1965.

Kee, Howard C. "Early Christianity in the Galilee: Reassessing the Evidence from the Gospels." Page 21 in *Galilee in Late Antiquity*. Edited by Lee I. Levine. New York: Jewish Theological Seminary of America, 1992.

Kerr, Colin M. "Andrew." Pages 122–23 in vol. 1 of *The International Standard Bible Encyclopedia*. Edited by Geoffrey W. Bromiley. 4 vols. Grand Rapids: Eerdmans, 1979.

Kingdon, H. Paul. "Who Were the Zealots and Their Leaders in A. D. 66?" *NTS* 17 (1970) 60–75.

Kiraz, Georg Anton. *Comparative Edition of the Syriac Gospels: Aligning the Sinaiticus, Curetonianus, Peshitta and Harklean Versions*. Vol. 1. New York: Brill, 1996.

Klein, Ralph W. *Textual Criticism of the Old Testament: The Septuagint After Qumran*. Philadelphia: Fortress, 1974.

Knox, Wilfred L. *Some Hellenistic Elements in Primitive Christianity*. London: British Academy, 1944.

Koester, Helmut. *History, Culture, and Religion of the Hellenistic Age*. Introduction to the New Testament. Vol. 1. 2nd ed. New York: Walter de Gruyter, 1995.

———. *History and Literature of Early Christianity*. Introduction to the New Testament. 2nd ed. New York: Walter de Gruyter, 2000.

Kruger, Michael J. "The Authenticity of 2 Peter." *JETS* 42 (1999) 645–71.

Kruse, Colin G. "Apostle." Pages 27–33 in *Dictionary of Jesus and the Gospels*. Edited by Joel B. Green et al. Downers Grove: InterVarsity, 1992.

Kuhrt, Amelie, and Susan M. Sherwin-White, eds. *Hellenism in the East: The Interaction of Greek and Non-Greek Civilizations from Syria to Central Asia After Alexander*. London: Duckworth, 1987.

Kummel, Banjoki Werner Georg. *Introduction to the New Testament*. Rev. ed. Translated by Howard Clark Kee. Nashville: Abingdon, 1975.

Lamsa, George M. *New Testament Origin*. Chicago: Aramaic Bible Society, 1947.

Langfur, Stephen. "Maresha/Beit Guvrin." http://www.netours.com/content/view/239/69/1/4/ (accessed June 24, 2013).

LaSor, William S. "Aramaic." Pages 229–33 in vol. 1 of *The International Standard Bible Encyclopedia.* Edited by Geoffrey W. Bromiley. 4 vols. Grand Rapids: Eerdmans, 1979.

———. "Palestine." Pages 632–48 in vol. 3 of *The International Standard Bible Encyclopedia.* Edited by Geoffrey W. Bromiley. 4 vols. Grand Rapids: Eerdmans, 1986.

Laughlin, John C. H. "Capernaum from Jesus' Time and After." *BAR* 19:5 (1993) 54–61, 90.

Levine, Lee I., ed. *The Galilee in Late Antiquity.* Cambridge: Harvard University Press, 1992.

Lieberman, Saul. *Greek in Jewish Palestine; Hellenism in Jewish Palestine.* New York: Jewish Theological Seminary of America, 1942. Repr., New York: Jewish Theological Seminary of America, 1994.

Lightfoot, J. B. *St Paul's Epistles to the Colossians and to Philemon.* London: Macmillan, 1879. Repr., Grand Rapids: Zondervan, 1959.

Liverani, Mario. "Semites." Pages 388–92 in vol. 4 of *The International Standard Bible Encyclopedia.* Edited by Geoffrey W. Bromiley. 4 vols. Grand Rapids: Eerdmans, 1988.

MacDonald, Dennis R. "Andrew." Pages 242–43 in vol. 1 of *Anchor Bible Dictionary.* Edited by David Noel Freedman. 6 vols. New York: Doubleday, 1992.

Malherbe, Abraham. "Gentle as a Nurse: the Stoic Background to 1 Thess. II." *NovT* 12 (1970) 203–17.

———. *Paul and the Popular Philosophers.* Minneapolis: Fortress, 1989.

Marshall, I. Howard. "Acts." Pages 513–606 in *Commentary on the New Testament Use of the Old Testament.* Edited by G. K. Beale and D. A. Carson. Grand Rapids: Baker Academic, 2007.

———. *The Gospel of Luke.* Exeter: Paternoster, 1978.

———. "Sanhedrin." Pages 363–64 in vol. 1 of *New International Dictionary of New Testament Theology.* Edited by Colin Brown. 4 vols. Grand Rapids: Zondervan, 1975.

Martin, Ralph P. "Gospel According to Mark." Pages 248–59 in vol. 3 of *The International Standard Bible Encyclopedia.* Edited by Geoffrey W. Bromiley. 4 vols. Grand Rapids: Eerdmans, 1986.

———. *Mark: Evangelist and Theologian.* Grand Rapids: Zondervan, 1973.

———"Mark, John." Pages 259–60 in vol. 3 of *The International Standard Bible Encyclopedia.* Edited by Geoffrey W. Bromiley. 4 vols. Grand Rapids: Eerdmans, 1986.

———. "Peter." Pages 802–7 in vol. 3 of *The International Standard Bible Encyclopedia.* Edited by Geoffrey W. Bromiley. 4 vols. Grand Rapids: Eerdmans, 1986.

Martin, Thomas W. "Matthias." Page 644 in vol. 4 of *Anchor Bible Dictionary.* Edited by David Noel Freedman. 6 vols. New York: Doubleday, 1992.

Marx, Werner G. "Luke, the Physician, Re-examined." *ExpTim* 91 (1980) 168–72.

Mayor, Joseph B. *The Epistles of Jude and 2 Peter.* Grand Rapids: Baker, 1979.

McFall, Leslie. "Hebrew Language." Pages 657–63 in vol. 2 of *The International Standard Bible Encyclopedia.* Edited by Geoffrey W. Bromiley. 4 vols. Grand Rapids: Eerdmans, 1982.

McKnight, Scot. "Matthew, Gospel of." Pages 526–41 in *Dictionary of Jesus and the Gospels.* Edited by Joel B. Green et al. Downers Grove: InterVarsity, 1992.

McRay, John. *Archaeology and the New Testament*. Grand Rapids: Baker, 1991.

———. *Paul: His Life and Teaching*. Grand Rapids: Eerdmans, 2003.

Meier, John P. "Matthew, Gospel of." Pages 622–41 in *Anchor Bible Dictionary*. Edited by David Noel Freedman. 6 vols. New York: Doubleday, 1992.

Meleager of Gadara. *Fifty Poems of Meleager*. Translated by Walter Headlam. London: Macmillan, 1890.

Metzger, Bruce M. *The Canon of the New Testament: Its Origin, Development, and Signification*. Oxford: Clarendon, 1987.

———. *The Text of the New Testament: Its Transmission, Corruption, and Restoration*. 3rd ed. Oxford: Oxford University Press, 1992.

———. *A Textual Commentary on the Greek New Testament*. 2nd ed. Stuttgart: Biblia-Druck, 1994.

Meye, Robert P. "Disciple." Pages 947–48 in vol. 1 of *The International Standard Bible Encyclopedia*. Edited by Geoffrey W. Bromiley. 4 vols. Grand Rapids: Eerdmans, 1979.

Meyers, Eric M. "Jesus and His Galilean Context." Page 63 in *Archaeology and the Galilee: Texts and Contexts in the Graeco-Roman and Byzantine Periods*. Edited by D. R. Edwards and C. Thomas McCollough. Atlanta: Scholars, 1997.

———. "Roman Sepphoris in Light of New Archaeological Evidence and Recent Research." Pages 321–37 in *The Galilee in Late Antiquity*. Edited by Lee I. Levine. Cambridge: Cambridge University Press, 1992.

———. "Yes, They Are." *BAR* 26 (2000) 46–50.

Meyers, Eric M., and James F. Strange. "Survey in Galilee, 1976." *Explor* 3 (1977) 7–18.

Meyers, Eric M., et al. "The Meiron Excavation Project: Archaeological Survey in Galilee and Golan, 1976." *BASOR* 230 (1978) 1–24.

———. *Sepphoris*. Winona Lake, IN: Eisenbrauns, 1992.

———. "Sepphoris, Ornament of All Galilee." *BAR* 49 (1986) 4–19.

Michaels, J. Ramsey. "Apostolic Fathers." Pages 203–13 in vol. 1 of *The International Standard Bible Encyclopedia*. Edited by Geoffrey W. Bromiley. 4 vols. Grand Rapids: Eerdmans, 1979.

———. "Peter, Second Epistle of." Pages 815–19 in vol. 3 of *The International Standard Bible Encyclopedia*. Edited by Geoffrey W. Bromiley. 4 vols. Grand Rapids: Eerdmans. 1986.

Millard, Alan. *Reading and Writing in the Time of Jesus*. Washington Square, NY: New York University Press, 2000.

Minkoff, Harvey, ed. *Approaches to the Bible: The Best of Bible Review, Composition, Transmission and Language*. Vol. 1. Washington, DC: Biblical Archaeology Society, 1994.

Mitchell, T. C., and R. Joyce. "The Musical Instruments in Nebuchadrezzar's Orchestra." Pages 19–27 of *Notes on Some Problems in the Book of Daniel*. London: Tyndale, 1965.

Momigliano, Arnaldo D. "Greek Culture and the Jews." Pages 357–58 in *The Legacy of Greece: A New Appraisal*. Edited by Moses I. Finley. Oxford: Clarendon, 1981.

Moo, Douglas J. *The Letter of James*. Pelican New Testament Commentaries. Grand Rapids: Eerdmans, 2000.

Morris, Leon. *The Gospel According to Matthew*. The Pillar New Testament Commentary. Grand Rapids: Eerdmans, 1992.

————. "John the Apostle." Pages 1107–8 in vol. 2 of *The International Standard Bible Encyclopedia*. Edited by Geoffry W. Bromiley. 4 vols. Grand Rapids: Eerdmans, 1982.

Motyer, Alec. *The Prophecy of Isaiah*. Downers Grove: InterVarsity, 1993.

Moule, C. F. D. "Once More, Who Were the Hellenists?" *ExpTim* 70 (1958–59) 100–102.

Moulton, James H. *Prolegomena*. A Grammar of New Testament Greek. 3rd ed. Vol. 1. Edinburgh: T. & T. Clark, 1908.

Mounce, Robert H. "Cana." Pages 584–85 in vol. 1 of *The International Standard Bible Encyclopedia*. Edited by Geoffrey W. Bromiley. 4 vols. Grand Rapids: Eerdmans, 1979.

————. "Nazareth." Pages 500–501 in vol. 3 of *The International Standard Bible Encyclopedia*. Edited by Geoffrey W. Bromiley. 4 vols. Grand Rapids: Eerdmans, 1986.

Muller, Dietrich. "Disciple." Pages 483–90 in vol. 1 of *New International Dictionary of New Testament Theology*. Edited by Colin Brown. 4 vols. Grand Rapids: Regency Reference Library, 1986.

Munck, Johannes. "The Acts of the Apostles." *Anchor Bible*. Vol. 31. New York: Doubleday, 1967.

Mundle, Wilhelm. "Rock." Pages 381–99 in vol. 3 of *New International Dictionary of New Testament Theology*. Edited by Colin Brown. Grand Rapids: Zondervan, 1935.

Murray, Gilbert A. *Five Stages of Greek Religion*. New York: Columbia University Press, 1925.

Mussies, Gerard. "Greek as the Vehicle for Early Christianity." *NTS* 29 (1983) 356–69.

————. "Greek in Palestine and the Diaspora." Pages 1040–64 in *The Jewish People in the First Century*. Edited by S. Safrai and M. Stern. Philadelphia: Fortress, 1987.

————. "Languages (Greek)." Pages 195–203 in vol. 2 of *Anchor Bible Dictionary*. Edited by David Noel Freedman. 6 vols. New York: Doubleday, 1992.

Myers, Jacob M. *I and II Esdras: Introduction, Translation, and Commentary*. New York: Doubleday, 1974.

Neusner, Jacob. "b. B. Bat. 21a." *The Babylonian Talmud: A Translation and Commentary*. Vol. 15. Peabody, MA: Hendrickson, 2005.

————. *Introduction to Rabbinic Literature*. New York: Doubleday, 1994.

————. *The Mishnah: A New Translation*. New Haven, CT: Yale University Press, 1988.

————. *Sifre to Deuteronomy: An Analytical Translation*. Vol. 2. Atlanta: Scholars, 1978.

Neyrey, Jerome H. *Paul, in Other Words: A Cultural Reading of His Letters*. Louisville: Westminster, 1990.

Nolland, John. *The Gospel of Matthew*. New International Greek Testament Commentary. Grand Rapids: Eerdmans, 2005.

Oepke, Albrecht. "Probleme der vorchristlichen Zeit des Paulus." *TSK* 105 (1933) 411–43.

Orchard, Bernard, and Harold Riley. *The Order of the Synoptics: Why Three Synoptic Gospels?* Macon, GA: Mercer University Press, 1987.

Ortiz, Steven M. "Archaeology of the Land of Israel." Pages 100–111 in *Dictionary of New Testament Background*. Edited by C. A. Evans and S. E. Porter. Downers Grove: InterVarsity, 2000.

Osborne, Grant R. *The Hermeneutical Spiral: A Comprehensive Introduction to Biblical Interpretation*. Downers Grove: InterVarsity, 2000.

Oswalt, John N. *The Book of Isaiah: Chapters 1–39*. Grand Rapids: Eerdmans, 1986.

Overman, Andrew. "Who Were the First Urban Christians? Urbanization in Galilee in the First Century." Pages 16–68 in *Society of Biblical Literature Seminar Papers*. Edited by David J. Lull. Atlanta: Scholars, 1988.

Packer, James I. "Inspiration." Page 693 in vol. 2 of *The Illustrated Bible Dictionary*. Edited by James D. Douglas. Leicester: InterVarsity, 1980.

Paige, Terence. "Philosophy." Pages 713–18 in *Dictionary of Paul and His Letters*. Edited by Gerald Hawthorne et al. Downers Grove: InterVarsity, 1993.

Painter, John. *Just James: the Brother of Jesus in History and Tradition*. 2nd ed. Columbia: University of South Carolina Press, 2004.

Parker, Pierson. *The Gospel Before Mark*. Chicago: University of Chicago Press, 1953.

Pearson, Brook W. R. "Alexander the Great." Pages 20–23 in *Dictionary of New Testament Background*. Edited by C. A. Evans and S. E. Porter. Downers Grove: InterVarsity, 2000.

Peisker, Carl H., and Colin Brown. "Open." Pages 560, 726–29 in vol. 2 of *New International Dictionary of New Testament Theology*. Edited by Colin Brown. 4 vols. Grand Rapids: Zondervan, 1986.

Perumalil, A. C. "Are Not Papias and Irenaeus Competent to Report on the Gospels?" *ExpTim* 91 (1980) 332–37.

Petersen, William L. "Review of the Gospel of Matthew According to a Primitive Hebrew Text." *JBL* 108 (1989) 722–26.

———. "The Vorlage of Shem-Tob's 'Hebrew Matthew.'" *NTS* 44 (1998) 490–512.

Pfann, Stephen, et al. "Surveys and Excavations at the Nazareth Village Farm (1997–2002): Final Report." *BAIAS* 25 (2007) 19–21.

Philo. *On the Confusion of Tongues*. Translated by F. H. Colson and G. H. Whitaker. 10 vols. Loeb Classical Library. Cambridge: Harvard University Press, 1968.

Placher, William. *A History of Christian Theology: An Introduction*. Philadelphia: Westminster, 1983.

Plumacher, Eckard. "Luke as Historian." Pages 398–402 in vol. 4 of *Anchor Bible Dictionary*. Edited by David Noel Freedman. 6 vols. Translated by Dennis Martin. New York: Doubleday, 1992.

Plummer, Alfred. *A Critical and Exegetical Commentary on the Gospel According to Saint Luke*. International Critical Commentary. Edinburgh: T. & T. Clark, 1986.

Polycrates. Early Christian Writings. http://www.earlychristianwritings.com/polycrates.htm (accessed February 19, 2013).

Porter, Stanley E. *The Criteria for Authenticity in Historical-Jesus Research*. Sheffield: Sheffield Academic, 2000.

———. "Did Jesus Ever Teach in Greek?" *TynBul* 44 (1993) 199–235.

———. *The Language of the New Testament: Classic Essays*. Sheffield: Sheffield Academic, 1991.

———. "Manuscripts, Greek New Testament." Pages 670–78 in *Dictionary of New Testament Background*. Edited by C. A. Evans and S. E. Porter. Downers Grove: InterVarsity, 2000.

———. "Septuagint/Greek Old Testament." Pages 1099–1106 in *Dictionary of New Testament Background*. Edited by C. A. Evans and S. E. Porter. Downers Grove: InterVarsity, 2000.

Qimron, Elisha, and J. Strugnell. *Qumran Cave 4.5: Misqsat Mase ha-Torah*. Discoveries in the Judean Desert 10. Oxford: Clarendon, 1994.

Rahlfs, Alfred, ed. *Septuaginta*. Vol. 2. Stuttgart: Deutsche Bibelstftung, 1935.

Ramm, Bernard. *Protestant Biblical Interpretation*. 3rd ed. Grand Rapids: Baker, 1970.

Redditt, Paul L. "Judas." Pages 1088–90 in vol. 3 of *Anchor Bible Dictionary*. Edited by David Noel Freedman. 6 vols. New York: Doubleday, 1992.

————. "Jude, Epistle of." Pages 1098–1103 in vol. 3 of *Anchor Bible Dictionary*. Edited by David Noel Freedman. 6 vols. New York: Doubleday, 1992.

Reich, Ronny. "They Are Ritual Baths." *BAR* 28 (2002) 50–55.

"Resurrecting Nazareth." *BAR* 25:3 (1999) 16.

Rey-Coquais, Jean-Paul. "Decapolis." Pages 116–21 in vol. 2 of *Anchor Bible Dictionary*. Edited by David Noel Freedman. 6 vols. New York: Doubleday, 1992.

Richard, Earl, ed. "Luke: Author and Thinker." *New Views on Luke and Acts*. Collegeville, MN: Liturgical, 1990.

Riesner, Rainer. "Archaeology and Geography." Pages 33–46 in *Dictionary of Jesus and the Gospels*. Edited by Joel B. Green et al. Downers Grove: InterVarsity, 1992.

————. *Paul's Early Period: Chronology, Mission Strategy, Theology*. Translated by Doug Scott. Grand Rapids: Eerdmans, 1998.

Rife, John M. "Greek Language of the New Testament." Pages 568–73 in vol. 2 of the *International Standard Bible Encyclopedia*. Edited by Geoffrey W. Bromiley. 4 vols. Grand Rapids: Eerdmans, 1982.

————. "The Mechanics of Translation Greek." *JBL* 52:4 (1993) 244–52.

Roberts, Alexander. *Greek: The Language of Christ and His Apostles*. London: Longmans, Green, 1888.

Robertson, A . T. "The Language of the New Testament." Pages 1826–32 in vol. 3 of *The International Standard Bible Encyclopedia*. Edited by James Orr. 5 vols. Grand Rapids: Eerdmans, 1955.

————. *Luke the Historian in Light of Research*. Edinburgh: T. & T. Clark, 1920.

Robinson, John A. T. *Can We Trust the New Testament?* Grand Rapids: Eerdmans, 1977.

Robinson, William C. "Apostle." Pages 192–95 in vol. 1 of *The International Standard Bible Encyclopedia*. Edited by Geoffrey W. Bromiley. 4 vols. Grand Rapids: Eerdmans, 1979.

Schleiermacher, Friedrich. "Uber die Zeugnisse des Papias von unsern beiden ersten Evangelien." *TSK* 5 (1932) 735.

Schmidt, Thomas E. "Taxes." Pages 804–7 in *Dictionary of Jesus and the Gospels*. Edited by Joel B. Green et al. Downers Grove: InterVarsity, 1992.

Schreckenberg, Heinz. "Josephus, Flavius." Pages 1132–33 in vol. 2 of *The International Standard Bible Encyclopedia*. Edited by Geoffrey W. Bromiley. 4 vols. Grand Rapids: Eerdmans, 1982.

Schultz, Samuel J. "Hezekiah." Pages 703–5 in vol. 2 of *The International Standard Bible Encyclopedia*. Edited by Geoffrey W. Bromiley. 4 vols. Grand Rapids: Eerdmans, 1982.

Schurer, Emil. A *History of the Jewish People in the Time of Jesus Christ*. Div. 2. Vol. 1. Translated by Sophia Taylor and Peter Christie. 1890. Repr., Peabody, MA: Hendrickson, 2009.

Schuster, Angela M. H. "Ancient Sepphoris." *Arch* 50 (1997) 64–66.

Schweitzer, Albert. *The Quest of the Historical Jesus: A Critical Study of Its Progress from Reimarus to Wrede*. Translated by W. Montgomery. London: Adam and Charles Black, 1910.

Schweizer, Eduard. *Lordship and Discipleship*. London: SCM, 2012.

Scott, Julius, Jr. "Matthias." Pages 288–89 in vol. 3 of *The International Standard Bible Encyclopedia*. Edited by Geoffrey W. Bromiley. 4 vols. Grand Rapids: Eerdmans, 1986.

Selby, G. R. *Jesus, Aramaic & Greek*. Doncaster, UK: Brynmill, 1989.

Septuaginta. Stuttgart: Deutsche Bibelstftung, 1935.

Sevenster, Jan N. *Do You Know Greek? How Much Greek Could the First Jewish Christians Have Known?* Translated by J. de Bruin. Leiden: Brill, 1968.

Sherwin-White, A. N. *The Roman Citizenship*. Oxford: Clarendon, 1939.

Shurkin, Michael. "Digging Up Ancient Tiberias." *BAR* 30 (2004) 12.

Silva, Moises. "Bilingualism and the Character of Palestinian Greek." Pages 205–66 in *Language of the New Testament: Classic Essays*. JSNTSup. Sheffield: Sheffield Academic, 1991.

Smelik, Willem. "The Languages of Roman Palestine." In *The Oxford Handbook of Jewish Daily Life in Roman Palestine*. Edited by Catherine Hezser. Oxford: Oxford University Press, 2010.

Smith, J. Payne, ed. *A Compendious Syriac Dictionary*. Repr., Oxford: Clarendon, 1994.

Soderlund, Sven K. "Septuagint." Pages 400–409 in vol. 4 of *The International Standard Bible Encyclopedia*. Edited by Geoffrey W. Bromiley. 4 vols. Grand Rapids: Eerdmans, 1988.

Sokoloff, Michael, translator. *A Syriac Lexicon: A Translation from the Latin, Correction, Expansion, and Update of C. Brockelmans's Lexicon Syriacum*. Winona Lake, IN: Eisenbrauns, 2009.

Stanton, Greg R. "Hellenism." Pages 464–73 in *Dictionary of New Testament Background*. Edited by C. A. Evans and S. E. Porter. Downers Grove: InterVarsity, 2000.

Stegner, William R. "Jew, Paul the." Pages 503–11 in *Dictionary of Paul and His Letters*. Edited by Gerald F. Hawthorne et al. Downers Grove: InterVarsity, 1993.

Stein, Robert H. *Studying the Synoptic Gospels: Origin and Interpretation*. 2nd ed. Grand Rapids: Baker, 2001.

———. "Synoptic Problem." Pages 784–92 in *Dictionary of Jesus and the Gospels*. Edited by Joel B. Green et al. Downers Grove: InterVarsity, 1992.

Steinmann, Andrew E. *Fundamental Biblical Aramaic*. Saint Louis: Concordia, 2004.

Stern, Ephraim. "Between Persia and Greece: Trade, Administration and Warfare in the Persian and Hellenistic Periods (593–63 B.C.)." Pages 432–45 in *The Archaeology of Society in the Holy Land*. Edited by Thomas E. Levy. London: Leicester, 1995.

Stewart, Roy A. "Esdras, Books of." Pages 143–47 in vol. 2 of *The International Standard Bible Encyclopedia*. Edited by Geoffrey W. Bromiley. 4 vols. Grand Rapids: Eerdmans, 1982.

Strange, James F. "Sepphoris." Pages 1090–93 in vol. 5 of *Anchor Bible Dictionary*. Edited by David Noel Freedman. 6 vols. New York: Doubleday, 1992.

Strange, James F., and Hershel Shanks. "Has the House Where Jesus Stayed in Capernaum Been Found?" *BAR* 13:16 (1987) 80–90.

———. "Synagogue Where Jesus Preached Found at Capernaum." *BAR* 9:6 (1983) 24–31.

Strauch, Alexander. *Biblical Eldership*. Littleton, CO: Lewis and Roth, 1995.

Strelan, Rick. *Luke the Priest: The Authority of the Author of the Third Gospel*. London: Ashgate, 2008.

Suetonius. *Divus Claudius*. Translated by J. C. Rolfe. 2 vols. Loeb Classical Library. Cambridge: Harvard University Press, 1914.

Swete, Henry B. *An Introduction to the Old Testament in Greek*. Cambridge: Cambridge University Press, 1902.

Tacitus. *Historiae*. Translated by Clifford H. Moore and John Jackson. 4 vols. Loeb Classical Library. Cambridge: Harvard University Press, 1925.

Thiselton, Anthony C. *New International Dictionary of New Testament Theology*. Edited by Colin Brown. 4 vols. Grand Rapids: Zondervan, 1975.

Thomas, Robert L., and Stanley N. Gundry, eds. *A Harmony of the Gospels*. Chicago: Moody, 1978.

Thompson, J. Arthur. *The Bible and Archaeology*. 3rd ed. Grand Rapids: Eerdmans, 1982.

Torrey, Charles C. *The Four Gospels: A New Translation*. London: Harper, 1953.

Tsuk, Tsvika. "The Aqueducts in Sepphoris." *Aqueducts of Ancient Palestine*. Edited by D. Amit et al. Jerusalem: Israel Antiquities Authority, 1989.

Turner, Henry E. W. *Historicity and the Gospels: A Sketch of Historical Method and Its Application to the Gospels*. London: Mowbray, 1963.

———. "Tradition of Mark's Dependence Upon Peter." *ExpTim* 71 (1960) 260–63.

Turner, Nigel. *Grammatical Insights into the New Testament*. Edinburgh: T. & T. Clark, 1965.

———. "The Language of Jesus and His Disciples." Pages 174–90 in *The Language of the New Testament: Classic Essays*. Edited by Stanley E. Porter. Sheffield: Sheffield Academic, 1991.

———. "The Language of the New Testament." Pages 659–64 in *Peake's Commentary of the Bible*. Edited by Matthew Black and H. H. Rowley. Edinburgh: Thomas Nelson, 1962.

———. *Style*. vol. 4 of *A Grammar of New Testament Greek*. Edited by J. H. Moulton. Edinburgh: T. & T. Clark, 1976.

Tyson, Joseph. *Images of Judaism in Luke-Acts*. Columbia: University of South Carolina Press, 1992.

Unnik, Willem Cornelius van. "Zur Papias-notiz uber Markus (Eusebius) H E III 39, 15." *ZNW* 54 (1963) 276–77.

VanderKam, James C. "Jubilees." Pages 600–603 in *Dictionary of New Testament Background*. Edited by C. A. Evans and S. E. Porter. Downers Grove: InterVarsity, 20.

VanderKam, James C., and J. T. Milik. "Jubilees." *Qumran Cave 4 VIII: Parabiblical Texts Part 1. Discoveries in the Judean Desert*. Vol. 13. Oxford: Clarendon, 1994.

Vermes, Geza. *The Complete Dead Sea Scrolls in English*. New York: Penguin, 1997.

———. *The Dead Sea Scrolls in English*. 3rd ed. London: Penguin, 1987.

Virkler, Henry A., and Karelynne G. Ayayo. *Hermeneutics: Principles and Processes of Biblical Interpretation*. 2nd ed. Grand Rapids: Baker Academic, 2007.

Voobus, Arthur. "Versions." Pages 969–83 in vol. 4 of *The International Standard Bible Encyclopedia*. Edited by Geoffrey W. Bromiley. 4 vols. Grand Rapids: Eerdmans, 1988.

Wachsman, Shelley, et al. "The Kinneret Boat Project: The Excavation and Conservation of the Kinneret Boat." *IJNA* 16 (1987) 243.

Walker, Larry. *New International Dictionary of Old Testament Theology and Exegesis*. Edited by William A. VanGemeren. 5 vols. Grand Rapids: Zondervan, 1997.

Wall, Robert W. *The New Interpreter's Bible*. 12 vols. Nashville: Abingdon, 2003.

Wallace, Daniel B. *Greek Grammar Beyond the Basics*. Grand Rapids: Zondervan, 1996.

Wallace, David H. "Nazarene." Pages 499–500 in vol. 3 of *The International Standard Bible Encyclopedia*. Edited by Geoffrey W. Bromiley. 4 vols. Grand Rapids: Eerdmans, 1986.

Waltke, Bruce, and M. O'Connor. *An Introduction to Biblical Hebrew Syntax*. Winona Lake, IN: Eisenbrauns, 1990.

Warren, David. "The Inspiration of the Bible." *Renewing Respect: Rediscovering a Forgotten Virtue*. Edited by Bell Bagents. Nashville: Gospel Advocate, 2009.

Waterman, Leroy, et al. *Preliminary Report of the University of Michigan Excavations at Sepphoris, Palestine in 1931*. Ann Arbor: University of Michigan Press, 1937.

Watson, JoAnn Ford. "Philip." Pages 310–12 in vol. 5 of *Anchor Bible Dictionary*. Edited by David Noel Freedman. 6 vols. New York: Doubleday, 1992.

Wegner, Paul D. *The Journey from Texts to Translations: The Origin and Development of the Bible*. Grand Rapids: Baker, 1999.

Weingreen, Jacob A. *A Practical Grammar for Classical Hebrew*. 2nd ed. New York: Oxford University Press, 1959.

Weiss, Zeev. "Sepphoris." *IEJ* 60 (2010) 98–107.

Wenham, John. "The Identification of Luke." *EvQ* 63 (1991) 3–44.

Werke, Eusebius. *Die Praeparatio Evangelica, Die Griecheschen Christlichen Schriftsteller der Ersten Jahrhunderte* 2. Berlin: Akademie-Verlag, 1982.

Wessel, Walter W. "Ebionites." Pages 9–10 in vol. 2 of *The New International Standard Bible Encyclopedia*. Edited by Geoffrey W. Bromiley. 4 vols. Grand Rapids: Eerdmans, 1982.

Wilcox, Max. "Peter and the Rock: A Fresh Look at Matthew xvi. 17–19." *NTS* (1975) 73–88.

———. "Semitic Influence of the New Testament." Pages 1093–98 in *Dictionary of New Testament Background*. Edited by C. A. Evans and S. E. Porter. Downers Grove: InterVarsity, 2000.

Wilkins, Michael J. "Bartholomew." Page 615 in vol. 1 of *Anchor Bible Dictionary*. Edited by David Noel Freedman. 6 vols. New York: Doubleday, 1992.

———. "Disciples." Pages 176–82 in *Dictionary of Jesus and the Gospels*. Edited by Joel B. Green et al. Downers Grove: InterVarsity, 1992.

———. "Discipleship." Pages 182–89 in *Dictionary of Jesus and the Gospels*. Edited by Joel B. Green et al. Downers Grove: InterVarsity, 1992.

Williams, Joel Stephen. "Inerrancy, Inspiration, and Dictation." *ResQ* 37:3 (1995) 158–77.

Willis, John T. *Isaiah*. The Living Word Commentary 12. Abilene: ACU Press, 1980.

Wilson, Walter T. "Hellenistic Judaism." Pages 477–82 in *Dictionary of New Testament Background*. Edited by Craig A. Evans and Stanley E. Porter. Downers Grove: InterVarsity, 2000.

Wise, Michael O. "Languages of Palestine." Pages 434–44 in *Dictionary of Jesus and the Gospels*. Edited by Joel B. Green et al. Downers Grove: InterVarsity, 1992.

Witherington III, Ben. *Conflict and Community in Corinth*. Grand Rapids: Eerdmans, 1995.

Wright, David F. "Ebionites." Pages 313–17 in *Dictionary of the Later New Testament and Its Development*. Edited by Ralph P. Martin and Peter H. Davids. Downers Grove: InterVarsity, 1997.

Wyatt, Robert J. "Hillel." Page 716 in vol. 2 of *The International Standard Bible Encyclopedia*. Edited by Geoffrey W. Bromiley. 4 vols. Grand Rapids: Eerdmans, 1982.

———. "Pharisees." Pages 822–29 in vol. 3 of *The International Standard Bible Encyclopedia*. Edited by Geoffrey W. Bromiley. 4 vols. Grand Rapids: Eerdmans, 1986.

Yamauchi, Edwin M. "Hellenism." Pages 383–88 in *Dictionary of Paul and His Letters*. Edited by Gerald F. Hawthorne et al. Downers Grove: InterVarsity, 1993.

Young, Bradford H. "Targum." Pages 727–33 in vol. 4 of *The International Standard Bible Encyclopedia*. Edited by Geoffrey W. Bromiley. 4 vols. Grand Rapids: Eerdmans, 1988.

Youngblood, Ronald F. "Gamaliel." Pages 393–94 in vol. 2 of *The New International Standard Bible Encyclopedia*. Edited by Geoffrey W. Bromiley. 4 vols. Grand Rapids: Eerdmans, 1982.

Zahn, Theodor. *Introduction to the New Testament*. Vol. 2. 3rd ed. Translated by John M. Trought et al. Edinburgh: T. & T. Clark, 1909.

Subject Index

Scripture Index